7/05

WITHDRAWN

Where Men Are Wives and Mothers Rule · *The History of African-American Religions Series*

Florida A&M University, Tallahassee
Florida Atlantic University, Boca Raton
Florida Gulf Coast University, Ft. Myers
Florida International University, Miami
Florida State University, Tallahassee
University of Central Florida, Orlando
University of Florida, Gainesville
University of North Florida, Jacksonville
University of South Florida, Tampa
University of West Florida, Pensacola

The History of African-American Religions
Edited by Stephen W. Angell and Anthony Pinn

This series will further historical investigation into African religions in the Americas, encourage the development of new paradigms and methodologies, and explore cultural influences upon African-American religious institutions, including the roles of gender, race, leadership, regionalism, and folkways.

WHERE MEN ARE WIVES

University Press of Florida
Gainesville
Tallahassee
Tampa
Boca Raton
Pensacola
Orlando
Miami
Jacksonville
Ft. Myers

Mary Ann Clark

AND MOTHERS RULE

Santería Ritual Practices and Their Gender Implications

Copyright 2005 by Mary Ann Clark
Printed in the United States of America
on recycled, acid-free paper
All rights reserved

10 09 08 07 06 05   6 5 4 3 2 1

A record of cataloging-in-publication data
is available from the Library of Congress.

ISBN 0-8130-2834-5

The University Press of Florida is the scholarly
publishing agency for the State University System
of Florida, comprising Florida A&M University,
Florida Atlantic University, Florida Gulf Coast
University, Florida International University,
Florida State University, University of Central
Florida, University of Florida, University of
North Florida, University of South Florida,
and University of West Florida.

University Press of Florida
15 Northwest 15th Street
Gainesville, FL 32611-2079
http://www.upf.com

Contents

Foreword

Over the course of several decades, practitioners and observers have shed light on the workings of Santería. These studies, both academic and popular, have been vital in developing a more complex understanding of the religious landscape defining the Americas. The elaborate ritual and doctrinal underpinnings of this rich tradition have been explored and explained. From studies of the historical development of the religion to more specialized discussions of the Orisha, various houses, and the aesthetic dimensions of the religion, interested parties are now able to tap into a good number of resources.

What has received less attention, however, is the issue of gender and gender implications surrounding the inner workings of Santería. That is, until now. We are pleased to have in this series on the history of African-American religion this text addressing gender and the implications of gender within Santería.

This study is informed both by Clark's deep academic familiarity with the religion and by her personal involvement as a priestess. Readers benefit from Clark's multilayered connection to Santería, a distinctive vantage point from which to challenge Western theological assumptions and the misogynistic attitudes that so often fuel the workings of mainstream religious communities.

Two central questions serve to frame much of what the author seeks to accomplish in this book: "How do our ideas of god (or the gods), human beings, and their interactions change in the light of gender awareness?" and "Does the normative male perspective incorporate the thinking and experiences of both men and women, and if not, how does the experience of women change our understandings of the great theological questions?" Drawing on the work of various scholars, Clark notes that the male perspective has typically served as the guiding framework for theological thought and ritual structures. What has been said about the gods and about human interaction with the gods in its various forms has assumed maleness as the normative stance, the characteristic mode of religious imagination and encounter. Yet, while this may be true for mainstream Christianity, Clark, through attention to central categories within Santería—possession, sacrifice, divination and destiny—points out the ways in which gender mixing takes place on various levels, adding "thickness" to notions of male and female as they function theologically and ritually within this religion. This is because, as Clark insightfully points out, Santería, unlike many "mainstream religions," is a female-normative system in which both men and women are expected to assume female gender roles at various points.

Regardless of the male point of view expressed in much of the literature, the beginnings of what would become Santería are marked by the organizational activities of women drawing from highly female-identified African traditions. While many of the books in this series are concerned with historical presentations of various dimensions of religion within the African Diaspora in the Americas, Clark's text provides an important contribution to the overall project of the series by suggesting a preliminary assessment of the contours of a theological system sensitive to the inner workings of Orisha traditions, one that seeks to use a concern with gender to unpack the conceptual framework underlying praxis within Orisha traditions. We believe readers of this book will enhance their understanding of Orisha traditions by addressing the issue of gender's influence on ritual thought and practice. It is a fine book and a significant addition to the ongoing conversation concerning Orisha traditions.

We are delighted to have the opportunity to offer this groundbreaking study in the History of African American Religions series.

Stephen W. Angell and Anthony B. Pinn, Series Editors

Acknowledgments

Maferefún Yemaya, Maferefún Eleggua, Maferefún Oshun, Maferefún gbo-gbo Orisha.

I am deeply grateful to all the people who have made this book possible, including my parents, Daniel and Marilyn Clark, who instilled in me a deep hunger to know just a little bit more, and my godparents Sandra Dillard (Ode Kan), who first introduced me to the Orisha, and Anthony DeQuinzio (Chango Ladé), who patiently answered my questions and helped me locate the theoretical material in the tangible world of practice. Although this book is not directly based on my dissertation, my committee, Edith Wyschogrod, William Parsons, Elias Bongmba, Patricia Seed, and Joseph Murphy, have provided invaluable guidance from the beginning of my academic career. I stand on the shoulders of giants.

This project has been helped immeasurably by a Rockefeller Residential Fellowship at the University of Florida and the wonderful people I met there, including Manuel Vasquez, Larry Crook, Joan Frosh, Sunni Witmer, and especially Martha Davis (Casa Marta will always hold a special place in the memories of my heart). I also owe a special debt of thanks to the Reference

Department at Rice University, which continues to support my work both monetarily and emotionally.

I met fellow student Alice Wood my first day in graduate school, on our way to pursuing our Ph.D.s in religious studies. Ever since, she has been a role model and steadfast companion on this fantastic journey. Thank you for listening to me think. Although Mary Curry died before I began this project, she continues to inspire and guide my work. I also want to thank those whose work I have found especially enlightening, including George Brandon, John Mason, J. Lorand Matory, Joseph Murphy, and Stephan Palmié.

Modupe to all the *santeros* and *santeras* who have welcomed me into their homes and hearts, especially Severiano "Junior" Bermudez, Greg Harrison, and all their godchildren, both in Houston and in New York. You wouldn't be holding this book without the encouragement of Tony Pinn, who supported me through several iterations of trying to find what I needed to say. Meredith Morris-Babb and her staff have shown extraordinary patience. I also want to extend a special thank-you to my reviewers Leslie G. Desmangles and Dianne Marie Stewart.

And finally, I cannot imagine where I would be without the love and support of my dear husband and companion, Art Gorski. I could never have done this without you, dearest. It's been a long and strange odyssey.

We are devoted to *òrìsà*; as for you, serve your god, but we will serve our *òrìsà*.

Olorisha (Orisha worshipper), 1877

CHAPTER 1 · Introduction

The philosophy of religion is generally understood to be the rational study of religious questions, including questions about the nature of god(s) and the place of mankind within the universe. Is there a god (or gods) and, if so, what can we know of the nature of the god(s) and his/her/its/their interactions in the world of humanity? Does our understanding of the nature of the god(s) affect our understanding of ourselves and our relationship with others? This study is also often called upon to answer questions of human meaning: Why am I here? What am I meant to do? Is there an ultimate meaning to human life in general and my life in particular? These philosophical and theological questions blend into questions of morality and ethics: How does one determine right from wrong action, and how does one decide on appropriate actions in the face of ambiguity? Ethics naturally leads to questions of theodicy: Why do evil people prosper while the good are left to suffer? And what is the appropriate religious response in the face of the evil in our lives and the lives of others? Underlying these questions of theodicy is a particular understanding of the nature of the gods. We ask, specifically, if god (or the gods) is good and just, why is there evil in the world?

These questions can extend beyond the nature of deity to ask not only why evil exists in general but also why evil strikes when and where it does. Why does the whirlwind take the one and leave the other? Such questions lead to more personal questions that can be summarized by the cry, Why me! Why am I made to suffer, and what can I do to alleviate my own propensity toward suffering? These questions lead in turn to questions of destiny: Is there a reason why I am here, at this place and in this time? Does my life have meaning beyond the needs of day-to-day existence? If there is a meaning to my life, how do I discover my destiny? And, if destiny can be manipulated, how might I assure the most positive destiny for myself and those I love?

Although within the Western philosophical tradition these questions have generally been asked and answered from the dominant male perspective, contemporary women have entered the fray, asking and answering these questions from their own perspectives. Thus one must ask one final set of questions: How do our ideas of god (or the gods), human beings, and their interactions change in the light of gender awareness? Does the normative male perspective incorporate the thinking and experiences of both men and women? If not, how does the experience of women change our understandings of the great philosophical and theological questions?

The Male as Normative

Much philosophical thinking assumes what is known as the "normative male perspective." Not only are the major thinkers across traditions men, but the descriptions of both the gods and human beings imply that maleness is the base case—that is, the gods and the people incorporated into philosophical thinking are presumed to be male unless they are specifically identified otherwise. In her 2003 article in *Cross Currents*, Rita M. Gross says that this preference for maleness over femaleness is one of the most deeply rooted problems in our cultural psyche and that it is "probably due in part to religious symbol systems that contain deeply misogynist elements and personify the most valued and ultimate symbols as masculine" (12). This has led, she says, to a belief that what is male is "normal," that everything deviating from stereotypical maleness is abnormal, and that men are unencumbered by gender, since gender is one of those characteristics that distinguish some human beings as outside the (male) norm. This deep-seated preference for characteristics that have been culturally constructed as male over those that have been constructed as female as well as over other cultural gender constructions has led to a general acceptance of women who want to act like men but a continued abhorrence of men who take on any characteristic that has been culturally defined as "female."

My intention in this book is to explore these issues of gender through the lens of the philosophy and practices of the Orisha traditions as they have developed in the Americas. My analysis of the beliefs and practices of the devotees of the Orisha suggests that, unlike the mainstream religions Gross alludes to, they exist within a female-normative system in which all practitioners, regardless of their own understandings of their sex or gender or sexual orientation, are expected to take up female gender roles in the practice of the religion. Although there are instances in which male roles are expected of both men and women in the religion, the more common situation is the adoption of female roles. How, then, might our perceptions of the philosophical and theological questions raised above be changed in a system that valorizes the female over the male, and how might the lives of the individuals caught up in a female-normative system change?

If what Gross says is true—and I believe that it is—this book will be extremely difficult for both scholars and practitioners of these Orisha traditions, because it challenges not only Western theological traditions but also misogynistic attitudes within communities of practitioners. In one way or another the questions we will be exploring have challenged human beings for millennia. However, for the past two thousand years, they have been most systematically analyzed within the confines of the Western Christian milieu. Even when Europeans began to investigate the ideas of non-Western religious systems, they generally worked from within a Western Christian foundation, so that, having developed a highly sophisticated theology based on biblical and Western philosophical traditions, they viewed the new religious traditions they found in Asia and later in Africa and the Americas through the lens of their understandings of Christian theology. Thus the literature of encounters between Europeans and the Others they found around the world is full of attempts by those Others and their conversation partners to describe their religious ideas in Western philosophical and theological terms.

This book is not an attempt to continue that (generally discredited) project. Rather, it is an effort to formulate the beginnings of a theology of the contemporary Orisha traditions using the Western philosophical and theological categories while approaching them from a different perspective. Although I am striving to answer the questions posed above, I will do so from the point of view of one who has become immersed in the Orisha traditions. Generally these traditions in the United States are based on the Afro-Cuban religious complex known as Santería. As we will discuss, Santería is understood to be a syncretization of the Orisha traditions brought to the Americas by enslaved Yoruba-speaking people and the colonial Catholic traditions they found when they arrived in the Americas. Although that is a misrepresentation of the tradition, it is important to recognize that contemporary practitioners of the Orisha traditions in the United States, Cuba, and even Nigeria have all been influenced by the Western colonial project and are familiar with at least the popular rendition of Western Christian theological and philosophical concepts. At the same time, it is important for scholars and practitioners to gain an understanding of this tradition and the ways in which its foundational ideas are different from those found either in the Western monotheistic traditions of Christianity, Judaism, and Islam or in the various polytheistic or atheistic Asian traditions—Hinduism, Buddhism, Shinto, and the like. Perhaps an example of one of those fundamental differences will be helpful at this point.

Christianity and Islam are generally considered salvational religious traditions. This means that among the fundamental beliefs is that, when one dies, one's life is judged worthy of punishment or reward. There are no second chances in these traditions. Once one dies, judgment is made and one's fate is determined. Within Hinduism and Buddhism, on the other hand, the idea of samsara prevails. Within these traditions one is continually born and reborn, each death leading to a new rebirth. The reward for a good life is rebirth at a higher level. The ultimate reward is nirvana, a stepping off the wheel of rebirth and an extinction of the "self." (*Nirvana* is a Sanskrit word meaning "extinction.") Continuing to be born and reborn is always a penalty; the goal is to elude rebirth altogether. Although they are different in many ways, all of these traditions see human life ("this world") as miserable, and all look forward to a future that is different from the everyday. Like Buddhism and Hinduism, Yoruba traditional beliefs include an idea of reincarnation, a belief that those who have lived before will live again. Significantly, among the Yoruba, reincarnation is believed to generally follow the family line—that is, the dead are reincarnated as their own descendants, often their grand- or great-grandchildren. However, the more important way in which the Yoruba understanding of reincarnation is different from the Asian traditions is the understanding that rebirth is a *reward* for having lived a good life. There is no idea of rising through levels of social hierarchy or of an ultimate reward of eluding rebirth altogether.

Only the most evil and warped human being is denied rebirth within the Yoruba tradition. This leads to (or comes from) a valorization of this life—the viewpoint that, in spite of the hardships of day-to-day living, life is good, this is where we all want to be, and death is only a temporary respite between lifetimes. This was summed up for me in the proverb "Life in heaven cannot be pleasant, otherwise people would not live so long and come back so quickly."

Each of these positions about the afterlife leads to different ways of acting and thinking. Each provides a different basis on which to answer such great theological questions as: How am I to live? How am I to react to the inevitable ups and downs along the way? We will examine the ways contemporary Orisha worshippers are encouraged to answer these questions and the ways this idea and others like it inform their idea of the good life. At this point what is important is a recognition that such differences exist and that they can radically change one's view of the world.

Santería: A Brief Overview

> My curse be on ye for your disloyalty and disobedience, so let your children disobey you. If you send them on an errand, let them never return to bring you word again. To all the points I shot my arrows will ye be carried as slaves. My curse will carry you to the sea and beyond the seas, slaves will rule over you, and you their masters will become slaves.
>
> Prince Adebo

The Orisha traditions in the United States are known variously as Santería, Lukumi (sometimes spelled Lucumí), Ifá, Regla de Ocha (Sp., Rule of the Orisha),[1] Yoruba Traditional Religion, or Orisha Religion.[2] Although this book is written from the viewpoint of traditional Santería (Lukumi) practice, much of what is said here also applies to these variants of Yoruba-based religion as well as to the Brazilian tradition of Candomblé. During the eighteenth and early nineteenth centuries, thousands of Africans were brought from the west coast of Africa to the Americas to work as slaves on the plantations created by European colonists.[3] After 1762 when the English captured the Spanish port of Havana, and after the Haitian revolution of 1794, the European passion for sugared foods was increasingly met by sugar from Cuban plantations. Hundreds of thousands of Yoruba-speaking people were brought to the New World to work these plantations. By 1888 nearly 10 million African men and women had made the Middle Passage to the Americas. It is estimated that between 500,000 and 700,000 of these Africans were brought to Cuba. During the final period of Cuban slavery, between 1850 and around 1870, slightly more than 34 percent of the slaves arriving in Cuba were designated as members of the Lukumi nation (actually the Yoruba language group), that is, Oyos, Egbas, Ijebus, and Ijeshas (Brandon 1993, 57–58, 55).

Although life on the sugar plantations numbed the mind and destroyed the body, slaves and former slaves living in the cities, notably Havana, had opportunities to learn trades and work for wages—and thus, according to long-standing Spanish law, to buy their own and their family's freedom. By the mid-nineteenth century more than one-third of the black population of Cuba were *gente de color* (Sp., [free] people of color), and they constituted one-sixth of the total population. For comparison, in Virginia at the same time free blacks were one-ninth of the black population and only one-thirty-second of the total population (Murphy 1993, 21–26; statistics from Klein 1967, 202, 236).

Even before the end of slavery, freed blacks and enslaved tradespeople living in the cities of Havana and Matanzas formed social clubs similar to the Spanish *cofradías* (brotherhoods), which they called *cabildos* from the word for church chapter house or town council.[4] These cabildos functioned not only as social clubs but also as quasi-political governmental bodies whose leadership was responsible for the behavior of their members to the Spanish city councils. By law and custom, the members of each cabildo were members of the same African "nation," whose dances, drum types, and songs were considered ethnically significant symbols. Since black servitude was known in Spain long before the discovery of the Americas, African-style drumming and dancing were better known and tolerated in Spanish colonies than in the English colonies of the New World.

In the mid-eighteenth century, the Catholic Church tried to bring religion into these clubs by providing an image of the Virgin Mary to each club and assigning a clergyman to direct worship and teach Catholic doctrine. Through a policy of guided syncretism that included injecting an African flavor into European Christian rites, the church hoped to sweep the Africans into the mainstream of Cuban Christianity so that they would eventually forsake their African customs. As was common in Spain, the members of the Afro-Cuban cabildos took part in religious festivals by bearing their saints' images in public processions. It was during these festivals that African-style dances were performed under the banners and images of Catholic saints. Within the walls of these cabildos, Africans and Afro-Cubans brought their own organizational and religious structures into being in the colonial environment. Along with their administrative functions, the cabildos also nourished distinctive religious functions separate from those provided by the Spanish clergy. In its Spanish form, the cabildo was responsible for the welfare of its members; in times of need, the cabildo provided clothes, medicine, charity, and a decent burial. The Afro-Cuban cabildos provided all these services to their members; however, most important for us, it was in these cabildos that scholars believe the Afro-Cubans were able to reconstruct their Orisha worship.

Among the Yoruba the worship of the Orisha tended to center on individual cult groups that worshipped either a single Orisha or a small number of related Orisha. While each lineage group had one or more deities accepted as "belonging" to that compound, in-marrying women and other "strangers" might bring additional deities to the compound. Any individual might worship a single Orisha, several, or none at all, although generally an individual worshipped five or six different deities (Bascom 1944, 23–24).

In Cuba the tradition of individual Orisha cults and lineage traditions could not be sustained.[5] Over time the founders of what was to become Santería reconstructed the Orisha cults into a single religious system in which all of the Orisha could be worshipped. Based on a tradition of cross-initiations, they established a system whereby a new priest was not only initiated into the cult of his or her ruling Orisha, he or she was also automatically initiated as a priest of a set of related Orisha. This style of initiation strengthened the developing religion, since the new priest would be able to initiate others not only into the cult of his or her primary Orisha but also into the cults of all the other Orisha received.[6]

Although much of the literature about this religion has been written from the viewpoint of male adherents, it is a religion that was organized and established during the cabildo period by women who based it on African religious traditions that were strongly female-identified. As Philip A. Howard suggests, in many cabildos the second most important officers were the *matronas* (matrons or queens). Although the slim literature on the early cabildos suggests that the responsibilities of these matronas was "more ceremonial than functional," we can suggest that these ceremonial roles were actually religious in nature (Howard 1998, 41, 42; see also Ortiz 1921, 6). In fact, Fredrika Bremer, a Swedish woman who traveled throughout the Americas in the 1800s, made the startling observation, "These cabildoes are governed, as I have already said, by queens, one or two, who decide upon the amusements, give tone to the society, and determine its extension. They possess the right of electing a king, who manages the pecuniary affairs of the society, and who has under him a secretary and master of the ceremonies" (Bremer 1853, 381; for a more accessible source, see Brown 2003, app. 1). According to Santería oral traditions, several women were influential in the early development of this new religion. Two who deserve special notice are Minga Latuan, a priest of Shango initiated in Africa, who arrived in Cuba in or around the 1840s, and María Towá, who has been called Queen of the Lukumi. These women are credited with instituting the position of *oriaté* (ritual specialist and diviner) and making the ritual that has come to be called *cuchillo* (Sp., knife) available to all priests. These two innovations are discussed in chapters 3 and 4 respectively. As we shall see, the Yoruba idea that the female is the ideal religious type continues to be manifested in the religious practice of contemporary practitioners of Santería.

Although tolerated early on, the cabildos and their members were severely oppressed during the early decades of the twentieth century as Cuba gained its independence from Spain (1895), established itself as a republic (1902), and was occupied by American troops twice (1898 and 1912).[7] Even though Cuba's republican constitution allowed for freedom of religion, Santería and Cuba's other African-based cults were persecuted during the period in an effort to "civilize" its citizens. However, the efforts to suppress these religions were unsuccessful, so that when Cuban refugees immigrated to the United States in the 1960s (after the revolution) and again in 1980 (the Mariel boatlift) they brought their African-based traditions with them. Here they have flourished in spite of continued opposition on a variety of fronts. Today estimates suggest that there are more practitioners of the Orisha traditions in the United States than in either Cuba or Nigeria.

The Nature of Deity

Western understandings of the nature of deity and the meaning of the word "God" are based on Hebraic thought as captured in the books of the Hebrew and Christian Bibles (the Old and New Testaments) and the Greek philosophical traditions.[8] This groundwork has been extended and refined by two thousand years of Christian theology and Euro-American philosophy. Most explorations of non-Judeo-Christian religious traditions continue to use the categories of thought developed within these theological and philosophical traditions, especially when the target traditions do not have a well-defined indigenous philosophical tradition. Embedded within these Eurocentric traditions is the view that "God" is the name given to the Ultimate Reality, a being who created and sustains the world, who acts as the protector and savior of individuals and nations challenged by evil. This being is the central object of worship and acts as the final arbiter for all human morality.

Often the biblical account describes God in anthropomorphic terms as a kingly figure with arms and legs as well as feelings and desires, as one whose will and mind engender purposive and creative actions. Examples of godly action include both constructive and destructive behavior: both the flooding of the entire earth and the protection of Noah and his family, for example. According to Christian understandings God is all-powerful, all-knowing, and absolutely moral; this godly morality is the standard against which all human action is measured and found wanting.

In addition to describing God in anthropomorphic terms, the biblical tradition uses abstract metaphors to describe the nature of God. In this view God is the beginning and the end of creation, everywhere present but untouchable, unknowable. Whereas the anthropomorphic metaphors bring God closer to his human subjects, the more abstract metaphors tend to emphasize the absolute difference between God and humanity. These metaphors express the nature of God as unique, eternal, absolutely Other.

Use of Greek philosophical thought further refined this second notion of God as an ideal being. Based on Platonic and Neoplatonic theories, God as the most perfect being must not be dependent on any other being, must be changeless, eternal, and unitary. However, these Greek notions of the immutable nature of God challenged the Christian belief in the Incarnation, the doctrine that God entered into the natural world through the person of Jesus. How could a unitary, unchangeable deity enter into time and be subjected to the vicissitudes of matter? This difficulty was finally resolved through the development of the most distinctive feature of Christian belief, the notion of the godhead as trinity—that is, as a union of three divine persons in one God. Much Christian theological thinking, particularly in the medieval period, was based on the need to resolve the differences between the God of revelation and philosophical concepts of what the nature of God should be.

In the modern and postmodern periods, theology was challenged in a different way by the alienation of the metaphysical from the natural world. Scientific theories and discoveries undercut theological notions about the origin and purpose of the material world and eliminated God from its order and design. This led to a more subjective theology. On the one hand, the godhead became defined in more abstract terms as the "ground of being," or "world-soul," and God became less static and more associated with the ongoing unfolding of the material world; on the other hand, thinking about the limitation of human knowledge relative to the godhead led to a negative theology (descriptions of what God is *not*) that suggested that God is ultimately unknowable.

Exposure to the cosmologies of non-Western peoples also drove theologians to ask what *kind* of God is found in Christianity. H. Richard Niebuhr suggested, among other things, that notions of God's transcendence undercut all human idols, including the Christian "idols" of church, Scripture, and even Christ. In addition, he suggested that the doctrine of the Trinity protects Christianity from a one-sidedness. The God of the Trinity, he said, is a fuller conception of deity than a God identified only as father, or only as son, or only as Holy Spirit (Fiorenza and Kaufman 1998, 149). In addition, feminist theologians, many of whom are familiar with the female deities of other traditions, have questioned the exclusively male-gendered imagery traditionally associated with the Christian godhead. Many have suggested that such images reinforce patriarchal cultural institutions. In an attempt to rectify such an imbalance, they have both drawn on the female imagery available within the Judeo-Christian tradition—for example, Elizabeth Schüssler Fiorenza's use of the feminine Sophia-God from the Hebrew Bible—and offered alternative images, such as Sallie McFague's reinterpretation of the Trinity as mother, friend, and lover (Fiorenza and Kaufman 1998, 149).

All of these notions of the nature of God and the appropriate ways to discuss and describe it either overtly or covertly influence accounts of non-Western, particularly indigenous, religious systems. Most practitioners and scholars of Orisha religions base their understanding of the religious cosmos of the Yoruba on the work of the Nigerian scholar and churchman E. Bọlájí Ìdòwú. Ìdòwú was the first patriarch of the Methodist Church of Nigeria and as such "played a key role in shaping and applying the concept of Indigenous African Christianity" (Ebisi 1994, vii). *Olódùmarè: God in Yorùbá Belief*, Ìdòwú's foremost work, was a revision of his doctoral thesis defended at the University of London in 1955. Basing his thought on the idea that the living God would have revealed Himself in some (perhaps imperfect) way to all people at all times, Ìdòwú posited that "God has spoken from the very beginning to every heart of all the peoples of the earth—all the peoples whom He has made and set in their places on the face of the earth—in a way which each understands" (Ìdòwú 1994, 31). Using his Christian theology as a foundation, Ìdòwú states authoritatively that "God is One, not many; and that to the one God belongs the earth and all its fullness. It is this God, therefore, Who reveals Himself to every people on earth and Whom they apprehended according to their knowledge of Him" (31). Ìdòwú goes on to describe Olodumare, the Yoruba "high god," according to classical theological criteria: he is the Prime Mover (32) or creator (39), the fountain of all benefits (53); he is the unique and incomparable King who dwells in the heavens (40); he is Omnipotent, All-wise, All-knowing, All-seeing (40, 41); he is the author of each person's destiny (53) and the final judge and disposer of all things (42); he is immortal, unchanging (42), and invisible (44); and he is holy, transcendent, and benevolent (46, 47).

Olodumare is not, however, alone. As Ìdòwú points out, it is not the worship of Olodumare that forms the basis of traditional Yoruba religion; rather it is the many divinities, called Orisha, who are the focus of the ritual attention of the Yoruba people and their religious descendants. Thus, although Ìdòwú describes Olodumare as similar to the Christian God, he must describe Yoruba religion as a "diffused monotheism"—that is, a monotheism that has been "attenuated through the many divinities [Orisha] whose cults form the objective phenomena of the religion" (204).

In Ìdòwú's view, the Orisha are the "ministers" of Olodumare who serve as mediators between Olodumare and humanity. But other researchers have questioned Ìdòwú's hierarchical model. Pierre Verger, the French anthropologist, suggested that the Orisha are actually separate and fully functioning deities more or less independent of Olodumare. Thus, he said, rather than describing the Yoruba cults as some sort of pantheism, they should more correctly be described as juxtaposed theisms or even juxtaposed monotheisms (McKenzie 1976, 190–91, quoting Verger 1957, 11, and Verger 1966, 24). Further, he suggested that the idea of *ashé* as "the vital power, the energy, the great strength of all things" (Verger 1966, 35) and not the idea of Olodumare best represents the Yoruba idea of God as the unknowable force that sustains the universe (38).

Based on his reading of Verger and extending Verger's conclusion from Yoruba cult groups to Santería, Joseph Murphy (1993) suggests that the world of the *santero* (Sp., Santería devotee) is a world constituted of and held together by ashé. He describes ashé as the movement of the cosmos toward completeness and divinity (130). It is "all mystery, all secret power, all divinity." It is without beginning or end; it cannot be enumerated or exhausted. It is not a particular power but Power itself (147n7, citing Verger 1966, 36; see also McKenzie 1976).

This view of ashé as the organizing power of the universe could lead to the understanding that Yoruba religion is monistic, or based on the belief that there is a single substance, ashé, underlying all of existence. Although it is possible to describe Olodumare as the personification of this underlying substance, a strict monism would be a-theistic: the substance underlying everything would be not an individual or personal being, but rather a force. This formulation would demote Olodumare from being the "high" god, as commonly perceived, to being merely one of the manifestations of the monistic substance.

The understanding that ashé encompasses every part of the visible and invisible worlds, that it is more than can be personified or portrayed, also leads to a religious viewpoint that eschews religious representations, particularly anthropomorphic representations. The Yoruba have never seen ashé and do not pretend to personify it. Thus, although we can suggest that Olodumare is the personification of ashé, we find no representations of Olodumare in either traditional Yoruba religion or its American variants.

In the Yoruba and Santería cosmological view ashé, the energy of the universe, is not homogeneous; it collects and forms into nodes of power we recognize as forces of nature (wind, the ocean, thunder), power sites (rivers, mountains), and aspects of human life (our roles as mothers, kings, warriors). In the Yoruba traditions these forces have been anthropomorphized and mythologized into a group of beings or demigods called the Orisha. The Orisha are multidimensional beings who represent the forces of nature, act as archetypes, and function as sacred patrons or "guardian angels." As the personifications of ashé and knowable aspects of Olodumare, they represent a level of power that is approachable through ritual action and so provide one very important focus for Yoruba religion (Lawson 1984, 57). And even though the Orisha are viewed as particular manifestations and personifications of ashé, a bit of this power seen in one of its numerous aspects (Verger 1966, 36), research suggests that the Yoruba were unlikely to create anthropomorphic representations of any divine beings. Thus, although the Orisha are represented in the mythology as having human characteristics, they are more likely to be represented by natural and manufactured goods than by statues or other sorts of images.[9]

The Orisha do have attributes and stories similar to the stories and attributes used to describe the ancient Greek and Roman deities. Their stories tell us how the world came to be the way it is (for example, why thunder and wind are often found together) and how to live a good life (sometimes you can persuade better with honey than with a sword). However, unlike the Greek gods, the Orisha are not remote deities living high on a mountain peak; rather they are living beings present in the everyday life of their followers. It is around the Orisha that most Yoruba and Santería religious activity focuses. In fact, as Peter R. McKenzie says (1976, 197), "the extraordinary richness of Yoruba religion lies in the profusion of its òrìsà, in the facility with which in the past an òrìsà has formed and gathered about itself a cult group."

Among the Yoruba, as with most polytheistic peoples, no one worshipped the entire profusion of Orisha, which are innumerable. Rather, any individual might worship a single Orisha, several Orisha, or even none at all, although according to the work of William Bascom, most Yoruba worshipped a group of five or six Orisha (Bascom 1944, 39, 23–24, 41–45).[10] In Cuba this worship pattern changed such that the group of Orisha commonly worshipped by practitioners was standardized. Although a profusion of Orisha remained, certain members of the pantheon rose to prominence and almost universal worship, while others fell to minor status.

Weaving the Web of Signification

I have suggested these Orisha form the warp of the memorative web that is created by santeros in the practice of their religion.[11] As each devotee weaves his or her own web of Orisha stories, attributes, songs, offerings, and prayers, he or she also shapes and creates an understanding of the Orisha and their religious system. As knowledge and understanding deepen, they begin to affect and shape the devotee's life. The world of Santería is symbolic, concrete, and experiential, shaped by each individual's experiences and his or her analysis of those experiences. This work began as an analysis of six of the major Orisha of Santería: Obatala, Shango, Yemaya, Oshun, Ogun, and Eleggua. These six Orisha are the most common of the Orisha in the Americas. They are found in the home of every santero, and it is to these six that the majority of ritual attention is paid. Although each santero worships a different part of the Orisha pantheon, everyone who has been initiated as a priest worships at least these six. Although the direct tie between these Orisha and this text weakened as it developed, they continue to form the warp of the memorative web I am attempting to weave. Although these chapters often leave the world of the specific behind in an effort to discuss the philosophical, theological, and symbolic, they are each formed by the experiences of Santería practitioners, santeros and santeras who have developed a personal relationship with these entities and who are attempting to live according to the way of the Orisha.

Although they are not usually regarded as the highest level of sacred beings, the Orisha are the most important of such beings in the Yoruba cosmology that is the basis of Santería. They are knowable aspects of Olodumare, the great god behind the gods, and represent a level of power that is approachable through ritual action. Thus they are the focus of religious practice both in Africa and the Americas. According to their stories, which form the bulk of the Yoruba mythological system, the Orisha are personalizations of the forces of nature and cultural ancestors. They also function very much as Jungian archetypes. While each Orisha is considered to be a complete deity, they are linked together in a relational community that is often symbolized by familial connections. Among the Yoruba in Africa there were an innumerable number of Orisha; the mythology says 201 or 401 or 4,001, as many as one can imagine— plus one more. Because they represent forces of nature and culture, there are Orisha associated with every natural and manufactured thing as well as every occupation and social relationship. Thus we can find Orisha in rivers, hills, forests, the ocean, and at the crossroads; we can find them in iron and wealth; and we can find them in occupations like blacksmith, farmer, and hunter as well as policeman, surgeon, and soldier. They are identified by colors, numbers, drum rhythms, dance steps, and their icons and images. The total number of Orisha is greatly attenuated in the Americas, as most devotees can name only fifteen or twenty, but many of the lesser-known Orisha continue to be worshipped in the New World.

All ceremonies and rituals begin with an invocation to the Orisha Eleggua, who is also called Eshu. He is the messenger among the Orisha and between the Orisha and men, the owner of the crossroads who must open the way for communication between the visible and invisible worlds. Eleggua is one of the most complex of the Yoruba deities. Christian missionaries, in their early encounters with Yoruba religion, tended to equate him with the concept of the devil, but this is most unfortunate and distorts his nature (Lawson 1984, 60). Eleggua is a trickster and a mischief maker, the one who punishes misconduct and rewards upright behavior. He is a source of wisdom and knowledge, as well as the one who can confuse situations in order to disclose the truth (60– 61). The Yoruba cosmology does not contain the duality of radically opposing forces such as good and evil, so Eleggua often appears ambiguous. His actions may appear evil because they test people's character as well as punish their misconduct. At the same time, it is Eleggua who rewards good character and correct conduct.

It was the Orisha Obatala who first created the earth as we know it. The name Obatala means Chief of the White Cloth. In this case white cloth is understood to represent the substance that forms the physical universe, the light energy that is transformed through the process of evolution into a planetary environment. Obatala is understood as the essence of this light. After Obatala created the earth with its oceans and forests, he invited the other Orisha to join him in living there. Most of the Yoruba mythology tells of this time when the Orisha lived upon the earth.

The stories of Orisha often serve as warnings to their human children.

Obatala, the symbol of wisdom, intelligence, and purity, was sent by Olodumare, the great god, to create the solid ground that became the earth as we know it. He was also instructed by Olodumare to mold the bodies of men and women so that Olodumare could breathe the breath of life into them. Unfortunately, while he was working he became thirsty and began to drink palm wine. As the liquor took effect, his hands became clumsy, so some of the figures he produced were twisted and malformed. When Obatala's intoxication wore off and he saw what he had done, he swore never to touch liquor again. To this day, priests of this most holy of Orisha avoid not only strong drink but all mind-altering substances. Among the Yoruba in Africa, Obatala's clumsiness explains children born with birth defects, albinos, hunchbacks, dwarfs, the deaf, and so on. These children are considered sacred to him and are marked as his worshippers. Children born in a caul or with their umbilical cords wrapped around their necks are also sacred to him (Bascom 1969, 81).

Strictly speaking, the Yoruba do not have a creator deity who is the equivalent of the Christian God, although Obatala embodies many of the elements associated with a creator god. As the king of white cloth, Obatala is seen as the master of the light-energy that forms the world. It is the Orisha Obatala, or another *funfun* (Yr., white) Orisha, who is credited with the creation of a habitable earth, and it is he who not only first formed the bodies of humankind but who continues to form the body of the unborn in the womb. As the ideal funfun Orisha, he represents ritual and ethical purity and thus is associated with the highest morality, holiness, and purity (Ìdòwú 1994, 73). In many ways Obatala conforms to Western notions of God. He is good and pure and wise. All of creation, both the natural world and its people, are attributed to him. He is considered the most holy, the most elevated of the Orisha. However, the worldview of both traditional Yoruba religion and Santería is non-dualistic—that is, there is no absolute good or evil. There is no purely evil being to counterbalance Obatala's goodness. Instead he is credited with a range of behaviors that exemplify both the best and the worst of his characteristics. His drinking, for example, has produced human suffering.

Although Eshu/Eleggua is often compared to the devil and Obatala is often seen as embodying the characteristics of God, both are ambiguous deities. Eleggua is not absolute evil, nor is Obatala absolutely good. Rather, both embody a range of behaviors. This leads us to suggest that this cosmos is not absolutist but relativistic and personalistic. Since each Orisha embodies both positive and negative qualities and there is no inherently evil entity in the Yoruba cosmology, this is a completely non-dualistic theological system. In the same way that some Christian theologians suggest that the Trinity and other images of God open up and expand their understanding of His nature, the multiplicity of named Orisha and the variety of characteristics associated with individual Orisha provide for an expanded understanding of the nature of deity and the workings of human life. While each Orisha represents a particular node of power, a specific archetype with definable attributes, each is also a fully functioning deity complete and powerful, able to provide for devotees across the religious spectrum. As McKenzie suggests (1976, 192–99), in the Yoruba context individual Orisha are considered full and complete deities in their own right.

Although Shango is a popular Orisha both in Africa and the Americas, he is considered to be a human ancestor who was the fourth *alaafin* (Yr., king) of the city of Oyo. Much of his mythology revolves around acquiring and maintaining a balance of power, particularly personal power. One of the stories says that he inadvertently caused a thunderstorm that killed his wives and children. Full of sorrow and remorse, he abdicated his throne and hanged himself. In another story he hanged himself after he was dethroned and expelled because of his abuses of power (Johnson 1921, 34). The act of contrition, represented by his self-imposed death, caused him to be raised to the level of Orisha, where his worship was syncretized with that of Jakuta, a thunder deity. As an Orisha, Shango is the essence of male sexuality, the power of the male to create new life. He is also associated with thunder and lightning, as well as with the power that can be unleashed against both others and one's self. To be able to control such power is power itself.

Just as Obatala is not all peace and calm, Shango is not all fire and lightning, power and sexuality. When his cult was assimilated into that of Jakuta, he also assimilated Jakuta's righteous attributes as the guardian of the Yoruba moral code. Ìdòwú calls Jakuta the "wrath of Olodumare" who was "The flashing of lightning free / The whirling wind's tempestuous shocks" (1994, 93). It was Jakuta who was first believed to punish wrongdoers by striking them dead with his lightning bolt. It is from this position as moral arbiter that Shango forbids lying, stealing, and other transgressions against ethical behavior (92–94).

Shango's support of a personal moral code is told in a story that is the favorite of Shango priests because it valorizes their guardian to the detriment of other Orisha:

At one time, a terrible famine fell over the land. Obatala called together the Warrior Orisha Ogun, Ochosi, and Shango. "You must go into the forest and bring back food for the people, else all will perish." The three went forth, each in a different direction, each determined to be the savior of the starving people. Ogun, whom we will explore more fully below, was the first to find game. After killing and dressing the bushbuck, he headed back to the village, but along the way his hunger overtook him. He stopped, intending to eat only a small portion of the animal. However, he kept eating and eating until he had devoured the entire beast. He continued toward Obatala's palace, certain that the others would return with food for the village.

After many days Ochosi caught and killed a small monkey. Like his brother Ogun, Ochosi cooked and ate his kill, certain that the others would have better luck than he did. Shango, more of a soldier than a hunter, was not very successful. Finally he caught a small bushrat. Famished, he cooked and ate it immediately, so that he would have the strength to return to the village.

At last the three erstwhile hunters stood in front of Obatala, barehanded. Both Ogun and Ochosi protested that they were unable to find any game and had barely made it back to the village. Shango, on the other hand, admitted that he had caught a bushrat but had eaten it to gain the strength to return, albeit empty-handed. Seeing through their stories, Obatala caused each of the failed hunters to vomit violently, and soon there appeared Ogun's bushbuck, Ochosi's monkey, and Shango's bushrat. For his honesty, they say, Shango was made a great king, while the others returned to their more humble professions of blacksmith and hunter.

Here we see Shango himself first suffering the humiliation of failure and then reaping the reward of honesty. Throughout the Yoruba mythology Shango is most often presented as arrogant and boastful, a liar and a womanizer, but this story exemplifies the other side of his personality—that of a great man too proud to lie even in the face of defeat and disgrace. Children of Shango and all santeros are warned against lying, and all the Orisha may punish moral lapses. However, among santeros it is said that Shango's punishment is particularly swift and effective. Unlike other deities who may be patient with human failings, Shango speaks only once, and the illumination of Shango's lightning serves both to punish the wicked and to warn observers who may be tempted to follow in their footsteps (Edwards and Mason 1985, 42).

Living at the boundary between town and bush is Ogun, the blacksmith, ironworker, and patron of all metals. Like Eleggua, Ogun is ambiguous. He is associated not only with surgeons, policemen, soldiers, automobiles, and railroads but also all acts of violence and war, especially those caused by metal implements—arrows, knives, swords, and later guns and cannon. Ogun represents the triumph of technology over raw nature. According to one story, when the Orisha first came to earth they were unable to pass through the dense thicket until Ogun opened the way using his trademark machete. For this reason he is often invoked "to clear the way" or remove obstacles to physical, emotional, or spiritual development. Because of his association with iron and all metal implements, Ogun has become the Orisha of war and sacrifice. It is said that one may construct an Ogun shrine merely by placing any two pieces of iron together and performing the appropriate sacrifice (Barnes 1980; Cosentino 1997). Thus every implement of war and violence is Ogun's tool of destruction.

The female Orisha Yemaya and Oshun are said to be sisters. They represent the complementary forces of female sexuality and maternal love and protection. Yemaya is seen as the great mother: her stories tell us that, in addition to her own children, she often raised the children of others, especially those of her sister Oshun, who as the goddess of love was more interested in the begetting of children than the raising of them. But Yemaya can be a stern mother. In some stories Yemaya is the real mother of Shango, while in others she is his adoptive mother. In one where she is his adoptive mother, they are separated for a very long time, so long that the great womanizer Shango does not recognize her when they meet at a drum party. Struck by her beauty, he suggests that they go off alone together. She agrees and proposes they go to her home. So the queen of the ocean takes the embodiment of fire in a small boat out in the middle of the water. When she causes a storm to rock the tiny boat, the great king, who cannot swim and is deathly afraid of water, is terrified. He is saved from her anger only when he recognizes Yemaya, repents of his incestuous desires, and promises to respect both the mother who bore him and the one who raised him.

Oshun, Yemaya's younger sister, is the divinity associated in the New World with the river and fresh water. She controls all that makes life worth living, including love, marriage, children, money, and pleasure, and is the essence of female sexuality. Unlike the warrior Orisha, Oshun uses the good things in life to win her battles. Once, the women of the world had separated themselves from the men and formed their own town. The king called upon the Orisha to bring the world back into balance by capturing the town and bringing the men and women back together. Each of the warrior Orisha tried and failed. Shango failed, Sopona failed. Egungun failed. Ogun failed. Even Oya, the woman warrior, failed.[12] Finally Oshun tried. But instead of attacking with sword and spear, she took a gourd and string and made a *shekere*—a musical instrument that has beads or shells woven around the outside of the gourd as noisemakers. Beating on the shekere, she danced into town singing, "Oshun is coming to play, Oshun does not know how to fight." Soon all the women joined in the dance and followed her back to where their men were waiting (Bascom 1980, 413–19). Thus did Oshun bring men and women together for the continuance of the world.

Rather than being based on absolute pronouncements, the Santería worldview as exemplified in the mythology values the maintenance of balance within one's life, one's family, one's community, the world at large, the fulfillment of each person's highest and best destiny. The summary of this view is embedded in the proverbs and *patakis* (Lk., stories) that have been preserved in the *diloggun* divination system. Many of the patakis tell stories of the Orisha highlighting the strengths and weaknesses of their different personalities. Most are teaching tales that suggest the consequences of certain types of behavior carried to the extreme. These stories form the basis of a Yoruba theological system.

Belief and Practice

"Faith" is often used as a code word for religion, especially Protestant Christianity but also any other religious system that can be reduced to a private creedal statement. This usage suggests that belief as formulated in a brief authoritative declaration is an essential feature of all religious traditions. Yet for many religious groups, if not most, it is practice—what one does—that is more important than any profession of faith or catalog of beliefs. Practice is certainly the most important element of Santería. Santeros don't generally speak of their beliefs but rather say that they "work" the Orisha. Rituals are "worked," spirits are "worked," devotees work with and for the Orisha while simultaneously expecting the Orisha to work for them.

This idea of worship being a kind of labor appears to have a long history among the Yoruba. In Peter McKenzie's analysis of mid-nineteenth-century Yoruba religious usage (1997), he consistently uses the phrase "to make òrìsà" to mean "to worship the deities." This seems to be based on the usage he found in the missionary record and is consistent with contemporary usage. The term "se òrìsà," which means "to make, do, or work the Orisha," is still used by Yoruba-speaking people in Nigeria to refer to the activities of Orisha worshippers. This emphasis on praxis rather than doxis has several implications for the development of Santería theology. First of all, since santeros are more interested in the work of the Orisha, they tend to emphasize ritual correctness rather than correct belief. Their discussions revolve around how one should behave in different circumstances and stories of the misbehavior of individuals, along with how a particular ritual should be done and critiques of rituals performed by themselves or others. Although certain understandings of the nature of the world and the Orisha underlie these discussions, there is little explication of the religious ideas behind these ritual practices and behaviors.

This same preference for praxis over doxis has also influenced the literature of Santería and related religions. Both popular and scholarly books tend to emphasize behavior to the detriment of any analysis of the concepts that underlie that behavior. In the following chapters I attempt to formulate the philosophical concepts underlying the various Orisha traditions. I do not pretend to present the definitive or final analysis of these Orisha concepts; rather, what I am presenting is a preliminary analysis of Orisha philosophy. My hope is to provide a foundation upon which other scholars can build. In the following pages I will begin an explication of what I think are among the most essential terms of Santería religious belief: destiny and divination, sacrifice, possession, and witchcraft. I will begin my discussion of Orisha philosophical issues, however, with an analysis of the gender anomalies embedded in Santería, because my analysis suggests that a unique understanding of gender and gender roles underlies much of Santería beliefs and practices.

In spite of more than a generation of feminist analysis, many people continue to have what Harold Garfinkel called a "natural attitude" toward gender, including the ideas that there are only two genders, that gender identity is invariant, and that the genitals are the essential sign of gender (Garfinkel 1967, chap. 5, esp. 122–28). As we shall see, such a natural attitude is not the best tool for analyzing the slippage between genders found within Santería and other Orisha religions. Many scholars have explored concepts of gender ambiguity and gender slippage within the religious milieu and in the larger environment. Few, however, can get beyond Garfinkel's natural attitude, and thus they tend to suggest that gender slippage is the result of gender confusion, a search for femininity, an effort at spiritual play, or a way of reinforcing or calling into question the binary gender scheme. None of these seems to be an adequate explanation for the types of gender ambiguity found in Santería. Oyèrónkẹ́ Oyewùmí's suggestion (1997) that the category of "gender" was completely absent from traditional Yoruba culture provides an alternative way in which to view personal relations not only within Yoruba culture but also in those subcultures based on Yoruba religious traditions. However, as exciting as is Oyewùmí's attempt to remove gender from the Yoruba worldview (worldsense, as she says), it does not provide an adequate explanation for the empirical data in both traditional Yoruba society and its American religious descendants. In chapter 2 I will suggest that while gender is not a strong category of analysis in these traditions, it does provide an important way to think about religious praxis. Thus I will show that the gender ambiguities found in Santería practice provide a nuanced way of thinking about the relationship between the visible and invisible worlds and are important to our philosophical project. Because of its importance, in each subsequent chapter we will use the understanding of gender relations developed in chapter 2 as one of the lenses through which we view the philosophical concepts found in Santería.

Important to an understanding of Santería religious practice are the concepts of destiny and divination. Like many Western psychologists, the Yoruba people believed that human beings are formed from a group of physical and nonphysical elements, the most important of which is *ori*, one's "head" or destiny. In the first part of chapter 3 I will use the work of Yoruba philosopher Segun Gbadegesin to explore the psychological and philosophical concepts embedded in the Yoruba concept of destiny. Gbadegesin says that although the broad outlines of one's personal destiny are fixed before birth, the destiny itself is not absolutely immutable; the choices one makes and the actions one takes are required to manifest the best portions of an auspicious destiny and can soften or ameliorate the most difficult portions of an unfortunate destiny. Although common sense, personal talents, and hard work can aid in the manifestation of one's best possible destiny, divination provides an aid in remembering the destiny one chose before birth and in making the best decisions and taking the best actions at important points in one's life.

This leads to the second part of chapter 3, a discussion of the ways in which different types of divination are used in contemporary Santería. All of the Orisha mythology is embedded within the various divination "texts" in the form of stories describing that time when the Orisha walked the earth, as well as stories of the lives of men and women and stories about anthropomorphic plants and animals. Although many of these stories are cosmogonic myths that tell of the creation of the world as we know it, others are fables in which people or animals either do or do not meet life's challenges, often aided by divinatory guidance. Under the guidance of a divinatory priest, one can learn how someone in the mythological past confronted a problem similar to one's own and either succeeded or failed to resolve it. Based on the divinatory model, one is guided toward the modification of one's own behavior in the hopes of resolving the current problem or furthering one's personal destiny.

Santería has embraced two divinatory systems with two different divinatory priesthoods. That one type of divination can be practiced by both men and women while the other is the exclusive dominion of men leads us back to the question of gender and the relationship between gender and religious beliefs and practices. That Ifá, the male divinatory system, has traditionally excluded not only women but also gay men raises questions not only of gender and gender ambiguity but also of the interaction between traditional Yoruba culture, which didn't have a vocabulary for discussing homosexuality, and the colonial and postcolonial Spanish and American cultures, which do.

In the history of Western philosophy, considerations of intersubjectivity often begin by positing, implicitly or explicitly, a monad, a singular, unique integrated self or being that can have experiences of another monad, the Other or double in the context of the social world. Even postmodern visions of a transitory, constructed self as proposed by Kenneth Gergan and others seem to assume some sort of perceived continuous existence. But not every experience of intersubjectivity has to be framed in terms of the Self/Other dyad interacting through continuously present bodies. In chapters 4 and 5 we will use the experience of priestly initiation and the phenomenon of trance possession to explore the ways in which the invisible can intrude into the visible world through the appropriation of the physical body of the Self by the second Other. We will examine the ways in which these experiences call into question concepts of Self and Other and the interaction between them, as well as the place of the Third as the witness to these transformations.

The fluidity in the areas of embodiment, gender, and power relationships presented by the Orisha traditions challenges our philosophical notions of body, self, and other. All portions of Orisha religion valorize bodies. Ritual action is always performative: bodies in action modeling the behavior appropriate to the moment (M. Mason 1994). But such embodiment is also fluid. Our analysis of initiation, possession, and Santería ritual practices will finally lead us to the suggestion that just as the "manly woman" formed the ideal of Christian female saintliness, qualities associated with being female form the ideal of Santería religious practice for both men and women. In chapters 4 and 5 we will explore the ways in which all priestly initiates are reinscribed as female, first in the course of their initiation and then as part of their ongoing religious practice. We will also explore how the Yoruba idea that the female is the ideal religious type is manifested in the religious practice of contemporary practitioners of Orisha religions.

Almost all divination sessions end with the requirement that the inquirer perform some sort of sacrificial ritual in order to invigorate or modify the current path of his or her destiny. In chapter 6 we will explore the place of sacrifice in the Santería religious complex. Sacrifice, particularly blood sacrifice, is one of the most challenging aspects of Santería ritual practice. Although santeros are more likely to sacrifice natural and manufactured items—fruit, flowers, food, cloth, liquor, candy—than living creatures, it is sacrifice in which the blood of various small animals is offered to the Orisha that catches the public's imagination. Since religious sacrifice is commonly paired with religious and nonreligious violence, I will begin chapter 6 with an exploration of some of the scholarship on religion and violence. Having analyzed religious violence in general, I will then turn specifically to Santería and its use of animal sacrifice. Santeros understand that sacrifice, the giving of natural and manufactured items to the Orisha or other spiritual beings, is essential for human well-being. Although they are often discussed according to the formulation *do ut des* (I give in order that you may give), offerings within Santería are not viewed in a purely mechanistic fashion. Rather, sacrifices of all sorts are seen as ways to solidify the relationship between a deity and the devotee so that help may be solicited and expected in times of need.

Blood sacrifices appear always to have a gender component to them as well. In most religious traditions sacrifice is solely the domain of men. In fact, Susan Sered (2002) says, "Cross-culturally, animal sacrifice is one of the most dramatically and consistently gendered ritual constellations" (13) and is "almost always a male dominated and oriented ritual activity" (15). Together with other scholars,[13] Sered suggests that sacrifice often functions in the service of patriarchal control or is somehow used to distinguish between the domain of women, which is focused on life-giving activities, and that of men, which is focused on death. Santería calls these analyses into question, since both men and women function as both sacrificer and sacrificator—that is, the person who actually performs the sacrifice and the person on whose behalf a sacrifice is offered. This chapter concludes with an analysis of the ways in which gender enters into Santería sacrificial practices.

Santería and the other African-based religions are often categorized as forms of *brujería* (Sp., witchcraft). Before we can accept or deny such categorization, we need to understand exactly what is meant by the term "witchcraft." That, however, is not a trivial task. The term has a long history in the study of European, African, and African-based societies. Even a cursory review of the literature of African and European witchcraft suggests that, in spite of their common designation, these cultural phenomena are based on fundamentally different views of the world. In chapter 7 we will explore how these different views of witchcraft have been incorporated into the Orisha-based cosmology to produce a unique view of the world and a response to the ills and misfortunes found there.

Many people come to the world of Santería and the other Orisha religions because of misfortunes in their lives. Because of the this-worldly orientation of these traditions, they promise to provide more than the cold comfort of a blissful afterlife. Although santeros generally do not attempt to cure illness better left to conventional medicine, healing rituals form an important part of many santeros' religious practice. A cosmological system that includes both visible and invisible beings and a theology that suggests that these beings can both harm and heal opens the way for a theodicy that not only explains personal misfortune but also provides healing even when a complete cure is impossible.[14]

Important to our analysis of the relationship between Santería and witchcraft are the concepts of brujería developed in Cuba during the Republican period and the relationships that have developed between Santería and the other Afro-Cuban religions of Cuba. Stephan Palmié says that Afro-Cubans developed a continuum along which the spirits of Palo Monte (another Afro-Cuban religion, based on the cosmology of the Bantu people of Central Africa) and its sister religions, the spirit guides and protectors developed in Kardecian Espiritismo,[15] the ancestral spirits invoked in Santería, and even the Orisha themselves were identified as increasingly more moral actors in the visible and invisible worlds. By suggesting that *paleros* (priests of Palo Monte) who worked with the amoral *nfumbi* developed an instrumental practice that could be juxtaposed against the expressive practices of santeros who work with the Orisha, Palmié allows us to explore the ways in which descriptions of these traditions have incorporated subtle gender attributes. Although the term "witch" is generally understood to describe a female practitioner of the "black arts" in both West African and European cultures, males can also participate in witchcraft. In chapter 7 I will explore these understandings of the workings of witchcraft, the gender implications, and the ways in which both European and African ideas of witchcraft have been incorporated into contemporary Santería.

In chapter 8 our analysis will come full circle. What began as an analysis of the category of gender within the Orisha traditions will conclude with a strong statement concerning the place of the female as the basis of Orisha practice. Throughout this book I will suggest that Santería is a female-based religion in that it valorizes female virtue and practice in such a way that the female, rather than the male, is normative, in spite of a patriarchal overlay from Spanish Cuban culture. In our concluding chapter I will pull together the various strands we have been exploring into the radical claim that, unlike many major religions and unlike its sister religions Palo Monte and Ifá, Santería is both female oriented and female normative.

CHAPTER 2 · Gender

When I first started studying the religion of the Yoruba people in the Americas and in Africa, I realized that gender designations were rather fluid in respect to both the deities and their followers. As they come to us out of Cuba, all of the Orisha are gendered beings. That is, every Orisha or Orisha path is assigned either a male or a female gender. This is not astonishing on its face. Americans (and Cubans) are used to all beings (and some or all objects) having gender assignments. We also expect these gender assignments to be more or less meaningful. However, a deeper look into the Orisha and their religion as it comes to us in Santería reveals a decidedly curious perspective—curious, at least, to contemporary American sensibilities—on gender among both the deities and their devotees.

A catalogue of some of these curiosities will perhaps whet our appetite in the exploration of these issues. First of all, although every Orisha or Orisha path is assigned a gender, several Orisha have both male and female paths.[1] When the early Afro-Cubans were setting up the correspondences between the Orisha and the Catholic saints, they were concerned about correspondences between the iconographies of the saint and the Orisha but, apparently, less concerned about keeping the gender consistent. Thus several Orisha are represented by saints of a different gender than that of their primary advocation.[2] It seems particularly interesting that female saints represent two of the major male Orisha but no female Orisha is represented by a male saint.

Priests also exhibit a form of gender mixing. When we look at the terms used to describe priests, we notice that initiates at all levels are given the title "iyawo" during the time frame of their initiation. *Iyawo* does not, as one might expect, mean "novice" or "initiate"; rather, it is a common Yoruba term meaning "wife, younger than the speaker." This implies that every initiate is gendered female during the duration of the initiation event.

In addition, every fully initiated Santería priest is crowned to a particular Orisha with whom he or she is often understood to share character and personality traits. In spite of a natural inclination, at least among Western observers, to associate male personality traits with anatomically male persons and female traits with anatomically female persons, an Orisha devotee is as likely to be crowned to a male as a female Orisha regardless of the priest's own gender (or sexual orientation).

Often, though not always, the characteristics of the ruling Orisha can be seen in their priests, so that a wise, placid individual may be associated with Obatala, while a wild man-about-town may be associated with Shango. The ruling Orisha is often spoken of in terms reminiscent of Jung's anima/animus archetype but without the cross-gender implications of Jung's theories. That is, a man is not given a female Orisha to "express his 'femininity'" nor is a woman given a male Orisha to gain access to her "recessive maleness" (terminology from Whitmont 1991, 189–90, 202). Although some researchers (for example, Palmié 2002, 345–54) suggest that gay men are more likely than straight men to be given a female Orisha, especially Yemaya or Oshun, that is not true in my experience or the experience of my informants.

Possession trance is an important part of Santería practice, and during certain rituals every priest is potentially the embodiment of his or her principal Orisha. Since there is no effort made to align the gender or sexual orientation of the priest with the gender of the Orisha when these relationships are determined, during a possession event the priest who may be male or female will exhibit the characteristic actions of the Orisha he or she is embodying. Thus male Orisha are often arrogant and combative, while female Orisha may flirt and primp regardless of the gender associated with the body they are inhabiting.

Additionally, ritual roles are dependent on initiation level rather than anatomy or gender or sexual orientation. With a couple of exceptions, all ritual roles are equally open to both men and women.[3] Although we will discuss these more completely below, the exceptions are worth noting. The best-known exceptions are the divination specialists known as *babalawo* (Yr., father of secrets) and the sacred drummers. Both manipulate sacred symbols that are understood to be female entities who do not want to be seen (in the case of the *odu* of the babalawo) or touched (in the case of *Añu*, the spirit inhabiting the sacred drum) by women. However, there are American women in training for both of these positions. A female divination priesthood, whose priests are called either *iyalawo* (mother of secrets) or *iyanifá* (mother of Ifá), parallel to the babalawo is becoming institutionalized in some religious communities. In Cuba and the United States, there is another type of divination specialist known as an *oriaté* (Yr., head of the divination mat). Oriaté are generally male, although historically there have been powerful female oriaté and there are women in training to become oriaté in the United States today. We will discuss these divination priesthoods and their impact on Santería practices in chapter 3.

The final example of a ritual role with a gender component is involved with animal sacrifice. Although both men and women priests are entitled to sacrifice the birds and other small animals classified as "feathers" and both men and women can receive the initiation known as *cuchillo* (Sp., knife) entitling them to use a knife to sacrifice the larger animals, premenopausal women generally do not use a knife in sacrificial rituals at all and postmenopausal women do not perform such sacrifices if a qualified male is available. We will discuss gender and sacrificial ritual in chapter 4.[4]

Little has been written about these seeming gender anomalies, which often amaze newcomers to the religion but become naturalized into the unconscious of Orisha devotees and cease to be points of interest. However, it appears that the Orisha and their followers can slip between gender roles, at least during periods of religious practice, in ways that confound contemporary American understandings of gender and gender roles. This leads to the question "What does 'gender' mean in such a fluid environment?"

Gender as Analytic Tool

The term "gender," of course, is itself slippery and problematic. However, even these short descriptions show how Orisha religious practice challenges what Harold Garfinkel calls the "natural attitude" toward gender. Included within this attitude are the ideas that there are only two genders, that gender identity is invariant, that the genitals are the essential sign of gender, that male/female gender dichotomy is natural, and that any deviation from these propositions is either a joke or a pathology (Garfinkel 1967, chap. 5, esp. 122–28). Both Yoruba culture and the religions it has engendered call this attitude into question.

In a 1997 essay in the feminist journal *Signs*, Mary Hawkesworth suggests that gender can be used as an analytical tool to illustrate certain critical cultural processes including individual gendering (how individual identity is constructed so as to correlate with sexual characteristics), the creation of gender structures (how gender dualisms are used to organize social activities), and the use of gender symbolism (how gender metaphors are used to categorize other types of dichotomies) (653). She says that scholars have developed a terminology of gender that distinguishes between such concepts as sex, sexuality, sexual identity, gender identity, gender role, and gender-role identity in order to challenge Garfinkel's natural attitude (656). Although all of the scholars Hawkesworth analyzes attempt to develop gender as an analytical tool, most return to the natural attitude in that they link gender to what she calls the "cunning of culture operating in the interest of reproduction" (680). That is, all of these scholars revert to an ideology of gender that assumes a functional basis of gendering grounded in biology and reproduction.

Scholars generally try to distinguish between sex and gender by suggesting that "sex" is biologically determined on the basis of one's physical features, including primary and secondary reproductive organs and, increasingly, one's chromosomes, while "gender" refers to the socially constructed behaviors assigned to persons based on their anatomy. Although we commonly speak as though there are only two sexes, male and female, a small percentage of the human population, including children born with ambiguous genitalia, do not fit neatly within this generally understood binary classification. And although gender is thought to map nicely onto sex as the socially determined characteristics of persons with certain anatomical features—those with male genitalia being classified as "men" and those with female genitalia as "women"—it is possible for societies to provide additional gender roles. For example, among certain Native American groups a person with male genitalia who assumes the dress and behaviors of a woman is considered as belonging to a third gender commonly referred to as "berdache."

Gender was originally a linguistic term used to describe classes of nouns that affect the behavior of words associated with them—that is, depending on the language, adjectives, verbs, adverbs, numerals, or even conjunctions must "agree with" their associated nouns. Thus, as Hawkesworth suggests, we might consider the ways in which gender describes how "categories of persons [are] constituted in and through the behavior of associated others." Although it is possible in both the linguistic and the cultural arena to have more than two genders, the concept can be described only in relational terms—by juxtaposing two or more concepts like masculine/feminine, male/female/nonsexed, human/animal/other, strong/weak (658).

It is possible to understand gender as a performance, a "'doing' that constitutes the identity it purports to be" (Butler 1990, 24, cited in Hawkesworth 1997, 663) or a "weaving of a structure of symbols" (Connell 1987, 79, cited in Hawkesworth 1997, 669). Since sexual characteristics are often hidden or disguised by clothing, and there is a general supposition that gender and sex correlate, it is common to make assumptions about people's anatomical sex based on their gender attributes. Suzanne Kessler and Wendy McKenna (1978, cited in Hawkesworth 1997, 669) identify these clothing and other gender attributes as "cultural genitals." We all use cultural genitals including such things as dress, hairstyle, and body language to categorize new people, and we find it disconcerting when our categorization goes astray. The use of cultural genitals to misinform observers highlights the constructed nature and the performance aspect of gender. Because gender is constructed, individuals can take on an "inappropriate" gender. European literature is full of stories of persons, generally anatomical females, who changed their cultural genitals in order to be accepted as belonging to a different gender, some so successfully that the fabrication was discovered only upon their death.[5] Contemporary cross-dressers are most commonly anatomical males who have assumed the cultural genitals of women. Cross-dressers study the ways in which their target gender is constructed and consider themselves successful when they are able to completely preclude recognition.[6] In the same way that other types of disguises can be complete or partial, gender-crossing can also be more or less comprehensive. Since the natural attitude posits a sexual dimorphism, there is a "natural" tendency not only to instantaneously assign a gender classification to everyone we meet but also to force everyone into one of the two stereotypical genders even if that means ignoring anomalous details (Hawkesworth 1997, 675, 676).

Many scholars have explored ideas of gender ambiguity. As William Parsons (1997) suggests, scholars of religion have often focused on the life of the Indian mystic Sri Ramakrishna to explicate gender ambiguity within a religious context. He says that their analysis of Ramakrishna's cross-dressing and other homoerotic behavior can most simply be described according to one of three formulas: (1) Ramakrishna is a "happy pervert" whose female clothing and other behaviors are the result of gender confusion; (2) Ramakrishna's appropriation of female attire is a way to develop his own "female element and allows him to experience his own 'femininity'"; or (3) Ramakrishna uses female clothing to reject a secular view of life "while emphasizing the ascendancy of *lila* (divine play) and the world as a 'mansion of fun.'" From another point of view, J. Lorand Matory (1994) begins his analysis of gender ambiguity in the Yoruba cross-dressing tradition by stating that ethnographic and cultural studies often suggest that transvestitism and transsexualism either reinforce the existing binary classificatory schemes and gender hierarchies or call attention to their "constructed" nature. However, within the Orisha-based ritual context, gender ambiguities do not seem to be the result of gender confusion, a search for femininity, or an effort at spiritual play. Neither do they seem to result in either the reinforcing or the calling into question of binary gender schema. It seems as though we need some other analytical lens through which to view these phenomena.

Gender as Prestige Structure

The historian Joan Scott has devised a two-part definition of gender that many scholars have found useful. First, she says, gender is "a constitutive element of social relationships based on perceived differences between the sexes" and, second, it is "a primary way of signifying relationships of power" (Scott 1986, 1067). In their classic book *Sexual Meanings: The Cultural Construction of Gender and Sexuality* (1981), Sherry Ortner and Harriet Whitehead suggest that in the majority of cultures the differences between men and women are conceptualized in terms of a set of metaphorically binary oppositions. These oppositions include nature/culture, self-interest/social good, and domestic/public. According to their thesis, women are associated with nature, while men are aligned with culture. Women are seen as tending to private and particularistic concerns, while men have a more universalist orientation; that is, women are mainly concerned with the well-being of themselves and their children, while men are more concerned with the welfare of the social whole. This leads to the idea that men control the "public domain," while women are confined to the "domestic domain" (7). They say further that the "sphere of social activity predominantly associated with males encompasses the sphere predominantly associated with females and is, for that reason, culturally accorded higher value" (7–8). They go on to argue that prestige structures show the ways in which gender symbolism is used to describe other types of interpersonal relationships. Prestige structures shape the ways a society evaluates individuals, and the social organization of prestige directly affects cultural notions of gender and sexuality. The fact that the gender system is a prestige structure means that the same concepts used to distinguish men and women in social worth are used to distinguish other social types as well as individuals within the same gender. This also means that prestige positions outside the gender realm are often rendered in gendered terms (16–17). Joan Scott says the same thing when she suggests (1986, 1067) that, because gender provides an array of culturally available symbols that can evoke a multitude of representations, gendered symbolism has often been used to express complex interpersonal connections even when those connections have no sexual connotations. Scott points to, for example, political relationships in which gendered symbolism is used to distinguish between the ruler and the ruled, nations and their colonial subjects, or members of one ethic group and another.[7]

However, since gender is, as Scott has suggested, one of the primary ways we signify relationships of power, it is also possible for individuals to appropriate some of the attributes of the gender of those whose place in the power relationship they want to emulate. Thus members of other groups can use the cultural genitals of the powerful to signify power. For example, American women (and minorities) who have moved into positions of power formerly limited to white men often appropriate their masculine power symbols as markers of their own positions. The American fashion industry, in its promotion of fashions for professional women, is constantly trying to negotiate ideas of dress as gender marker oscillating between "femininity" (bits of lace, stiletto heels), which conjures up one type of gendering, and "power" (tailored suits, sensible shoes), which invokes another. Without engaging in complete gender-crossing one can use generally understood gender symbolism to take on the attributes and enjoy the cultural prestige of the members of the preferred group.

The Nature of "Woman"

Along with an analysis of the natural attitude toward gender, contemporary feminist theory has developed two important, but contradictory, viewpoints about the nature of gender and sexual roles in both Western and non-Western cultures. The first is that the categories "male" and "female" are essential features of humanity from which we can extract certain commonalties; the second suggests that all experiences of gender and sexuality are cultural constructs and as such are open to change and reconstruction. This has become known as the essentialist/constructionist debate.[8] Some scholars suggest that there is an intrinsic and universal female (or male) self that is described by the term "woman" (or "man"). They suggest that there are intrinsic and universal characteristics associated with female (and male) anatomy that are found across cultural boundaries and that these characteristics have been used in all known cultures to limit the choices of women to those roles that dovetail with their responsibilities as mothers, caretakers, and nurturers while expanding the choices of men toward roles of power and control. Although characteristics included as part of the essential nature of "women" (and "men") have been expanded in modern times, many feminists continue to attempt to discover and describe the essence associated with the female (or male) body. While it could be argued that essentialists are merely promulgating the natural attitude, what they are doing is actually subtler than that. What they are suggesting is that the combination of one's physical characteristics provides a frame within which one's life is lived. Differences in hormonal levels, interior and exterior genitalia, and the like form a base on which one's gender, sexuality, and other characteristics can be built.

Constructionists, on the other hand, suggest that the role of "woman" (and "man"), like all social roles, is produced at the intersection between the individual and the cultural milieu. According to this viewpoint, simply living in a female (or male) body is not enough to make one a woman (or a man). One's gender identification is constructed through the interplay of social and historical circumstances. Especially important in this constructive activity is the role of the abstract concepts embedded in language and the culture in the formation of the social categories of "woman" and "man." Whether one is seen as a man or a woman depends, in this view, on the ways these terms are constructed by one's society. As social constructs and linguistic terms, they are subject to redefinition as the social values of the society change. Thus characteristics that are defined as "manly" in one time and place may be defined as "womanly" in another. Rather than an absolute or physical attribute, gender is constructed according to certain cultural concepts and abstract notions.

Both of these positions draw strongly on people's lived experience. On the one hand, we each feel as though there is some portion of our selves that is foundational, essential, and that our lived experience as beings with certain anatomical features is part of that essential self. On the other hand, the constructionist position provides us with insights into the ways in which our views of others and ourselves are formed by the society into which we happened to have been born. Particularly when we study societies in which femininity and masculinity are constructed differently, we begin to see how we have been taught to act and react in certain gender-appropriate ways. And even though we may rebel against that teaching, these cultural norms continue to haunt our understanding of ourselves.

Anne Klein (1994) argues that the tendency of these two positions to valorize either personal experience (the body) or the abstract world of language and culture (the mind) replicates the Western cultural tendency to bifurcate one into a body and a mind. She says that both of these theories threaten the "individual," either by favoring the general to the detriment of the particular or, conversely, favoring the particular and losing the general. Each theory depends to a certain extent on the other; neither can exist in the other's absence. The challenge of contemporary feminist thought is finding a place "between the two" (9), a way of framing the debate to include a synthesis of the two positions, an answer to the question "how can we suggest a female sense of self that is neither overly essentialized nor so contingently constructed that its existence is in question?" (9–10).

In Mark Taylor's *Critical Terms for Religious Studies* (1998), Daniel Boyarin approaches the subject of gender in the study of religion not through the lens of feminist theory but by exploring the ways in which the category "woman" has been explicated in two religious traditions. Focusing on the creation of humanity in the book of Genesis, he looks at the way early Christian and rabbinic thinkers used this text to formulate their ideas of personhood, gender, and religious and cultural ideals. Using the work of Philo, one of the foundational thinkers of the version of Judaism that became Christianity, he argues that Christianity developed a view of humanity that juxtaposed the spiritual to the physical. In this view the "earth-creature" created in the image of God in Genesis 1:27–28 and 5:1–2[9] is different from and superior to the earth-creature formed from the dust of the earth in Genesis 2.[10] Philo sees the first Adam as a purely spiritual being who is noncorporeal and "both male and female"—that is, without gender. The second Adam, created from the dust of the earth, is physical, carnal. This Adam needs a helpmate, so God engages in a third act of creation, drawing the first woman from the rib of Adam. Philo thus sees two "races" of man, one spiritual and made after the Divine Image, the other material and molded out of earth stuff. It is from this second man that wo-man is formed as a subsequent creation. It is only through the creation of woman that gender is created. Thus for Philo and those who followed him, the spiritual is ontologically privileged. The "true self," the spiritual self, exists *before* the creation of gender (117–20).

In this view, because it is corporeality that separates a person from this true self, both men and women could approach the spiritual through the renunciation of the physical. For women this meant renouncing that which made them specifically female: sexuality and childbearing. It follows that the category "woman" was formed only in relationship to the material conditions of marriage and childbearing. Thus virgins, free of the constraints of marriage, could attain the status of spirituality that is "neither male nor female." In the early church, virgins were seen as androgynes, representations of purely spiritual, nongendered, presocial human beings (124). But as Boyarin says, virgins, although like Adam "neither male nor female," were not completely without gender: through her acceptance of "celibacy the female could cease to be a woman and become a man" (125). Just as the deity was gendered male, so too the normative "transcendent androgyne is [also] male" (122). Thus when a female renounced her womanly nature she became a manly woman, a virtual man. Using our feminist vocabulary, this is a constructionist reading of the Creation, which proposes that gender was constructed along with the construction of carnal bodies. By renouncing the body one can be reconstructed on the spiritual plane, as a transcendent being, a being like God who is always already male.

In the early rabbinic literature, however, the story of the Creation was read differently. The dominant rabbinic interpretation of Genesis saw in the first creation story the creation of a fully sexed hermaphrodite who, in the latter account, is separated in the manner of conjoined twins. Similar to the tale told in Plato's *Symposium*, this account saw the primordial Adam as having the genitals of both sexes in a single body, thus "both male and female." When that body is later split in two, man and woman emerge simultaneously. In this account there is no secondary creation of woman, no separation between the material and the spiritual. Here humanity is marked by sexual difference from the beginning, and the twoness of humanity is essential, from God, so to speak (128–29). However, even though rabbinic Judaism managed to resist the essentialist dualism of Western philosophy that associated the spirit with the masculine and the body with the feminine, it still prescribed women's roles in oppressive ways and failed to provide a method by which women could transcend femininity and participate in the physical, intellectual, and spiritual realms set aside for men (128–32).

Boyarin suggests that the essentialist/constructionist debate continues to problematize gender studies. On the essentialist side, women become locked into certain roles based on their biology, while constructionism—which he characterizes as transcendence—is always predicated on the denigration of the body and invokes a normative male-modeled androgyny. He suggests that these two theoretical positions form a dialectic for which a third term, a Hegelian synthesis, has yet to appear (132–33). Perhaps looking at the Yoruba sense of the world and the way that world-sense is embodied in contemporary understandings of the Orisha will offer an alternative position and the synthesis he is looking for.

Difference without a Distinction

In her 1997 book *Invention of Women*, Oyèrónké̩ Oyewùmí, herself a Yoruba woman, argued that "there were no *women*—defined in strictly gendered terms—in [traditional Yoruba] society," that "the concept 'woman' as it is used and as it is invoked in the scholarship is derived from Western experience and history," and that it has been inappropriately applied to Yoruba society (xiii). Looking specifically at the traditional religion, she says that anatomical "distinctions did not play any part, whether in the world of humans or that of the gods," that gender was not a category, and the roles of Orisha, priests, and ancestors were not gender dependent. Specifically she cites four examples of gender independence in Yoruba religion: (1) Olodumare, the great god, had no gender identity; (2) although the Orisha, the focus of Yoruba religious worship, were both male and female, "this distinction was inconsequential . . . best described as a distinction without difference," since male and female Orisha could have similar attributes and the gender of the Orisha was rather fluid, with an Orisha sometimes being gendered male in one location and female in another; (3) both male and female ancestors were venerated and acknowledged in the Egungun masquerade; and finally (4) the priesthood of the various gods was open to both males and females (140).

Focusing on language usage and social custom, Oyewùmí argues that relative age rather than body type forms the basis for the hierarchical organization among the Yoruba. Impressed by Oyewùmí's argument, we can begin to explore the gender anomalies in Yoruba religion on both sides of the Atlantic with the Yoruba "world-sense" she suggests rather than the Western "worldview." Focusing on her statement that the gender assigned to the Orisha was a distinction without a difference, we can begin with the question of why the

Orisha were gendered at all. It is generally understood that Olodumare, the great god, is perceived as above, beyond, and without gender (140), so it seems possible that the Yoruba could have conceived of the Orisha, the ministers of Olodumare, as also ungendered. Because the Yoruba language is ungendered and without gendered pronouns, it would certainly be possible to speak (and conceivably think) of the Orisha in nongendered terms. However, exactly the opposite is the case. All of the Orisha have at least one gender and many have both male and female variants that appear to have different characteristics in their male and female forms. Significantly, although there are many different lists of Orisha (the actual number of Orisha appears to be infinite), in all of the lists that I am familiar with, the preponderance of the Orisha are gendered male. This suggests a male-normative system and leads to the question, What is it about those Orisha that are gendered female that makes them different from the other members of the pantheon?

Oyewùmí suggests that the only time the Yoruba distinguish between anatomical males and anatomical females is in respect to reproduction; the terms *okùnrin* and *obìnrin*, which are generally translated "male" and "female," are used only when issues of procreation and intercourse are being discussed and they indicate only those physiological differences, not differences of social privilege (32–33). Actually, she suggests, the distinctions signified by these terms are superficial in that the terms are "not elaborated in relation and opposition to each other, they are not sexually dimorphic and therefore are not gendered." Referring back to the precolonial period, she says that these terms did not connote social ranking or express notions of masculinity or femininity, since these "categories did not exist in Yoruba life or thought." In sum, the difference between okùnrin and obìnrin, between anatomical males and females, is a distinction that makes a difference only within the realm of reproduction and does not extend beyond these issues (33–36).

We might expect, then, that those Orisha gendered female are those most involved with issues of reproduction, either as givers of children to barren women or as producers of children of their own within the mythological corpus. We are disappointed on the first point, as Oyewùmí correctly states that both male and female Orisha are "specifically worshipped for their ability to give [their followers] children" (116). The second point, the place of female Orisha as childbearers, is more complicated.

At first glance, it appears that what distinguishes the female Orisha from their male counterparts is their participation in women's reproductive activity. Female Orisha are generally numbered among "the mothers," and even Oya, whom Oyewùmí highlights as a "wrathful" warrior, has among her praise names "mother of nine," alluding not only to the relationship between her river (the Niger) and its tributaries but also to a divination story in which as a barren woman she petitioned for children and was able to birth nine off-spring.[11] But not all of the female Orisha are known for their childbearing. Several, including the Olokun worshipped in Ile-Ife and at least one advocation of Yemaya in the Americas, are described as childless (Abogunrin 1989, 277; H. Drewal 1997, 39; Ogun Tolle, personal communication, 1999). And even for those Orisha strongly associated with motherhood there is little in the mythology that specifically alludes to their child-raising duties. In fact, the majority of the divination stories are focused on the adult-adult relationships of all the Orisha.

Perhaps some Orisha are gendered female in order to provide models for women's roles as wives and mothers.[12] On the one hand, the stories of the female Orisha can be used to support the traditional roles of wife and mother among their female devotees; on the other hand, they provide a myriad of alternatives for those who find these roles constricting or who need a different type of personal power. Many stories of female Orisha valorize the essential female activity of reproduction. Both in the mythology and in the practice of the religion the "female" virtues of "coolness," calm, devotion, and caretaking as exemplified by the maternal role are emphasized, particularly for those who identify with these Orisha. Yet none of the female Orisha are merely or only mothers. Individually and as a group they offer a wide range of additional roles for women. Yemaya dyes cloth, farms, and goes to war with her husband; Oya is known as a warrior but she also runs the marketplace and manages the spirits of the dead; Oshun divines, sews, works with her husband at the forge, and manages those forces called the *aje* or sometimes "our mothers," the witches; Obba, best known as the jealous wife, is also credited with inventing navigation and commerce and is said to be a superb warrior who taught her husband Shango the use of the sword and cutlass. Each of these Orisha has been constructed to provide more than a maternal role model, and the various stories show the ways each constructed herself to meet a particular range of needs.

Using female Orisha as marital role models is particularly problematic. Judging from the Yoruba mythological record, marriage is not a very important relationship among the Orisha. Although just about every Orisha has a marital relationship with every Orisha of the opposite gender, marriage as an institution seems to have little value in the mythological corpus. The Orisha join together casually and part from their partners just as casually. Since both male and female Orisha maintain their own compounds, a male is as likely to move to the compound of his female partner as she is to move to his, in complete disregard for marriage practices among the Yoruba people themselves. Unlike marriages between actual men and women, which are generally unbalanced in that the male partner is older, often much older, than the female partner, liaisons between Orisha are unions of equals, with little hierarchical differentiation within Orisha pairs. Thus sexual relationships among the Orisha seem to be much more egalitarian than among their devotees.

And women are not limited to these female Orisha for role models. Because the Orisha as archetypes are gendered but not gender-specific, any Orisha can serve as a role model for any devotee. As we shall see in chapter 6, priests are assigned to the Orisha without regard to their own or the Orisha's gender. Because of the assumed correspondence between priest and Orisha, priests often take on or emphasize the characteristics associated with their Orisha in their personal behavior regardless of the gender role normally associated with that behavior. In addition, a devotee might invoke any of the Orisha to justify or embody the stereotypical characteristics of that Orisha. Thus one might invoke Shango's nature as the champion of justice and fair play as one is attempting to fight for one's own or another's rights.

Women in Traditional Thought

Although her analysis of traditional religion is accurate as far as it goes, Oyewùmí's descriptions seem to have ignored facts that suggest that among the Yoruba certain characteristics are attributed to women particularly in their roles as mothers and that these characteristics have an important place in the understanding of traditional religion in Africa and among Orisha worshippers in the Americas.[13] Several scholars of Yoruba traditional religion have suggested that women and the female body shape are important in Yoruba religious thought. As Rowland Abiodun suggests (2001, 15), "there may have existed [an] ancient set of female-related attributes" that form the core attributes of the female Orisha and the place of the female body in traditional Yoruba religion.

Among the Yoruba many religious accouterments have an identifiable female shape or include an actual female figure. Often this figure is of a woman, nude, kneeling holding her breasts or in the position known as *ikunle abiyamo* (Yr., the kneeling posture of a woman in labor). This posture is considered the most effective for approaching the Orisha because it is sacred and exemplifies a woman's ability to honor, soothe, and cool the deities so that they will be most beneficent to their devotees (Abiodun 1989, 111–13). The kneeling woman also represents the ideal devotee, kneeling in worship, soothing the deities, and speaking with the power of their ashé. It is only through the ritual actions of Orisha devotees, the majority of whom are women, that the worship of the Orisha can be maintained and continued. That these female images are naked is also significant. Although adult nakedness is generally considered inappropriate among the Yoruba, according to Rowland Abiodun (2001, 26–27) a woman's nakedness is believed to give her utterances additional clout in both the visible and invisible worlds, so much so that "a Yoruba man will be quite disturbed if his wife threatens to undress during a disagreement," as this would give her word "causative power." Thus we can suggest that the female body, particularly in its most exposed form, serves as a metonym of women's childbearing function and extraordinary powers. In addition, since reproduction may also represent characteristics attributed to women and to women's generalized power, these religious images and ideas display the deeply religious significance of reproduction (Ogungbile 2001, 195). At another level, it appears that the female represents the ideal religious type. That is, since the ideal devotee is represented by the female in a physical position particular to women, one approaches that ideal through an identification with these female attributes. At the same time, there is no understanding in Yoruba cosmology that bodies, particularly women's bodies, are inferior, dirty, or unspiritual. In fact, as we have seen, although nakedness is generally considered inappropriate, even contemporary Yoruba believe that a naked woman possesses particularly powerful ashé.

Often the more prominent way power is expressed is in terms of men's power over women, and there are certainly instances of such power inequality among the Yoruba. However, as Oyewùmí suggests, power dynamics among the Yoruba are primarily based on seniority rather than body type, so one's place in any hierarchy is largely independent of whether the other members of the hierarchy are male or female. Nonetheless, there is also an understanding that women as a group have access to a particular type of power that is different from the powers available to men.

One of the best-known stories in the Ifá divination corpus tells of when the first Orisha, characterized in some versions of this story as the sixteen Odu, were coming from heaven to earth to prepare it for habitation by both their fellow Orisha and human beings. Along with the sixteen presumably all-male Orisha was a seventeenth, the female Oshun. A home—that is, a place of power—was prepared for each of the sixteen other Orisha, but no provision was made for Oshun. Rather than demanding her rights as one among equals, she sat quietly and watched to see what would happen. As the sixteen began their work, ignoring the woman who was plaiting her hair and admiring herself in her mirror, they discovered that their labor was coming to naught. What they built fell down; what they planted died; nothing was successful. Finally they returned to heaven to consult with Olodumare, who surely would not have commissioned them to form the earth without giving them the means to succeed. When the sixteen appeared before Olodumare to describe their troubles, the great god asked about their companion, the seventeenth Orisha, Oshun. Then they realized that Olodumare had made Oshun the keeper of all good things, the one with the power of success and failure, the one from whom all the Odu were derived. Only when they returned to earth to pacify and appease Oshun could the work of creation proceed and prosper (Abiodun 2001, 16–18; Bádéjo 1996, 2–3).

In his analysis of this story, Abiodun suggests that Oshun's female nature must have special significance for her ability to obstruct the work of all the other sixteen Orisha. Here the power of a single person explicitly described as female is sufficient to overturn the power of sixteen presumably male beings. Abiodun suggests that the "ashé of the female Orisha is inherently different from" and "perhaps even antagonistic" to that of the male Orisha (18). He also suggests that men are ambivalent toward women's power because women of all ages are assumed to possess aje, which he translates as "bird power." He says that the power of the aje, like Oshun's power in the story, is the power to aid or hinder, the power "that enables women to accomplish whatever they wish" (18–19, 11).

The female Orisha represent another way in which power is attributed to beings with female bodies. These female Orisha are often called "queens" in the literature, in parallel with the many Orisha that are "kings" or rulers of particular towns or regions. The Yoruba oba is the term generally translated "king" and used to describe both human and divine rulers. One Orisha, Obatala, even carries his kingly nature in his name, which translates as "king of white cloth." In parallel with designating Obatala and other royal Orisha as kings, is it common to designate female Orisha such as Yemaya, Oshun, Obba, and Oya as queens. The English word "queen" has two distinct meanings: the wife of a king or a female sovereign in her own right. These two different types of queens represent different levels of power. As a female sovereign, the queen is the most powerful member of her society, with the same rights and responsibilities to rule as a male counterpart. However, the person who wears her queenly title as the consort of the king, while powerful with the reflected status of her husband, has only a ceremonial role with no imperial rights. Consequently we need to distinguish between Queen Elizabeth II, the current monarch of England, and her mother, the wife of King George VI, who could never have ascended to the throne.

However, here again we are confounded by Yoruba social structure. Because Yoruba is a nongendered language, there is no word in Yoruba for "queen" in either sense of the English word. Rather the Yoruba have a single word, *oba*, for a sovereign, whether male or female. Because the Yoruba are polygamous, a male sovereign could have many wives, *aya*. However, all of the palace women, including his own wives, the wives of the previous oba, the current oba's birth or adopted mother, and the mother of the previous oba if still alive, were called *ayaba*—the palace women or, literally, wives of the king. These women were very powerful and often served as the domestic ministers of the oba, but no single one of them could be called the queen according to our understanding (Johnson 1921, 63–67; Bascom 1969, 29–41, 49–54; Oyewùmí 1997). Any female ruler would also have many of these kinds of women in her entourage, but none of them would be her queen either.

Similarly, although every female deity has one or more consorts, she does not gain her power from them. Female Orisha are deities in their own right, not because of relationships with male deities. In many cases, female Orisha are rulers in their own right as well; for example, Oya is the ruler of Ira, and Oshun is the owner/ruler of Oshobo. They are always queens in the first sense of the English word (monarchs) and never in the second (consorts of a king).

Priesthood as Successive Gendering

Oyewùmí also says (1997, 140) that the gender independence of traditional Yoruba religion can be found in the fact that the priesthood of the various gods was open to both males and females. Setting aside for a moment the sweeping overgeneralization of such a statement, the place of actual human beings in the religious system may provide additional ways to deconstruct our own ideas of gender and religion. However, before we can deconstruct priestly titles and relationships, we need to make a short excursus into the world of Yoruba familial relationships.

The typical Yoruba household in the precolonial period consisted of a compound that housed a group of people who claimed descent from a common ancestor. Members of this lineage group, the *omo-ile* or "children of the house," were ranked according to their birth order. Since residency was generally patrilocal, upon her marriage a woman usually moved into the compound of her partner, leaving behind her birth compound. Such incoming women, the *aya-ile*, were ranked according to their marriage date rather than their birth date. Individually all omo-ile were ranked higher than all in-marrying aya-ile regardless of age. Although the term *oko* is normally translated "husband," as a group the omo-ile regardless of anatomical sex are oko relative to the in-marrying women. Thus Oyewùmí suggests that "insider/owner of the house" would be a better translation of *oko* than "husband," since "insider/owner" doesn't carry any gendered connotations; likewise, "outsider/nonowner" would be a better translation of *aya* than "wife," since it describes the status of these in-marrying women in their conjugal household (44; see also Bascom 1969, 49–54). It is also important to realize that when a woman marries she does not lose her rights as a child of her birth compound. While she is aya to all the siblings, male and female, of her conjugal partner, she remains oko to all the conjugal partners of her brothers.

Thus, according to Oyewùmí, there is no understanding of an essential female (or male) nature among the Yoruba even in matters of marriage relationships. In the same way that one can simultaneously be a mother and a child, a Yoruba woman can be at once a husband (oko) and a wife (aya). Rather than constructing roles relative to others in the community according to anatomy, the Yoruba construct these roles according to constantly changing interpersonal relations and a hierarchy of seniority.

Viewed as a power relationship, any iyawo or new in-marrying woman is conceptually younger and less powerful than any of the "husbands" in her new compound regardless of their chronological age or social status. It is only after the woman bears children, thereby bringing new insiders to the household, that she gains (indirect) power through them. Thus older women may have considerable power in a household, both by being senior to later in-marrying women and by being the mothers of the children of the household, especially as their husbands die and their children gain control of the compound.

It is important to note, however, that by focusing on the experience of women, Oyewùmí misses an important distinction between male and female children: the male child generally is born, lives, and dies in the same household, while the female child leaves her natal household to provide reproductive services for another household. A woman lives in two different worlds, that of her natal family and that of her marital family. Men can only be "insiders," while women can be "insiders" and "outsiders" simultaneously. If a man should move to the compound of his conjugal partner, he would not become aya relative to his wife's family but rather would maintain his status as an in-law. In terms of familial relationships, the anatomical male lives within a single hierarchy, that of his birth family, while the female experiences two, the hierarchies of her birth family and of the family she joins upon marriage.

That Orisha priests on both sides of the Atlantic are given the title "iyawo" in the course of their priestly initiations invokes all of these connotations in respect to the "household" of the Orisha. As the more powerful member of the deity-priest dyad, the Orisha, whatever its gender attributes, is oko/insider relative to the priest, who is always iyawo/outsider. Not only is the initiate, regardless of anatomical sex, placed in the position of a new wife relative to his Orisha; he is also subordinate to all of those who have gone before him into the service of the Orisha. In terms of power and authority, all priests are female relative to the Orisha and are both male and female relative to the other priests of the community, depending on their tenure in the religion.

Within Santería this insider/outsider terminology becomes even more complex, as all Santería practitioners experience a mix of Oyewùmí's insider and outsider status relative to the Orisha. Although all devotees are considered *omo*, children of the Orisha, a new priest is designated as *iyawo* and an older priest who initiated others ("birthed" new Orisha) is known as *babalosha*, father of Orisha, or *iyalosha*, mother of Orisha, depending on his or her anatomical sex. Drawing on Oyewùmí's description of the multiple roles of women in traditional Yoruba society, we can suggest that, just as a Yoruba woman can be both an insider in her family compound and an outsider in the compound of her conjugal partner, a santero can be both *omo-Orisha* and *iyawo-Orisha* simultaneously. It is also interesting to note that, although all initiations of santeros require two priest sponsors because "reproduction always requires two," the anatomical or religious genders of the two priests are inconsequential. That is, any two priests, regardless of their own or their Orisha's genders, may sponsor a new initiate.[14]

However, the relative power relationships are inverted from those suggested by Oyewùmí. Omo-Orisha that have not been initiated into the priesthood, although they are insiders according to Oyewùmí's analysis, are always hierarchically below initiated priests, so that the "youngest" iyawo (an outsider, according to Oyewùmí) is always considered superior to all of the uninitiated devotees regardless of their chronological age or length of time as a devotee. It may also be significant that these terms become more gendered as one advances within the religion. From a Yoruba point of view, an omo-

Orisha is not gendered in any significant way. The term just means "child of the Orisha" and carries no gender connotation. On initiation into the priesthood, the devotee takes on the title of iyawo and is placed in the position of an anatomical female relative to all the members of her conjugal household. In the religious milieu, this is movement from an undifferentiated state to one with some gendered connotations. The priest who has matured and begun to initiate others into the religion can then take the title "iyalosha" or "babalosha," regaining her or his reproductive gender based on anatomical sex and becoming a fully adult member of the Orisha household as the mother or father of new Orisha initiates. The priest even gains some power over the Orisha, as it is the iyalosha or babalosha who decides whether or not to initiate new devotees and consequently whether or not to "birth" new Orisha. Thus even the Orisha are dependent on these priests for the continuation of their worship.

As one gains gendered designations, one becomes a more powerful member of the devotional community; as one becomes a more powerful member of the devotional community, one gains (or regains) one's anatomical gender designation. All of these designations, of course, are based on Garfinkel's "natural attitude" in that the title of iyalosha or babalosha is dependent solely on anatomical sex rather than on any gender or sexual orientation that may deviate from that standard.

Significantly, among the Yoruba a newly married iyawo has the lowest status in her husband's household, since she is considered younger than even the youngest child. By calling new priests iyawo, Orisha worshippers are subjecting them to the status loss experienced by every new bride. However, both males and females ultimately gain status within the community when they become the brides of the Orisha—that is, when they take on a female gender relative to the deity. In contradistinction to other religious and cultural forms, which require anatomical females to renounce their feminine nature in order to gain religious and spiritual status, within the Orisha-worshipping community men must take on female-identified roles in order to become priests and raise their status. By becoming wives of a deity, both male and female priests are accorded higher status than nonpriestly members of the religious community. Thus, taking on a wifely gender designation increases rather than decreases a man's prestige. Although it is dependent upon his relationship with his Orisha husband, his position as the embodied representative of a powerful being gives the priest both status and its corresponding power.

Conclusion

Unlike Oyewùmí, who says that there was no idea of gender among the Yoruba in the precolonial period, I would advance the less absolute but still challenging idea that, within Orisha religion, gender is a weak category that provides a model for certain kinds of relationships based on a fluid concept of gender construction. Both Yoruba culture and the religions it has produced call Garfinkel's natural attitude toward gender into question while refusing to challenge its basis directly. That this gender fluidity continues, however covertly, among contemporary practitioners of Orisha religion in the Americas, who include both those who have a sophisticated understanding of contemporary theories of gender and sexuality and those who portray an aversion to all examples of gender ambiguity outside the ritual context, suggests the strength of its force within the religious environment. However, within contemporary Orisha religions this gender fluidity is embedded within a rigid hierarchical scheme. Paralleling Oyewùmí's description of Yoruba culture as primarily based on seniority rather than gender, prestige within Orisha religions is also built on a structure of hierarchical relationships. Santería is not an egalitarian religion; rather, all relationships are based on a system of spiritual age-grading that is independent of gender, physical age, or other characteristics. Everyone involved in the religion is deeply embedded in this hierarchical system, in respect not only to the deities but also to every other practitioner. As I have suggested elsewhere (Clark 2003a), it is these relationships that American practitioners find most difficult. Perhaps because they lack a deep understanding of the metaphoric fluidity behind that hierarchy, their participation in this religion often challenges their ideas of power and the role power plays in human relationships.

The analysis in this book will follow Scott's definition of gender described above by first looking at the ways in which gender is used as a constitutive element of social relationships and then looking at how gender is used to signify relationships of power. In the remainder of this book we will be exploring contemporary Santería practices with an eye to the ways in which they both challenge and buttress our ideas of gender and gender symbolism. On the one hand we will keep in mind these scholarly understandings of sex, gender, and gender roles, while on the other hand we need to also keep in mind that practitioners of Orisha religions both in the contemporary environment and historically have an unsophisticated understanding of the terms sex and gender that harks back to Garfinkel's natural attitude. According to this viewpoint, the term "gender" represents those roles and characteristics assigned to members of society on the basis of their anatomy and their place within the biology of reproduction, such that femaleness/femininity is reserved for those who can become pregnant and bear children, while maleness/masculinity is reserved for those whose role in reproduction is as the maker and bearer of sperm. In spite of this invocation of the natural attitude, the religion is permeated with gender ambiguity. Reconciling these two aspects of the religion will be part of our challenge.

CHAPTER 3 · Destiny and Divination

Once upon a time, the storytellers say, an oracle warned a Greek king that his newborn son presented a danger to both himself and his throne. Wishing to save himself and protect his kingdom, he gave the child to a shepherd to expose on a nearby mountain. Taking pity on the boy, the shepherd gave him to a fellow shepherd, who gave him to a childless king, who raised him as his own. When the child became a man, he consulted a second oracle, who predicted that he would kill his own father and sleep with his mother. Horrified, the young man refused to return to his (adopted) home and headed off in the opposite direction.

Half a world away, another king's son was brought before a great and wise sage, the former teacher of his father. "Here is my son," the king said. "Tell me of his future." Examining the child, the sage said that he would become a very great teacher. Later other sages predicted that if he chose to rule, the young prince would be a great king, and if he chose the religious life, he would be a great teacher. To keep his son at home, the king built for him a great palace so that his life should never be troubled and he would never consider the religious life.

In Nigeria a young couple presented their newborn child to the babalawo, the divination priest, for the ritual known as Stepping into the World. In the course of the divination, the parents were told that the spirit of their son dwelled very near the lagoon, a symbol of prosperity, and if he was raised well he would prosper as a fisherman or "catcher" who could easily acquire the bounty of the sea. However, his father should not be wasteful and his parents should not quarrel or his spirit might become disillusioned—that is, the baby might die. The next day the baby's father went fishing and, as predicted, caught more than his family could eat, and so in the spirit of his son's divination he shared the bounty with his friends (M. Drewal 1992, 52–55).

Butter Bean and Itchy Bean went to the diviner because they had no children. They were told to make a sacrifice of cowries, a cock, camwood, a giant rat, and lots of palm oil because of people who would want to eat their children. Butter Bean believed that she would have so many children that people could not eat them all, and refused to make the sacrifice. Itchy Bean, on the other hand, did not want the people to eat even one of her children, so she made the sacrifice (Bascom 1980, 267–69).

Oracles have been used around the world and throughout history. People have often consulted oracles at the important points in their lives. But people are often unhappy with the words of an oracle, and mythology is full of stories of people who attempt to reverse, delay, or forestall a portion of the predicted future. Oracular sayings and divinatory speech are considered to be messages from some extraordinary source informing humans about the future or some other unknown circumstance. Among the Yoruba it was very common for people to go to a diviner before any major activity. Marriages, travel, the birth of children were all seen as turning points in life, points at which destiny might be manifested. However, the Yoruba were unusual in that their divination process was based on the concept not only that one could determine one's destiny but also that knowledge combined with action might soften or change a difficult destiny. Thus their mythological stories not only tell tales of divination and the playing out of destiny but also tell their characters, and by extension their listeners, what they can do to manifest the best possible version of their destiny. These stories form the basis of the divination corpus each diviner learns so that the mythological stories can be used to advise a client on the best course of action at the current point in that client's own life.

Divination is generally broken down into two types: technical or inductive divination, which depends on the interpretation of certain signs, lots, dreams, and the like, and natural or intuitive divination, which is based on direct inspiration of the practitioner through trance or visions. Many forms of divination are based on a cosmological view that God, the gods, spirits, or demons can speak through the divination process or that one can gain insight into the general course of events. Although inspirational divination through the medium of possession trance is an important part of Santería practice, in this chapter we are going to focus on the various forms of inductive divination, including the divination system of the babalawo, called Ifá, and the coconut and seashell divination that can be practiced by the majority of initiates. These divinatory practices are of the form called lot divination, in which the random heads-or-tails fall of a set of objects is supposed to express the will of a spiritual being. Queries brought to coconut divination must be in a yes/no form, while shell divination allows for a more elaborate set of responses. Ifá is a still more sophisticated form of divination performed by a priest specially trained in its methods. Divination is an important method for obtaining insight or information that is generally unavailable through more conventional or rational means. Diviners are often consulted when one has a vague or amorphous concern or when one is facing a decision fraught with peril or uncertainty. By consulting a diviner, one attempts to reduce the risks inherent in all human experience.

Many books about Santería include a compilation of spells or magical formulas for making changes in one's life and affecting one's destiny. These spells tend to focus on gaining and keeping one's health, wealth, and mate. There may also be spells that allow one to work one's own will on others, although these are fewer in Santería than in books about other types of magical systems. What is not apparent from most of these books is that within the Santería cosmology one cannot just work a spell because one needs a job or wants to restrain a wandering spouse. All such "magical" work must be preceded by a divination session that inquires into one's destiny at the current moment and elicits the cooperation of an Orisha or other spiritual being who will ensure the efficacy of the prescribed procedure. Santeros speak in terms of the *ebo* or sacrifice required to soften an unfortunate turn in one's destiny or to enhance the manifestation of a fortunate one. Many of the divination texts are stories in the form so-and-so went for divination, was told to perform such-and-such an ebo, and either performed the ebo and was happy or failed to perform as required and suffered the consequences. Never in either the stories or a divination session is an inquirer left without some action. Orisha religion is inherently pragmatic, so that unlike the fathers of Oedipus and Siddhartha, who were left to their own devices in their desire to affect their children's destinies, those who consult one of the Santería oracles are always given possibilities for the remediation of a difficult destiny or, as in the case of the young Yoruba father, the manifestation of a favorable one.

Within the divination texts the ebo required often gives the inquirer the tools needed to bring about the best destiny for the situation. In the story of Butter Bean and Itchy Bean, one of the things the future mothers are asked to sacrifice is a giant rat. Later, when the people are hungry, they begin eating Butter Bean's children. They find them so tasty that they don't even wait for salt to flavor them. After they have eaten all of Butter Bean's children, they turn to the children of Itchy Bean. But Itchy Bean's children are covered with the hairs of the rat she sacrificed. These hairs are so irritating that they repel the hungry people and protect Itchy Bean's children from being eaten. Here we see an example of the practicality of Orisha divination: not only does the sacrifice ensure the cooperation of invisible beings and perhaps function as a form of sympathetic magic, the items from a sacrifice are actually available to protect the sacrificer and her children.

Sometimes the ebo entails a form of sympathetic magic that enacts metaphorically the intended action. It is common not only to treat the client personally with this form of sympathetic magic but also to use the agency of a ritually enhanced object. For example, several years ago a young woman, a fellow graduate student who was having problems keeping a pregnancy, asked my godfather for help. Based on a cowry shell divination session, the three of us (the mother, my godfather, and I) placed a small doll in a hollowed-out pumpkin. After the requisite number of days, when the doll had symbolically gestated, it was "birthed" and placed for the duration of the pregnancy under the protection of an Orisha identified in the divination. The accompanying rituals implored the Orisha to watch over this child "as if it were his own" and not to let it enter the world prematurely. In this case the doll was invested with the ashé, or power, to act in the place of the unborn child so that it could be placed in a healing relationship with an Orisha. After the birth of the baby, a robust boy child, we performed other rituals to strengthen the tie between the child and his protectors. The doll, as the physical embodiment of the boy's spirit, was included in these rituals.

Like many Santería rituals, the ebo required to create the best possible outcome in this case involved both material objects (the pumpkin and the doll) and ritual action (the inserting and removing of the doll from the pumpkin and subsequent rituals). Although no blood was spilled in the course of these rituals, energy in the form of both time and money was expended to acquire the necessary items and to perform the requisite ceremonies over a several-month period. Often, as in this case, the objects and ceremonies required are metaphorically related to either the perceived cause of the problem or the anticipated result or both.

Destiny in Yoruba Thought

I do not know where people with good *ori* choose their *ori*,
I would have gone to choose mine there;
But no! We choose our *ori* from the same source.

Traditional Yoruba song

Even when personal destiny is not mentioned as influential in a particular problem or its solution, as in the case of Butter Bean and Itchy Bean, all Yoruba-based divination depends on a certain view of human destiny. The Yoruba, like many Western psychologists, believe that human beings are formed from a group of physical and nonphysical elements. In his book *African Philosophy: Traditional Yoruba Philosophy and Contemporary African Realities* (1991), Segun Gbadegesin presents a systematic view of Yoruba psychology based on mythology, language, and other oral sources. He describes the traditional understanding of a human being or *èniyàn* as having several constituent parts, which he names in Yoruba as *ara* (body), *okàn* (heart), *èmí* (breath), and *orí* (head).[1]

The component of the human being that is of most interest to us is ori. On one hand, the word *ori* refers to the physical head and recognizes the head's important physical character. On the other hand, it refers to the spiritual ori that is the bearer of a person's destiny. Ori is also considered one's personal divinity. Among the Yoruba, offerings are made to ori, and it has the power to guard and protect (38). It is also understood that one's ori, the bearer of one's destiny, is the key to success or failure in life. Indeed, a proverb says that if your ori is against you, there is no question of success, but if your ori is with you, there is no possibility of failure (48).

In the Yoruba understanding of the creation of new life, after a child has been given her ara and okàn, her body and heart, she kneels in front of the great god Olodumare and chooses her ori (head) for this lifetime.[2] This head encompasses her intelligence, competence, personal limitations, and capacity to defend herself; it is her personal destiny. She must choose her destiny in the absence of full information. Gbadegesin says (1991, 50–51) that some destinies are "overburnt" or not properly done; some are beautiful on the outside but full of worms; some are ugly on the outside but solid and neat. Each person chooses her own destiny, but choosing a destiny is like choosing lottery numbers or picking a spouse who is appealing today but whose future is unknown.

Ori is often described as a container whose contents are unknown until the choice is made. The song that begins this section is the conclusion of a story of three youngsters who must choose a destiny before coming into the world (that is, before being born). While one child delays to consult a diviner, his two friends go on ahead to the home of Ajalamo, the maker of heads. There they see many beautiful heads and each chooses one he thinks he will like. Having chosen, they continue on the journey to the world. Their friend, Afuwape, by following the advice of the diviner, wins the favor of Ajalamo, who tells him that many who choose the most beautiful heads do not succeed in the world or are surrounded by jealous enemies. Ajalamo helps Afuwape choose an appropriate destiny. When Afuwape has grown into a wealthy and successful man, his friends sing, "If I knew where Afuwape chose his head / I would go and choose my own again" (Beier 1980, 4–6). But of course all chose at the same place; all got their destinies from the same source.

One's destiny is also associated with a guardian Orisha. It is this Orisha that "owns one's head," as santeros say, and it is to this Orisha that one will be initiated should one choose to become a priest. Within Santería the relationship between the guardian Orisha and the individual is described in terms of familial relationships. Everyone is the child of a ruling Orisha. And just as one exhibits certain characteristics inherited from one's natural parents, it is believed that one also exhibits the characteristics, both positive and negative, associated with one's personal Orisha (Canizares 1991, 372). By understanding the foibles of the different Orisha—understood here as different personality types—one can recognize not only one's own strengths and weaknesses but also those of the people one meets in daily life. Understanding one's destiny means understanding that it is through the interaction between one's will, one's head, and one's Orisha guardian that one can realize the fullness of one's personal destiny.

Since this destiny is represented by a specific energy pattern, it can be discovered through divination. Among the Yoruba and their Santería descendants each individual's destiny can be represented by one of the 256 *odu* or sacred "letters" that embody the oral scriptures of Ifá. These scriptures are contained in a set of verses telling the stories of the Orisha and are used to guide practitioners. By knowing one's birth odu, one can begin to remember the agreement between one's ori and Olodumare and to make the life choices that are in harmony with that agreement. At the same time, each destiny is also associated with an Orisha. Each Orisha represents a particular energy pattern, a particular force of nature. These energy patterns might be thought of in terms of Jungian archetypes. Although each of us manifests the energy of several archetypes, one predominates. This dominant archetype can be personified as a particular Orisha. In order to embody fully this archetypal energy and live in harmony with one's destiny, this Orisha becomes the focus of one's worship. From another viewpoint, we might think of this Orisha as the expression of one's higher, truer consciousness (Murphy 1993, 132). This is the Self that Jung suggests is each individual's drive toward wholeness.[3]

This idea of destiny and the need to learn the forces of one's destiny active at any particular time led to the use of divination among the Yoruba. In this worldview, destiny forms the general outlines of one's life path, while divination is the means by which one learns both the fundamental contours of that destiny and the ways one's destiny is manifesting itself in the current situation. Destiny determines when and to whom one will be born, when and how one will die, and the broad sweep of one's life. However, the Yoruba do not believe in a strong, unalterable destiny. Rather, they understand that individual actions can modify a personal destiny for better or worse. Not only can other forces, including witchcraft and the ill will of both visible and invisible beings, influence that destiny, each of us has the opportunity to maneuver within the general allotment of our destiny.

If one has chosen a difficult destiny, one can soften it and enhance the possibility of enacting the best possible scenario within that destiny. On the other hand, if one has chosen a fortunate destiny but refuses to engage one's Legs (industry) and Brain (intellect) in the manifestation of that destiny, it will remain unmanifested. Character, industry, sacrifice, and dynamism are all required to realize the success encased in the most fortunate destiny.

Through divination one can begin to remember the agreement between one's ori and Olodumare and to make the life choices that are in harmony with that agreement. As one moves through life, one makes choices that enhance certain inherent skills and abilities while neglecting others. Choosing a particular school may require moving to a town far away from family and friends; time spent studying can't be spent perfecting one's free throw. Divination, as well as familiarity with one's guardian deity, is used to determine whether these choices are consistent with one's destiny and in harmony with one's inner balance. Divination provides ways to return to the path chosen by one's ori so that one can live in harmony with one's self, one's family, the community, and ultimately the world.

Divination also provides communication between the invisible and the visible world. Many people come to Santería in a last-ditch effort to solve some personal or familial problem. In Hispanic communities it is common to combine Western-style medical treatment with spiritual baths and other treatments recommended by various types of divination, and even nonbelievers will visit a santero or a babalawo for a consultation when they encounter serious situations that appear intractable by other methods. The young woman described above, for example, was encouraged to follow the advice of her doctor and midwife, whose work was understood to be enhanced and strengthened by our protective ritual for her unborn child.

Divinatory Techniques

The simplest form of Santería divination uses coconut pieces to get answers to yes/no questions. So-called coco divination is normally used for simple questions and to confirm actions. More complicated problems might be addressed through cards of various types. Questions or problems addressed directly to a particular Orisha use a set of cowry shells dedicated to that Orisha. The most difficult problems and questions provoked by simpler forms of divination must be brought to a babalawo for resolution.

Coco divination uses four pieces of unpeeled coconut, white meat on one side, dark rind on the other. When the pieces are dropped on the ground, they fall in one of five dark/light patterns: all white, one, two, three, or four dark sides showing. This is a form of divination by lots in which each combination is read as "yes," "no," or "throw again." By asking a series of yes/no questions, a person can determine the will and pleasure of the Orisha or *egun* (Yr., dead ancestor) consulted and discern a plan of action.[4] Coconut divination is used at strategic points in ritual to determine that the denizens of the invisible world are happy and satisfied with the ritual to that point and, if not, what needs to be done to achieve such satisfaction. It can also be used to get quick answers from the ancestors or the Orisha outside the context of other rituals. However, if one has severe problems or requires a detailed answer, one of the more complex divination systems is employed.

Many santeros use one of the European divination systems when dealing with clients. They may read cards, use a crystal ball, or gaze into a candle. However, when they want to speak directly to an Orisha, they use cowry shells. Each time a person is initiated to an Orisha, he or she is given a set of small seashells that are the divination set for that Orisha. These shells have a natural "mouth" on one side, while the back of the shell is removed so that it will lie flat. Sixteen of the shells are cast onto a reed mat, and the resulting number or series of numbers is interpreted according to the client's problem and the Orisha whose shells are being read. Since each "throw" produces a set of two numbers between o (no shells mouth up) and 16 (all shells up), there are many possible combinations,[5] which the diviner must be able to interpret. Although shell divination, known as diloggun, is of African origin, it is less popular in contemporary Nigeria than in the Americas, where it is an important form of divination in both Santería and Candomblé communities (Bascom 1980, 3).

One story says that the diloggun originally belonged to Orula (Orunmila), the divine seer, who used them to determine the cause and solution for the problems that beset both the Orisha and human beings. Through observation and intelligence, Yemaya, his wife, was able to learn the secret of the shells. One day, when Orula was away, she began divining on her own. The mythology says that she read the shells with exquisite aptitude and was able to mark the most effective ebo to solve her clients' problems. The long line waiting their turn outside her door certainly attested to her skill. Orula, however, was enraged when he returned and discovered that she had appropriated his power. From that moment he eschewed the use of the shells and developed a different divination system, one that only men could read. Yemaya (or Oshun, who is named in many versions of this story as Orula's wife) took the divination shells and shared this oracle with the other Orisha. Thus today all of the Orisha speak through the shells except Orula, who speaks to his priests, the babalawo, only through the Table of Ifá.

Any santero who has learned the verses and stories associated with the various combinations of throws can "read the shells," but santeros do not normally interpret falls with thirteen or more mouths up. It is believed that those throws require recourse to a still higher level of divination that only a babalawo, Orula's divination priest, can perform. Using the kola nuts or the divining chain called the *opele*, the babalawo speak the will of Olodumare through the mouth of Orula, their patron Orisha. Mythology tells us that Orula is present when each ori is chosen, hence he knows each person's past, present, and future. Through Ifá divination, Orula indicates one of 256 possible odu or letters. Each letter is associated with a set of poems. Although the odu Ifá are similar to the numbers generated by the diloggun, they use a different set of sayings and poems or assign the same sayings and poems to different numeric combinations. Orisha worshippers in both Africa and the Americas believe that the solution to their problem, the secret of their destiny, is contained in these poems. It is the responsibility of the babalawo to know and be able to interpret the poem or poems associated with the odu and recommend a course of action to the client.

All of Yoruba mythology is embedded in the Ifá and diloggun divination stories. One of these stories says that during the earliest times, when there was no barrier between heaven and earth, Orunmila was often summoned to heaven by Olodumare to use his wisdom to help solve problems.[6] One day Orunmila, annoyed at an insult given him by one of his children, decided to remain in heaven. In his absence the earth was thrown into great confusion, neither crops nor women reproduced, famine and pestilence raged. The people of the earth sent the children of Orunmila to beg him to return. He refused, but gave his sons sixteen palm nuts and taught them his style of divination so that they could communicate with him. The spiritual descendants of Orunmila's children are the priests of Ifá, the babalawo. Unlike the priests of the other Orisha, who were very often women and whose primary ritual event involved possession trance, the priests of Orunmila have almost always been men who knew of Orunmila's secrets through the complex divinatory system of Ifá and were never possessed by their deity.[7] Although both Ifá and diloggun divination are forms of interpretative divination, diloggun specialists will often talk of also receiving intuitive messages from spirits of the dead or other Orisha during the divinatory session.

Many suggest that diloggun, as the simpler and more widely available system, developed as an offshoot of Ifá. But 'Wande Abimbola, who is widely known for his scholarly exposition of the Ifá corpus, suggests that in reality Ifá is based on diloggun, which is the more ancient system. He also suggests that babalawo should not look down on diloggun, as it has its own ashé from Olodumare (Abimbola 2001, 150; see also Abimbola 1976, 94). We will discuss the relationship between the practitioners of the two divinatory systems further below.

Orisha as Archetypes

Within Santería the relationship between a devotee and the Orisha that owns her head is often described in terms of familial relationships.[8] That is, each individual is believed to be the child of a particular Orisha. As a child of the Orisha, she is believed to exhibit the archetypal qualities of that Orisha. And it is through the interaction between her head or destiny and her Orisha guardian that she can manifest the fullness of her destiny, or, as Jung would say, achieve individuation.

Although the association with an Orisha isn't solidified until the time of initiation, there is much theorizing among devotees about the identity of this Orisha, and many solicit knowledge of "their" Orisha in anticipation of eventual initiation. Outside of formal divination, one can hypothesize a person's Orisha by correlating the person's personality and the known characteristics of the Orisha.

It is important to remember that the classification of individuals according to these archetypal categories is inexact, largely because of the overlap between and among categories. We can identify a group of characteristics that are typical of a particular Orisha-archetype, but it is unlikely that any *one* characteristic can be invoked as a definitive trait that excludes the possibility of a different Orisha-archetype. For example, both Yemaya and Obatala are considered wise and benevolent, while both Shango and Oshun are associated with sexuality and reproduction. A preponderance of characteristics linked to a particular archetype may be enough to suggest a person is the child of an Orisha, but exceptions preclude absolute certainty (Segato 1995, 177, 181).

At the same time, we must understand that one does not choose one's primary Orisha, nor is that Orisha assigned by others. Rather the Orisha that owns one's head is determined through divination, the throw of cowry shells or kola nuts. Devotees believe that an individual is chosen by an Orisha to be its worshipper and priest. An Orisha may claim an individual for a variety of reasons. Although the personality one brings to the divination session may predispose one to an alliance with a particular Orisha, some individuals are chosen by Orisha in opposition to their personal characteristics. And to the outside observer some associations seem completely arbitrary, neither supporting nor challenging the devotee's personal self-concept. Thus there doesn't appear to be any *necessary* relationship between the personality of the individual and the Orisha guardian.

It is also important to mention that the Orisha and the archetypes they represent are distributed without regard to the gender or sexual orientation of the human participants. That is, an individual is equally likely to be given a male or a female Orisha. Because the personality of the priest often correlates with the type of the Orisha, one would expect that gay or effeminate men as well as most women would be associated with Oshun, the goddess of love and sexuality, or Yemaya, the maternal Orisha. However, in the communities with which I am familiar and those of my informants, this correlation does not generally hold. In fact, there are many gay men with male guardian Orisha, many straight men with female guardian Orisha, and many women whose guardian Orisha do not correlate with either their own gender or their sexual preference. In addition, the gender attributes associated with the Orisha are not universally projected onto the devotee. That is, male Oshun priests are not necessarily perceived as effeminate, nor are female Shango priests necessarily seen as overly virile.[9] Using a Jungian vocabulary, this means that one's Orisha does not necessarily function directly either as one's Self or as an anima/animus archetype. Jung understood that gendered archetypes functioned differently for men and women, serving different purposes in the development of a fully individuated personality. This, however, does not seem to be the understanding among Santería practitioners. Rather, everyone has access to the archetypal characteristics of all of the Orisha regardless of gender designations. In fact, gender correlation between one's ruling Orisha and one's self does not seem to be important at all. I mention this only in passing now. The phenomenon and some of its implications will be explored more fully in chapter 5, "Possession Phenomena."

Phenomenological Descriptions

Much more could be said about the relationship between the individual Santería practitioner and his or her Orisha. But at this point I want to describe how these relationships are used within the Santería community. The determination of one's Orisha guardian is of great interest to the community. Of course, for all initiated priests this Orisha has been determined and has been firmly "attached" to the individual as part of the initiation ceremony. However, as soon as one becomes involved in the religion and long before initiation is contemplated, there is a hunger for this piece of knowledge. In the same way that those who know astrology feel that they know something about a person when they know the birth sign, Santería practitioners believe that knowing someone's Orisha guardian gives them insight into the person's personality. Independent of the divination session, practitioners speculate on which Orisha "owns" a newcomer's head. Correspondences between the personality of the individual and the archetypal characteristics of the Orisha govern this speculation. Someone who is brash and forward may be associated with Shango, while someone who is even-tempered, calm, and cerebral may be the child of Obatala. Motherly types are thought to belong to Yemaya, while Oshun is thought to govern someone who is always impeccably and fashionably dressed. A popular book (Neimark 1993) actually has a checklist to determine which Orisha might be one's guardian, although, as suggested above, this determination is often contradicted by experiential encounters with actual priests.

Many practitioners are quick to take their new followers or "godchildren" to the diviner to determine this interesting piece of information. Although within the Santería complex the determination of the guardian Orisha serves little function until initiation is imminent, learning their personal guardians is for many people an important part of their socialization into the Santería community. Once people learn which Orisha "own their heads," they have a strong tendency to attribute behaviors to this correspondence. Even those without children will begin to look for maternal feelings after being identified with Yemaya. Or those who have a problem controlling their temper or sexuality may attribute their failings to their association with Shango, the great womanizer among the Orisha. Practitioners will dig into the mythology to explain certain types of behavior. For example, in one story Ochosi, the hunter Orisha, accidentally kills his mother because he thinks she is a thief. A priest of Ochosi might find in this story an explanation for her own problems with her mother.

It is at the time of priestly initiation that the determination of the ruling Orisha is most important, because each new priest is initiated as a priest of that particular Orisha.[10] Initiation does more than solidify the relationship between Orisha and devotee. During the initiation process the Orisha is firmly seated "in" the devotee's head, so that she is not only the child and priest of the Orisha but also its vessel, since after initiation the new priest can manifest the Orisha directly through possession trance. During the possession event the priest becomes her Orisha guardian in a uniquely intense way. It is during this event that we find the archetype tangibly manifested for the worshipping community. During this time what was internal and psychological becomes external and physically available to the community. The archetype comes alive in the body of the priest. The embodied Orisha can bless members of the community, offer healing, or counsel devotees in a particularly personal and physical way. For the duration of the possession event, it is the Orisha that actually speaks and acts using the body of the devotee. Much more can be said about this phenomenon, which we will discuss in chapter 5, but we must note now that during a true possession (the community acknowledges that false or faked possessions are possible) the personality and awareness of the priest are completely absent. That is, a priest can become the archetype only *in absentia*; she can *never* have the experience of being the Orisha.

This relationship between Orisha and worshipper is hard to understand, even for Santería participants. The priest not only is the worshipper of the Orisha but also carries the archetype "in her head." During the possession event, her words and actions are the words and actions of the deity and are treated as such by the worshipping community. Although a priest's words and actions outside the possession event are not considered to be those of the Orisha, the community acknowledges that the special relationship between a priest and her Orisha continues to exist. On the one hand, during the possession event the priest is expected to manifest the archetypal behavior of the Orisha inhabiting her body. In many cases, this behavior exaggerates particular characteristics of the archetype: Shango may be inordinately virile, Oshun charming and seductive, Eleggua playful and mischievous. On the other hand, much of the behavior that is expected *during* the possession event is not acceptable *outside* the ritual context. However, because of the close association between priests and their ruling Orisha, they and others are liable to explain or excuse certain everyday behaviors as the manifestation of that Orisha archetype. This is especially easy in those cases where the personality of a priest closely parallels the characteristics of the Orisha. Thus when a priest of Yemaya acts in a maternal fashion toward others or when an Oshun priest is being coquettish, they are said to be manifesting the characteristics of their guardian Orisha. Even the behavior of individuals not crowned to a particular Orisha might be framed in terms of an Orisha archetype. This can become a problem in the community when a priest chooses to explain unacceptable behavior in this manner. All Orisha have behaviors that exemplify the negative aspects of their archetypes: on the individual level the great mother archetype, Yemaya, may lead one to become smothering, while the cool detachment of Obatala can lead one toward obsessive or compulsive behavior. Priests of Shango are especially noted for excusing unacceptable behavior by appealing to their archetypal Orisha. Shango, the arrogant manly Orisha with hundreds of wives and a quick temper, is often used to provide an excuse for his priests to exhibit the worst of these characteristics. "I can't be faithful to my wife. I'm a son of Shango, after all," or "Pardon my quick temper. It is Shango who speaks through me."

Older priests, who see such behavior as the excuse it is, will often counter with the reply "But you are *not* Shango" to remind the offending priest that, while he may be the embodiment of Shango during possession, he himself is not the deity and is not allowed to excuse his behavior in this manner. Priests are reminded that many of the mythological stories are teaching tales and not guides to behavior. As instructional stories, these anecdotes suggest the best and worst aspects of individual archetypes while pointing out the results of inappropriate behavior. Thus one might be reminded that Shango lost his wives and children because of his arrogance, or that Obatala spent six months in jail because of his cool reserve. By telling a young priest that he is *not* the personification of his Orisha archetype, the elders are telling him that, outside of the controlled environment of the possession event, he is still expected to manage his own behavior and to follow the general norms of the community, *not* the inappropriate examples of the mythological corpus.

Gender Analysis

If I have money
It is my Orí I will praise
My Orí, it is you
If I have children on earth
It is my Orí to whom I will give praise
My Orí, it is you
All the good things I have on earth
It is Orí I will praise
My Orí, it is you.

'Wande Abimbola, *Ifá: An Exposition of Ifá Literary Corpus*

Unlike the seers who divined for the fathers of Oedipus and Siddhartha, Yoruba and Santería diviners offer ways to avoid the traps exposed in the course of their divination. Within Yoruba-based cosmology everyone bears an individual fate, but that fate is not absolute. Through the divination process one is given a plan of action that will help to realize the best possible fate within the boundaries of one's destiny. Through personal action (ritual and sacrifice) one can manifest a favorable destiny or mitigate a difficult one. But such action isn't magical; not all portions of one's destiny can be changed. Leg (industry) and Brain (intellect) must join Head (destiny) in the manifestation of one's best and highest destiny.

Such a view resonates with the American view that one can determine one's own destiny. While recognizing that different people come into the world with different gifts and advantages, the great American myth suggests that all people can achieve whatever they want if they are willing to work hard to get ahead. Divination offers Orisha worshippers the possibility of improving their chances for success by delineating the boundaries of their innate potential and by providing a plan of action for the highest achievement within those boundaries. Although the story of Oedipus is rich and deep, one moral of the story is that one's destiny is fixed and immutable, that no action by the child's parents or by Oedipus himself could deter the inevitable working out of that destiny. The Yoruba cosmological system offers a different viewpoint. Yes, one may be born with a difficult destiny. Like the children of Butter Bean and Itchy Bean, we might be destined to be destroyed by forces beyond our control, to be "eaten" by those around us. But wider possibilities exist. The tale implies that Itchy Bean's children are as tasty as those of Butter Bean, but in spite of their tastiness they escape the fate of Butter Bean's children because their mother followed the divinatory advice. All such stories encourage inquirers to follow the advice of the diviner, but they also present a particular worldview, a worldview that promotes personal achievement without promising the highest level of achievement to everyone. Such stories encourage the inquirers to consider their own destinies and the ways they have applied industry and intelligence toward the achievement of those destinies.

Although most of what is written about destiny seems to assume a normative male, in fact there is no gender bias in the general understanding of destiny among the Yoruba. Everyone, regardless of anatomical body type, chooses a destiny and then tries to discover and live out the best version of that destiny. The sexual characteristics of the body with which one is born affect the playing out of that destiny as much as all the other givens of one's birth, including the place and time of that birth, one's parents, lineage, family dynamics, and inborn skills and abilities. As Oyewùmí explains (1997, 66–68), genitalia are not the most important of these factors. In fact, she suggests, traditionally many trades were lineage based and in some cases required the familial ashé in order to be successful, which means it would have been difficult for one to take up such a trade outside one's own lineage. However, if divination determined that one should engage in a profession not associated with one's own lineage, there were ways in which such a destiny could still be fulfilled.

Transplanted to the Americas, this view of destiny and its manifestation also provides for a high level of tolerance of individual differences. Because everyone "comes from heaven" with different characteristics and a different destiny, there is no push for everyone to act or be the same. Everyone must work out his or her life according to a unique destiny. Since Yoruba traditional religion and its New World descendants are focused on the manifestation of each individual's destiny, the tolerance for a variety of personal choices and lifestyles seems to be higher than in many of the more mainstream religions. As Robin Horton discusses in his 1983 essay "Social Psychologies: African and Western," the Yoruba idea of "a multiplicity of different paths to self-realization" leads to the understanding that there are many different "states of normal adjustment" and that often the disturbances in one's physical or mental state are the result not of an inability to achieve normal adult adjustment but rather of attempting to pursue a type of normality that is, given the individual's own inner potential, simply the wrong one for that person (80–81).

Particularly striking is the fact that issues of sexuality and sexual difference seem not to come under the level of scrutiny that they incur in other religious groups. On the one hand, practitioners are conservative in their opinions. Marriage, fidelity, childbearing, and traditional families are highly regarded within the mythology and among practitioners. On the other hand, individuals whose destiny leads them along another path are not severely censured. We can suggest that this is one reason why many gay men and lesbians have found acceptance within these traditions. In fact, according to one knowledgeable source, more than 30 percent of the Santería initiates (priests) in the United States are gay men or lesbians (Afolabi 1999; see also Lemmon 1998). Since priests are selected and confirmed by the Orisha rather than by human beings, individuals are generally not denied initiation because of race, gender, nationality, or sexual orientation. In the best understanding of Yoruba psychology, sexual orientation is merely one aspect of a person's full destiny, a destiny that has been chosen for this lifetime and must be pursued diligently in an effort to achieve a personal state of normal adjustment.

This is not necessarily true of all the African-based traditions that come to us through Cuba. Both the priests of the divination cult of Ifá, which we will discuss below, and of the Bantu-identified cult of Palo Monte are much more concerned with adherents' "manly" nature than are the priests of Santería. Although there have been some women initiated as diviner-priests in Ifá in recent years, they are still considered unusual and are excluded from the highest initiatory levels. Palo Monte accepts both men and women initiates, but many women consider it too masculinist in its orientation. Both of these cult groups not only categorically exclude gay men from their ranks but have a pronounced homophobic atmosphere.

To be sure, these issues of cultural import find their way into Santería in the same way they do in other religious or social groups. Although gay men and women have played a role in Santería from as early as the 1800s and have been among the most powerful of its early leaders, their presence has often caused the religion to be denigrated as "overly refined" and associated with women and "womanly" men, in contrast to the more masculinist Afro-Cuban religious traditions. "Outsiders," whether they are English-only speakers in a predominantly Spanish-speaking religious house, whites in an Afrocentric house, or gay men in a house led by a homophobe, may not feel or be welcomed. However, there is no doctrinal sanction within Santería for the kind of exclusionary practices found in some other traditions. All people carry the vitality of Olodumare in their breath and are protected by their Orisha guardians. And all have personal destinies that lead them on unique paths, paths not to be denigrated by others since they have accompanied their newborn owners from *orun* (Yr., heaven, the invisible world). If divination suggests that a person has been called by an Orisha to be a devotee, then mere humans cannot close the door. As much as it may pain some people that the Orisha has called a person whose race, gender, nationality, sexual orientation, or any other characteristic they find uncomfortable, they cannot, within the confines of the religion, exclude that person from practice. Priests may choose not to initiate or participate in the initiation of one whose calling they disapprove of, but they cannot deny that person's initiatory status after the fact.

What this means is that the religion of Santería has become a haven for women and gay men. All different types of people find acceptance in the religion, and few roles are closed to individuals because of their body type or other characteristics. Today some houses in the United States are intolerant of gay practitioners—this is particularly true of babalawo-centric houses—but because of the preponderance of gay men in positions of authority in the religion, it is difficult if not impossible for the homophobic and misogynistic to avoid working with women and gay men. Particularly in its philosophical openness to all people regardless of their anatomy or sexual orientation, Santería closely follows Oyewùmí's suggestion that Yoruba culture does not maintain the categories of thought necessary to establish exclusionary practices. However, there are exceptions, and those exceptions suggest a more subtle view of gender and sexuality than Oyewùmí's analysis allows. As we continue, we will note those areas where women and gay men are subjected to special qualifications, since they point to these more subtle understandings of gender and sexuality.

Divinatory Priesthoods

The two types of divinatory practices used in Santería reflect the two types of priest found among the Yoruba. Often these are distinguished in the literature as divination priests and possession priests. These two groups were interdependent but not hierarchically associated with each other. Orisha cults that regularly used possession trance to communicate with the Orisha were generally open to both men and women, although women often predominated because it was thought that women were better trance mediums. It is not surprising that cowry shells, the currency of the precolonial West African marketplace and of the petty traders, who were most often women, should also be the divination tools of these priests. Specialized cults that did not depend on trance, of which the cult of Orunmila is the most widely known, generally limited their priesthood to men.[11] Although both types of priests helped to sustain the welfare of the people, each provided a distinct style of practice.

The earliest records of Yoruba religion, letters and reports produced by missionaries working in the Yoruba region of Africa, note the differences between "Ifá priests," whom the missionaries seemed to respect, and "fetish priests," upon whom they heaped their unalloyed contempt. In these early records the *babalawo* were generally seen as religious professionals, sophisticated men with whom missionaries could engage in learned discussion, while *aworo*, the so-called fetish priests or *olorisha* (Yr., owners of Orisha), were presented as corrupt and ignorant, deceivers of the people who enriched themselves on the superstitions of others.

In a 1990 article in *Religion* Rosalind Shaw suggests how this characterization of the babalawo as the "high priest" of Orisha religion might have initially come about. She suggests that Christian missionaries may have favored the cult of Ifá diviners over that of the possession priests because of the similarities between the Ifá cult and Christianity. These similarities, including the hegemonic claims of the Ifá cult, its association with the high god, and its male-dominated priesthood, both distinguished it from other Yoruba cults, which as female-dominated tended toward a diversity of beliefs and practices, and preadapted it to a mutually respectful interaction with Christianity (Shaw 1990, 343, citing Peel 1990). In addition, since a majority of the early researchers into Orisha religion both in Africa and the New World were men who seemed to have preferred to work with male practitioners, one should not be surprised if the babalawo they consulted described themselves as the high priests of the traditions and suggested that they were responsible for the preservation of these traditions in Cuba and throughout the Americas. That olorisha were often women, or men who were gendered female in relation to their deities,[12] only provided a further division between them and the all-male Christian clergy. As missionaries—and, later, missionary-trained scholars—constructed the religion of the Yoruba, it was the babalawo and the cult of Ifá rather than that of the olorisha that became central (Peel 1990, 342–47). Consequently much of the literature about Yoruba religion valorizes the work of the babalawo while ignoring the place of the olorisha. In their descriptions of both African and New World Yoruba religious systems, scholars often describe the babalawo as the "high priest" of the religion while ignoring or devaluing the work of the olorisha, priests and priestesses of the other Orisha.[13]

The earliest works on the religion focused on the place of the babalawo. Joseph Murphy's groundbreaking *Santería: African Spirits in America* says that the preservation of Orisha religion can be credited to the wisdom of the babalawo whose memories contained the entire Ifá corpus, the "entire language of the Òrìshàs," the divination verses, prayers, songs, and praise names of the Orisha, as well as the knowledge to conduct every ritual, to organize the herbs, foods, and sacrifices, and to advise and prescribe in times of misfortune. He suggests that because of the extensive knowledge of the babalawo the enslaved Yoruba were able to reconstruct their religious traditions in Cuba (105–6, 62).

Citing Murphy, David Brown (1989) suggests that many scholars and priests assume that it was the babalawo who founded and disseminated the standard, canonical practice of Orisha religion in the New World. According to his informants, all subsequent practice, faithful or divergent, pure or bastardized, right or wrong, comes directly from that source (88). He also says that the American babalawo themselves believe that African and Cuban babalawo and their Ifá texts are "central to the strength and resilience of Lucumí [the New World Yoruba] tradition" (90). Since much of the research on Yoruba religion in the New World, particularly on its development in the United States, is based on information provided by babalawo, it is not surprising that this story of babalawo primacy has become a central theme. However, there is an alternative scenario.

Although everyone in Yorubaland used the services of the babalawo, and a babalawo might conduct a divination to recommend a person's initiation into a particular priesthood, the direct participation by precolonial babalawo in the worship of the other Orisha is under dispute. In the New World, the babalawo have become intimately involved in Santería and the world of the Orisha, but their authority and participation is not the same in all Santería communities or houses.

In his descriptions of Santería communities (2003, 19–20), David Brown discusses two different organizational styles, which we can call oriaté-centered houses and babalawo-centered houses. An oriaté is the ritual specialist who presides over the initiation of the priests of all the Orisha—except priests of Orula/Orunmila, whose initiation is solely the responsibility of the babalawo. He or she is also an *italero*, a highly trained diviner in diloggun. As described above, diloggun divination uses cowry shells and can be learned by any Orisha priest. Each set of diloggun shells is dedicated to a particular Orisha and is considered the mouthpiece of that Orisha. In an oriaté-centered house a babalawo is not used for any portion of the initiation process and is usually consulted only when his special type of divination is required. In these communities it is the oriaté who presides not only at the actual initiation but also at all the preliminary rituals—determining the guardian Orisha, making the warriors, and so on—as well as at the *matanza* (Sp., sacrifice) afterward.

In babalawo-centered houses, on the other hand, a babalawo determines the guardian Orisha of the initiate, makes the initial set of warriors, performs other divination sessions before the initiation, and performs the matanza that feeds the new Orisha. He will generally also give members of the house the entry-level initiation into the cult of Ifá through a ceremony called the Hand of Orula. However, since babalawo cannot participate in some portions of the Orisha initiatory process, in babalawo-centered houses these initiation activities, including the *asiento* (Sp., ritual initiation of new priests) and the dilog-gun-based divination afterward, must also be presided over by an oriaté.[14] In addition to these ideal forms, there are other ways in which the responsibility for the different activities can be distributed between the babalawo and the oriaté.

Although only a babalawo can perform Ifá divination, Ifá divination is not required for an Orisha initiation. Thus an oriaté can conduct an entire initiation from start to finish without the assistance of a babalawo. Although the role of oriaté is a New World innovation, such exclusive use allows oriaté-centered houses to initiate new possession priests in the absence of any members of the divination priesthood. The inability of babalawo to perform a complete initiation, particularly the diloggun-based divination known as *ita*, calls into question their valorization within contemporary Santería.

This brings us to the second and more troubling objection to the babalawo-as-religious-source myth. Since African babalawo did not seem to participate in Orisha initiations and New World babalawo cannot conduct Orisha initiations, it is unlikely that they could have had "the knowledge to conduct every ritual." Rather we can suggest that it was the possession priests of the Orisha, who were more likely to be women than men, who carried the knowledge of their own rituals to the New World. Most of the earliest leaders of the religion in Cuba were women; there were few active babalawo until the twentieth century, and it was not until the 1930s that they did more than perform their trademark divination and the requisite ebo (Brown 2003, 291). Only after they began marrying successful and renowned priestesses did they begin participating in rituals like the asiento (Ramos 2000).

Several respected Cuban priestesses, among them a priestess of Shango named Latuan who was one of the first to use the title "oriaté," were responsible for introducing substantial changes into the evolving Orisha cult that we now call Santería.[15] Perhaps the most important of these changes was presentation of multiple Orisha to their initiates and organization of the diverse rituals into a single process. These senior priestesses would have had the knowledge to conduct all the different rituals for their own Orisha and others into whose cults they had been initiated. Because these priests would not have been able to maintain their independent traditions in Cuba, they must have worked together in the cabildos, negotiating among themselves to create a way of continuing their various priesthoods in a new and alien environment. Working behind closed doors, away from the eye of both the colonial master and the historian, priests from a variety of related but rival African religious groups came together to create a new method of practice.[16]

This new religion enabled the continuation of the core of each of their individual religious systems based on ideas of ashé, the stories and mythology, sacred herbology, songs, dances, ritual elements (and perhaps the direct input of the Orisha themselves as they spoke through the mechanisms of possession and divination). What they reconstructed was not a single "African" or "Yoruba" religion—there had been no such thing—but a new religious system using the shared elements of the Orisha complex along with the rituals and practices of each Orisha cult. Over time, knowledge of these practices was further standardized by a highly trained group of Orisha priests, the original oriaté, who became the ritual specialists who knew how to "make" or initiate priests for all of the Orisha (Brown 1989, 94–95; J. Mason 1996, 18–19). As traditional Yoruba cultic practice would lead us to expect, the earliest oriaté were women.

When Africans initiated into the mysteries of Orula/Orunmila—that is, babalawo—came to Cuba, they were met by a thriving Orisha religious community. Although that community welcomed them, the cult of Orunmila was incompletely integrated into the new united Orisha tradition. Whereas priests of all the other Orisha had established a system of cross-initiation that enabled the priest of an Orisha to fully participate in the rituals of all the other Orisha, the priests of Orunmila were limited in their participation. Babalawo cannot directly participate in any initiation ritual; they cannot act as godparents in any rituals from the simple giving of Orisha necklaces to the priestly initiation of *kariocha*. Although babalawo make warriors and give them to their own godchildren, these Orisha icons cannot be used in the kariocha, and a new set of warriors must be made for the initiate by a santero. Because babalawo are precluded from divining with cowry shells, they cannot perform ita or speak directly to the Orisha; they are limited to accessing the Orisha through the intermediary of Orula and Ifá divination. Because babalawo are precluded from participating in possession, the Orisha cannot speak through them in possession trance. Any santero who acts as godparent or second godparent (*yubona*) in any Santería ritual is forever afterward barred from initiation into

Ifá. Conversely, a man who is initiated as a babalawo without first participating in the kariocha cannot even enter into the sacred space of initiation as an observer.

Although Orula/Orunmila is the Yoruba god of divination, it is Eleggua's shells that are normally used for day-to-day divination among santeros. Orula is the divination divinity par excellence, but Eleggua is the ubiquitous Orisha who knows much of what is going on in the world. As a matter of fact, in one story Orula complains, "Where do you get your knowledge? If I had your sources of information, I wouldn't need an oracle to divine the future." Throughout the mythology we see Eleggua as the perpetual secret agent, the one who just happens to be standing in the doorway or beneath the window or on the other side of the tree, watching and listening. In another story, Orula can gain the right to use the Table of Ifá only after passing a test devised for him by Olodumare. Because he does not yet own the divination equipment, he gets the correct response from Eleggua, who learns it by spying on Olodumare, the great god. As the Orisha who "knows all and sees all," Eleggua continues to participate in Ifá divination. It is his face that is carved on the *opon Ifá*, the Ifá divination board. Within the Ifá mythology it is often Eleggua who decides whether the Orisha will come to the aid of a devotee and how that aid will be manifested. Frequently in the divination texts we find him checking to see if the appropriate offering was made before coming to the aid of a supplicant.

Although few sources state it explicitly, it is important to realize that the diloggun, not Ifá, is the core of Santería ritual and practice. Whereas it is possible to continue the worship of the Orisha without access to Ifá, as has happened among Candomblé practitioners in Brazil and certain purely oriaté-centered houses in the United States, it is impossible to carry on the full rituals and practices of Santería without the diloggun. Not only is it impossible to communicate directly with an Orisha without the set of shells dedicated to that Orisha, it is impossible to initiate new priests or present devotees with Orisha icons without the appropriate set of diloggun. As every new iyawo is told, everything you have received as part of your initiation can be replaced—the *soperas* that are homes of the Orisha, the stones and other items that are concealed inside the soperas and that form the embodiment of those Orisha, all the accouterments of the religion can be recreated—but the diloggun, the mouthpieces of the Orisha, are irreplaceable. If a priest's diloggun are lost or stolen or misplaced, that priest can no longer speak directly to the Orisha, cannot initiate other devotees, can no longer practice as a priest of the Orisha.

Similarly, if a santero puts aside his diloggun to take up the practice of Ifá and be initiated as a priest of Orula, he must give up all of his rights as a priest of the other Orisha. He can no longer use his diloggun as a divination tool, nor can he initiate others into the worship of those Orisha, since the initiating priest's diloggun are an indispensable part of the ritual. He may continue to worship his Orisha privately, but he can no longer actively participate as a priest of those Orisha.

Conclusion

It is the errand Ori has sent me on that I am running.
It is the path that Orisha has laid out that I am following.

Traditional Yoruba saying

An analysis of destiny reveals two important points concerning Santería practice and the place of gender in the religion. On the one hand, the concept of destiny provides an opening for each individual to manifest the best possible life within the circumstances of his or her birth and to act in unconventional ways as long as these are consistent with the person's own perceived destiny. This understanding of personal destiny opens up each individual's life to a vast array of possibilities. Both within the religion and in the larger mundane world, one's role possibilities are limited not by anatomy or racial category or social status but by choices made at the feet of Olodumare and choices made in the living out of one's destiny.

On the other hand, by valorizing women's roles and powers, the practice of Santería provides extraordinary openings for women (and men). This analysis of gender within Santería, since it juxtaposes the powers and roles of olorisha with those of babalawo, provides a counternarrative to the standard understanding of the babalawo as the "high priest" of Orisha-based religion. In this narrative, the olorisha who has initiated many others into the religion and the oriaté who has presided over many rituals are the priests who have the most important roles in the religion. Without these priests the cults of all the Orisha (except Orula) would have died out. In chapter 5 I will return to this discussion of the valorization of women in the religion and the ways in which that valorization is being undermined by the narrative of babalawo as high priest.

CHAPTER 4 · Initiation

Mircea Eliade tells us that "hierophany" is the act of manifesting the sacred in the world of the profane. He suggests that when a stone or a tree is worshipped, it is no longer simply stone or tree but rather something sacred. And in becoming sacred, the stone or the tree becomes *ganz andere,* wholly other. Yet, even as it manifests the sacred, the stone or the tree continues to be itself, for it continues to participate in the surrounding (profane) world (Eliade 1959, 11–12).

Santería is an initiatory religion. This means that devotees become involved in the religion and advance within it by means of initiations. The most important of these is the kariocha ceremony that inducts one into the Santería priesthood. There are lower-level rituals that bring one into the religion and involve a less intense level of participation, and there are other initiations that enable one to perform additional roles for the community. But the kariocha ceremony is the central initiation in Santería. It is only through initiated priests that the Orisha can be made present in the visible world either through their icons or through the vehicle of possession trance, and it is only through initiated priests that the tradition can continue. Through their manipulation of "stones, blood and herbs" (Bascom 1950, 64–65), priests pass on the religious tradition to a new generation of devotees, vivify the Orisha icons, including the cowry shells used for divination, and empower others to serve as the embodiment of the Orisha during possession events. From the moment of their initiation, priests function as points of the sacred manifested in the profane world. This is most obvious during the initiation event itself and the subsequent period known as the *iyawoage*,[1] and during those radical manifestations of the sacred called possession trance. Just as a variety of material objects can be seen as a series of signifiers for religious beliefs, the body of the initiate serves as the expression of the sacred. It is this most important work of santeros that will be the focus of this chapter.

I will divide my discussion into two sections. First, I will focus on the kariocha ceremony and the way it not only provides a gateway for the sacred to manifest itself in the profane world but also serves to call into question some of our most closely held notions of what it means to be an individual self acting in the world. One of the most important effects of the initiation ceremony is to strengthen the ori of the newly initiated priest so that he or she can become the embodiment of an Orisha through the medium of possession trance. During the course of the possession event, the priest ceases to be him- or herself and becomes instead the living, breathing embodiment of an Orisha. To accept the actuality of the possession event is to hold in abeyance all traditional Western ideas of an individual as a continuous, if not unitary, self. The second portion of this chapter will explore possession trance, focusing especially on the slippages between self and other and the ways these slippages further challenge our notions of self and other.

Making the Sacred Manifest

In this section I want to explore the ways the iyawo, as a newly initiated Santería priest, embodies the sacred in his or her body. I will look at the person and persona of the iyawo and at the proscriptions of the iyawoage as points of hierophany that manifest a portion of the sacred. Like Eliade's stone, the iyawo becomes wholly (holy) other while continuing to participate in the world of work, school, shopping, and all the other minutiae of daily life. I will also suggest that, as part of the initiation process, the Santería priest learns to be able to move between the various concepts of self—including different concepts of a gendered self—required for this signification process. Rather than a being that is always already shaped into a unified self, Santería metaphysics understands being as flexible and permeable, dynamic without being fragmented.

Although this section will include some first-person accounts of being iyawo,[2] I will not be exploring the experience of the iyawoage from the perspective of the new initiate. In his essay on religious experience (1998), Robert Sharf rightly criticizes the use of the internal and mystical in the study of religion owing to the subjective, personal, and private nature of such reports. However, Santería is an initiatory religion. As Jacob Olupona suggests (1991, 14), it is participation in ritual and ceremonial activities rather than doctrinal purity or belief that is the focus of religiosity for santeros and other participants in Orisha religions. Because of this orientation, internal or mystical experience is underemphasized. What is important is not inner "feelings" but the correct performance of ritual requirements. Even in the case of possession trance, as we shall discuss in the next chapter, devotees do not talk about what is happening in the inner world of the medium, the person entranced, but what is happening in the outer world of the community and its interaction with the purported Orisha. At the same time, it would be too simplistic to say that devotees' inner experiences have nothing to do with their practice of Santería. As a matter of fact, it is the devotees' personal experience with the Orisha that brings them to and keeps them in the religion. Without some kind of personal connection or experience, most people would not continue in this, or any, religion. Yet much of that personal connection is also external, as devotees see the touch of the Orisha in their personal lives. Many "fateful" events—the unexpected, either positive or negative—are attributed to the action of the Orisha. Personal experience is important, but these experiences are physical rather than mystical. One must actually endure the initiation event and the rigors of the iyawoage, have one's hair cut, eat, sleep, and live in the prescribed way in order to enjoy the benefits of initiation. There is no mystical substitute for "the real thing." Although there are some who claim self-initiation, they are outside the general community.

As discussed in chapter 2, *iyawo* is a Yoruba term meaning "bride younger than speaker." It is used in Santería to designate a person who has completed the asiento ceremony and has been initiated into the priesthood. For a full year after the ceremony the new santero dresses in white, is subject to a wide number of taboos, and is generally "in training" toward his (or her) eventual position as a fully certified priest.[3] Typical of many rites of passage, the initiation into the Santería priesthood consists of three phases: separation, margin, and reintegration. During the first week of his initiation the iyawo is taken out of his old life and confined to a single room. It is in this room that the new priest is "made" by the Santería community. During the rest of the year the iyawo's status is ambiguous. He is both the most helpless of beings and one of the most powerful. As the year progresses, the restrictions that surround him are loosened or lifted so that the new santero is slowly reintegrated into both communities. However, it is not until the completion of the iyawo period that the initiate is accepted as a fully functioning member of the religious community and reintegrated into his previous secular life.

In Lukumi, the dialect of Yoruba spoken by practitioners of Santería, this ceremony of initiation is called kariocha, to place the Orisha in or on the head.[4] A quick review of the seven-day ceremony will help us see the theological background of this ritual (Murphy 1994, 96–104; M. Mason 2002, chap. 4). Like its African antecedents, the kariocha takes place in a simulated grove. A house or apartment is transformed into an African village. One room becomes the *igbodu*, a sacred grove separated from the rest of the house by a white sheet, a raffia skirt, and a chain of okra. A throne area is built in one corner of this room. A mat on the floor and a canopy overhead define the portion of the room that will be the initiate's home for the next week. It is in this room that he will be reborn as a iyawo and that the Orisha will be "made." The remaining portions of the house become sleeping quarters for the various attendants, a common kitchen and dining room, a corral for the animals awaiting sacrifice, and indoor and outdoor gathering areas. On the evening of the first day the initiate, who has already lost his name and is simply called "iyawo," is taken to a local stream, where he is bathed in the waters of Oshun, the Orisha of the river. Alongside the stream his old clothes are torn from his body and he is washed of the impurities of his old life. Then he is dressed in white clothes, his head is covered with a white cloth, and the white beaded necklace of Obatala, the Orisha of clarity and serenity, is draped around his neck. These actions are said to clear his head and prepare the way for the upcoming rituals. The next day he will be led blindfolded into the igbodu, where his head will be shaved in preparation for the installation of the Orisha.

From that moment at the river it is the head of the initiate that becomes the overriding concern of those supervising both the initiation and the following liminal year. From that moment the head is sacred. It is kept covered except when it is the focus of ritual attention. As the imminent seat of the Orisha, it is cleansed and purified on several occasions. After the guardian Orisha has been enthroned in it, it is pampered, blessed, and cared for as one of the most sacred of ritual implements.

As discussed in chapter 3, according to Yoruba cosmology the head is the seat of one's personality, one's metaphysical self. It is said that before birth a child kneels in front of Olodumare and chooses a "head" for this lifetime. This head encompasses the individual's intelligence, competence, personal limitations, and capacity for self-defense. It is symbolized by the physical head and is associated with the guardian Orisha. It is this guardian Orisha that is said to "own one's head." And it is this Orisha that is enthroned onto the initiate's head during the asiento. But more than merely intensifying the relationship between one's guardian Orisha and oneself, the initiation opens the pathway between the inner head and the guardian Orisha so that the new iyawo not only is associated with the Orisha but, in a very clear sense, becomes the embodiment of that Orisha. The tureens that house the implements of the Orisha can be broken and the implements themselves lost or destroyed, but the relationship between the Orisha and the head of the iyawo cannot be undone.

When the guardian Orisha and the other Orisha included in the initiation ceremony have been seated in the head of the initiate, the newly made Orisha, housed in their individual tureens, are fed the blood of their favorite animals. As each of the four-legged animals is brought forward for sacrifice, the iyawo will touch his head to the head of the animal. After saluting each animal he will watch as it is decapitated and its blood is fed to his Orisha. In his description of the initiation of Shango priests in Africa, J. Lorand Matory (1994) suggests that this gesture identifies the victim with the sacrificator so that the subsequent decapitation severs the head of the novice, the iyawo, by proxy. "Much as worldly husbands purchase the 'heads' of their brides with bridewealth, Shango demands the 'head' of his new bride" (133). No longer is the head of the iyawo his own; it has been both conquered and purchased by the Orisha. For the rest of his life, but especially during the iyawo year, the head will be the focus of particular attention. A iyawo's head must be covered during the novitiate period; it is blessed and cooled periodically by the initiating priest, the iyawo's godparent. If the iyawo should injure his head, the godparent must be notified immediately so that appropriate action can be taken. Although the body of the iyawo should not be touched by anyone, certain close family members are exempted, including the children, spouse, and members of the iyawo's immediate religious family. However, except for the godparents, no one may touch the iyawo's head under any circumstances, because the head belongs to the Orisha, is the altar upon which the Orisha have taken residence. The iyawo has become a walking temple, his head a mobile sacred site.

Marriage Symbolism

As we have said, the term used to describe the priests of the Orisha in both Africa and the Americas is "iyawo," a Yoruba word meaning new wife, younger than the speaker. Among the Yoruba "iyawo" describes more than one member of the reproductive dyad of husband and wife. When a woman marries into a Yoruba lineage, she is bride not only to her spouse but also to all the members of his lineage who preceded her entry into it, including her senior co-wives, the brothers of her spouse and their wives, and any daughters of the lineage. Even children born into the lineage before her marriage are considered to be her oko, "husband," and are entitled to call her "iyawo." As she ages and as additional women are brought into the household, she will be not only bride to all those who preceded her into the lineage but husband to those newer than herself. These terms, husband and new wife, oko and iyawo, express her place relative to the other members of the lineage (Bascom 1969, 51–52).

Upon initiation a new priest stands in the same position relative to the Orisha as a new bride does in relation to her husband. At the same time, the priest's relationship to the religious community is similar to a new bride's relationship to the household she joins upon marriage. This relationship holds true regardless of the nominal sex of either the initiate or the deity. The titles "husband" and "wife" indicate not so much a sexual relationship as the possession of certain productive and reproductive rights by all the "husbands" of the new bride. In the African case, a wife is nominally younger than and subordinate to her husband; by extension, human initiates are always subordinate to the god they manifest and to the other santeros in the religious family.

The initiate's first relationship to the Orisha, however, is that of a child to a loving parent. Two different phrases are used to describe the guardian deity: "So-and-so owns my head" and "So-and-so is my father/mother." Before they ever reach the point of initiation, most followers of Santería have discovered the name of this Orisha and have begun to make associations between their own life and personality and those of the guardian Orisha. It is expected that such knowledge will help them coordinate their conduct with the personality chosen before birth. Thus usually the early relationship with the primary Orisha is one of familial kinship.

To this parent-child relationship the asiento ceremony adds one symbolized by marriage. Now the Orisha is not only parent and ruler, it becomes lover and spouse. This relationship is not like an egalitarian American-style marriage but is based on the more hierarchical African social model in which the husband is the senior and more powerful party. Although the Santería initiate belongs to the Orisha, he is also tied by a variety of relationships to all the other members of the *ilé*, the religious household. Regardless of his actual sex, the iyawo assumes a female position in that household. He is addressed as "iyawo" throughout his novitiate year and must prostrate himself to every member of the household and of the larger community whose initiation predates his own. All iyawo are expected to perform certain types of physical and spiritual work for the household; after the first three months, when they are treated as infants, they are at the beck and call of the other members of the household. One often sees a iyawo in the kitchen washing dishes, cleaning up a godparent's home or apartment, or performing other types of personal service.

The liminal period of a Santería initiation lasts well past the time the new priest leaves the igbodu. For a full year after his birth "en santo," the iyawo is subject to a wide-ranging list of prohibitions. He must always dress in white; must not visit bars, jails, cemeteries, hospitals, or other places of contamination; must not drink alcohol or use recreational drugs; must not use profane language; must not shake hands or eat with a knife and fork. A female iyawo may not wear makeup or curl, cut, or dye her hair; a male must be clean shaven. All iyawo must keep their heads covered and may wear no jewelry except their Santería necklaces and bracelets. For the first three months after the initiation, the iyawo may not use a mirror, even to shave. In addition, during that initial period he must eat all meals while seated on a mat on the floor using only a spoon and his own set of dishes. During the entire year, the iyawo loses his name and is simply addressed as "iyawo" by his family and friends. At three-month intervals some of these restrictions are lifted, until at the end of the year the iyawo completes his iyawoage and becomes an olorisha, a "fully crowned" santero who is mature enough to relate to the outside world. At this point he can present the Orisha he carries within himself to godchildren of his own. After the final ritual of the iyawo period he can put aside his white clothes and return to his regular life. But even after the end of the iyawo period, the santero cannot simply return to his old life. Restrictive regulations both positive and negative continue throughout his life, and at death he is returned symbolically to the igbodu when his body is dressed in his coronation clothes and portions of the hair that was removed to seat the Orisha are returned to him.

After the completion of his iyawoage and as he matures in the service of the Orisha, the new priest may initiate others into the religion. Those who have initiated one or more godchildren are given the title "iyalosha" or "babalosha," mother or father of Orisha. Now the priest stands not only as a child and wife of the Orisha but as one who has given birth, as the spiritual parent of new devotees and their Orisha icons. This suggests a movement toward an increasingly gendered view of devotees, who begin as undifferentiated children (omo), become wives (iyawo) upon priestly initiation, and finally are fully gendered parents when they "reproduce" or create new members of the ritual family. However, priests always remain iyawo-Orisha, wifely followers of the Orisha whom they serve. Thus it is of particular interest to explore the ways in which priestliness is concurrent with womanliness—that is, the ways in which the feminine is considered the most appropriate metaphor for religiosity.

As Daniel Boyarin's analysis of Christianity has suggested, maleness serves as a norm of spirituality for that tradition. God is generally conceived of as male, the highest functionaries are male, and it is only by repudiating her femaleness that a woman can achieve high levels of spiritual development. In other traditions as well, it appears that male anatomy and roles are valorized in the performance of religious rituals.[5] However, our analysis has suggested that it is both female anatomy and female behavior that are valorized in the performance of Orisha-based traditions.

As both Oyewùmí and Matory have indicated, a iyawo is not simply part of a gender dyad, since each new wife has a group of people she calls oko, husband. Outside of the religious environment, it is only those with female anatomy who are denominated iyawo. A man who leaves his natal home to live in the compound of a wife or who is acquired as a slave or servant to join another lineage is not iyawo. It is only women brought into the lineage for reproductive purposes and priests of the Orisha who are given that role title. Since "iyawo" has a specifically gendered connotation in the Yoruba cultural environment, we can suggest that it involves a type of gendering in the religious environment as well. New wives not only provide reproductive labor to the lineage of their husbands, they also provide labor to the household as a whole. Beyond their responsibility for their own food and clothing, wives are expected to participate in many kinds of work. They must maintain their own quarters as well as the common areas of the compound, they must help their husbands on their farms as well as planting and harvesting from their own plots, they often raise small animals, and they cook for themselves and their children, as well as for their partner in a rotation with his other wives. Many Yoruba women are also traders, buying and selling in the marketplace, cooking for sale on the street, and producing and selling merchandise. If a woman comes from a family with a specialized skill, she may continue to engage in the work of her own lineage after her marriage. Or she may participate in the specialized work of her husband's lineage.

Iyawo-Orisha perform a similar series of services for their Orisha and the community of worshippers. Santería priests must maintain the shrines of their Orisha, "feeding" them and providing other offerings as appropriate. They look after the spiritual—and often emotional and material—well-being of their spiritual families while maintaining the well-being of themselves and their physical family members. They may perform divination for their religious household and others who need their services. They generally also perform the rituals and sacrifices called for during divination sessions. If they have a skill or ability that can be used in the production of Orisha goods, they may work at the production of the *herramienta* (tools) and other accouterments of the Orisha. They participate in the round of ritual events in their communities, and even when they themselves are not initiating new priests, they will be called upon to work at the initiation rituals of others.

All of these activities come under the rubric of "working" the Orisha. The idea of worship as "work" seems to have a long history in Orisha religion. Not only do contemporary Yoruba people characterize the religious activities of Orisha worshippers as work by speaking of them under the rubric "ṣe òrìṣà" (to make, do, or work the Orisha), but Peter McKenzie (1997) consistently uses the phrase "to make òrìṣà" to refer to such activities among mid-nineteenth-century Orisha worshippers. Spanish-speaking santeros call the kariocha "hacer el santo," to make the saint, and both English-speaking and Spanish-speaking santeros consistently use "work" to describe their own religious activities.

The Yoruba people were not the only ones who were able to reconstruct their religious traditions in Cuba. The Bantu-speaking people from central Africa were brought to the island as early as the sixteenth century (Palmié 2002, 162). The so-called Kongo religious traditions that were developed in Cuba are generally gathered under the descriptive umbrella of Palo and include Palo Monte, Palo Mayombe, Kimbisa, and others. Whereas the Yoruba cosmology is focused on the Orisha, the cosmology of these traditions focuses on the spirits of the dead, which are captured and placed in iron cauldrons. Although there was a good deal of antagonism between the practitioners of these traditions and the later-arriving Yoruba-speaking peoples, the two traditions continue to form a religious continuum, as many contemporary practitioners are initiates of both systems. Chapter 2 of Stephan Palmié's *Wizards and Scientists* (2002) is one of the few scholarly works about these religious systems. In his comparison between Ocha (Santería) and Palo, Palmié suggests that the practice of Ocha focuses on reciprocal interchange and divine initiative while that of Palo is cast in terms of wage labor and payment, dominance and potential revolt, which he characterizes as expressive and instrumental orientations respectively (25). Although Palmié doesn't make explicit the association of instrumentalist practice as masculine and expressive as feminine, the terms often carry such gendered connotations.[6] As Eugen Schoenfeld and Stjepan Mestrović suggest (1991, 365, citing Parsons 1962), fundamentally different system needs can be represented by gender difference in religious practice. According to their analysis, instrumental needs "represent the polity and the rational-level aspect of society" and thus are associated with male tasks, while the activities associated with expressive needs "solve cathartic problems and are rooted in the problems of gratification" which are traditionally met through the performance of roles typically associated with the female (366). Ethically male experiences and personality attributes are typically associated with justice, while female experiences lead to an emphasis on qualities of caring (366, citing research of Gilligan, esp. 1982). Their Weberian analysis suggests a division between *"ritual-centered* priestly religion" and *"moral-centered* prophetic religion," which are also genderized such that a ritual focus is considered rational and thus masculine while a prophetic focus is considered subjective, imaginative, emotional, sensual, and thus feminine (369). Instrumental-rational religion emphasizes a "nonemotional approach to prayer" while expressive religion places "primacy on prayer as emotional expression" (369). Thus Schoenfeld and Mestrović suggest that a religion that is caught up in ideas of justice, military prowess, and market dominance can be characterized as instrumental and masculine, while religious expression that is associated with care, mercy, and mutuality, the nonrational and noncalculating side of being human, can be described as expressive and feminine (369).

As we will discuss in chapter 7, Palmié (2002) invokes these connotations when he suggests that "ocha and palo stand to each other like religion and magic, expressive and instrumental forms of human-divine interaction" (193) and that the primary ritual events of Ocha are "stately even royal displays" (194), while ignoring all the activities that make such displays possible as well as all of the other religious work that santeros perform. Palmié claims that sociological factors lead to the association of instrumental "magic" with Palo Monte while expressive "religion" is reserved for Ocha (190), yet he too seems to associate the instrumental with the more masculinist form while suggesting that expressive practice is more female in orientation. Although he suggests that the practice of paleros is "morally ambivalent and potentially malignant" (165), it also tends to be valorized as more powerful and effective than Ocha in achieving the ends of practitioners. Whereas paleros can be characterized as the masters of the spiritual forces they control, santeros are wives who work with and for their Orisha and the religious families they have created. Since many santeros are also paleros, there is not an absolute division between these two modes of practice. Rather, practitioners are able to move between masculine-instrumentalist forms and feminine-expressive forms according to their perceived needs and their relationship with the spiritual entities involved.

Priestly Womanliness

While our reading of Oyewùmí in chapter 2 suggested that gender is a weak category among the Yoruba, the roles played by women in traditional families seem to have provided a model for religious practices and relationships both in the African and American contexts. In a cultural system in which women's reproductive powers are essential for the continuation of the lineage and where women's speech and hidden behavior are considered especially potent (Abiodun 2001, 26–27) but where gendered terminology is limited to women's roles as wives and mothers, it is surprising neither that the female serves as the ideal religious type within the Orisha traditions nor that those few gendered terms available are appropriated to describe religious relationships.

Though it may be true, as Oyewùmí suggests (2000, 1096), that "wife is a four-letter word" throughout African society and among the Yoruba people because it symbolizes the subordination of one person by another, Orisha priests on both sides of the Atlantic have chosen to use this terminology to identify themselves in their priestly roles. And, in spite of her contention that "*Mother* is the preferred and cherished self-identity of many African women" (1096), Orisha priests have regenderized their terminology when referring to their religious reproductive behavior, preferring to invoke anatomical differences for senior practitioners and eschewing the feminized terminology developed for the initiation experience. That is, although all priests are gendered female as iyawo-Orisha, they recover their gender and metaphoric sexuality as iyalosha or babalosha, in spite of the identical function of these roles. Thus, contrary to what Oyewùmí's analysis might lead one to expect, all priests take on the pejorative title "iyawo" while limiting the more valorized title "iya" (mother) to anatomical females.

Let us consider first why men might be willing to take on the disparaged title of iyawo in conjunction with their religious practice and then consider why they might choose to drop the female attribution on other occasions.

As discussed in chapter 2, a majority of cultures structure gender relationships according to a set of metaphorically binary oppositions that associate women with nature and the private domain and men with culture and the public domain. Since the domain of men encompasses that of women, it is accorded greater prestige and higher social value (Ortner and Whitehead, 7–8). Thus in most cultures men, husbands, and masters have more status than women, wives, and servants. Yet, as we have seen, within Yoruba society male Orisha devotees gain status when they become the brides of the Orisha, that is, take on a female gender relative to the deity. How, we should ask, is it possible for an individual man to achieve a higher status by taking on a gender role normally associated with women?

Although men generally have more prestige than women do, in many societies the women associated with certain highly placed men have a higher status than some other men in that society. Among the precolonial Yoruba, the women of the palace, the *ayaba*, often called the king's wives, were accorded higher status than men not associated with the king. These palace women were government functionaries and royal advisors who stood as intermediaries between the king and his subject chiefs. High status was also accorded to certain functionaries of the king called *ilari*, whose ranks included both men and women. An indication of both the ilari's status and function as royal representatives was their appropriation of the title of ayaba, or "wives of the king" (Matory 1994, 9).

Similarly, the priest as iyawo, as "wife" of the Orisha, appropriates some of the status of his spirit-husband and is accorded a higher position than other members of the religious community. Thus for both the ilari and the iyawo-Orisha, taking on a wifely role increases rather than decreases a man's prestige. The possession priest—and all priests in the Santería/Lukumi tradition are potentially possession priests—acquires some of the status of his Orisha not only by association but also by becoming the direct representative of that Orisha during possession events. Although his status is dependent upon his relationship with his "spirit-husband," being the embodied representative of a powerful being gives him, as the "wife" of the Orisha, both increased prestige and authority.

However, this ascribed status is not the only reason for the feminization of the priesthood. As we will discuss more fully in chapter 6, the work of Orisha devotion parallels a wife's work in a traditional family. Both wifely and priestly work is concerned with the well-being of others. Its responsibilities include procuring and preparing food, maintaining the living area, monitoring the health of the family and caring for the ill, and guarding the family from both visible and invisible hazards. Although both men and women may perform cooking tasks, generally it is women who are responsible for the feeding of their families, especially their children. Ritual feasting on both sides of the Atlantic requires the work of many women over many days to prepare both the sacred and the secular food. Even when the performance of the sacrificial act falls to men, it is women who transform the sacrificial carcasses into tasty dishes for both human and divine consumption.

All of these "wifely" tasks can become incorporated in the terminology of iyawo as a new priest, much like a new wife, learns how to satisfy both his spirit-husband and the community he has joined. If the principal work of the iyawo (bride) is to become iya (mother) through the medium of sexual inter-course, that of the iyawo-Orisha is to bring the Orisha into presence in the religious community. There are two principal methods for accomplishing this task: the possession trance and the initiation of new devotees. Both involve the penetration of the sacred into the physicality of an individual. During the possession event the spirit-husband "mounts" and controls the body of his wifely devotee just as a human husband mounts and controls his wife's body in copulation; through initiation new priests are made along with a new set of Orisha icons which form the most accessible point of contact between the Orisha and their devotees.

By convention there are no limits on who may be initiated, and after initia-tion there are few limits on who may become possessed. This means that any-one regardless of age, sex, gender identity, racial identity, or socioeconomic class may be called by the Orisha to serve as priestly wife. And anyone who has had the appropriate initiations may become possessed by his titular Orisha. However, initiation always makes the initiate a iyawo, a wife, regardless of the anatomy of the new priest and regardless of the gender ascribed to the possess-ing Orisha. All of the Orisha can "mount" their mediums, penetrating and dominating their bodies. Thus by convention both initiation and possession turn men into women and sometimes, when the possessing Orisha is gen-dered male, women into men.

Conclusion

Priestly initiation both valorizes and overturns essentialist views of gender. On one hand, all of the metaphoric usages draw on a stereotypical and essentialist view of the female wifely role and the relationship between wives and their husbands and families. Priestly wives, like many of their cultural counterparts, are younger than their spirit-husbands; they are responsible not only for their relationship with those spirit-husbands but also with all members of the religious family both visible and invisible; they must assume the caregiving burden of feeding, clothing, and ministering to both their Orisha-husbands and their extended religious families. On the other hand, both anatomical males and females are regularly initiated into this priestly role without regard for any conception of cognitive dissonance between one's "essential" anatomy, gender, or sexual orientation and one's priestly gender roles. In spite of a very stereotypic view of sex and gender, Orisha devotees routinely enact an underlying belief that gender can be constructed according to the demands of their religious practice. Thus one is "made" iyawo in the initiation room and becomes Orisha through the possession ritual without any respect for one's "everyday" gender and without any necessity to change one's genitals or one's sexual orientation.

Gender crossing is integral to the practice of Santería. Both male and female devotees, in their relationship with the Orisha, are given the chance to adopt roles and characteristics typically assigned to the opposite gender as well as their own. To the extent that the Orisha serve as archetypes of human behavior, they can be used by both men and women to explore the nuances of those archetypes without respect to the ostensible gender of the Orisha or their own gender or sexual orientation. Thus even men may incorporate aspects of the great mother Yemaya into their personalities, and women can use Ochosi to explore their own inner warrior or hunter aspects. Although all of the female Orisha have warrior aspects which a woman in search of her own empowerment can explore, she is not limited to the aspects of those Orisha who share her gender. Thus a woman might look to the stories of Shango, Obatala, or even Ogun for developmental models. Similarly, men not only can experience the feminine in their roles as iyawo-Orisha, but they can also look to the stories of female Orisha such as Yemaya, Oshun, Oya, and Obba for edification. One need not be a crowned priest of an Orisha to explore the meaning of that Orisha's energies in the unfolding of one's destiny.

At the same time, a woman need not repudiate her female nature in order to explore a wide range of roles and characteristics. Within the Orisha mythology she can find female Orisha that were not only wives and mothers but also warriors, rulers, workers, wise advisors, and the like. In addition to appearing in stories as mothers and consorts, each of the female Orisha is also known as an oba, a ruler in her own right. Thus just as femaleness serves as the model for priestly behavior, it also can be embodied in a wide range of cultural roles and behaviors, without limitation. If one's destiny is to be a leader, one's biology may have an effect but never stands as an absolute impediment. Not only can an anatomical female embody a male Orisha during possession trance, becoming the King of the White Cloth or the great Shango, she may also rise to the highest leadership roles within the religion as the head of her own spiritual household or as an esteemed elder in the tradition. Although, as we have discussed, in the contemporary period the oba oriaté are generally male, there is no structural requirement forbidding women from training and taking on that role. Even as the earliest oriaté were strong women, so today a new generation of female oriaté are being developed. Leadership need not be a gendered concept. Not only can men be wives, but women can rise to the highest ranks and become oba, leaders and kings.

CHAPTER 5 · Possession Phenomena

Maya Deren (1953, chap. 7) called it the "white darkness"; French psychiatrist Levy-Valensi saw it as the "ante-chamber of the asylum" (Lewis 1971, 179); many people consider it the second most challenging aspect of Santería after animal sacrifice (which we will discuss in chapter 6). Possession trance, the state of being entranced and dominated by another being, is an important part of Santería religious practice. Possession trance not only allows practitioners to talk to their deities and other spiritual beings but also allows those beings to talk back, to respond in a clearly material fashion. In this chapter we will explore three important aspects of Santería possession phenomena. First we will challenge the suggestion that Santería and its sister religions have no mystical or prophetic element by suggesting that the possession phenomenon is a communal mystical experience that provides devotees with a direct revelation of divine will; then we will look more deeply into the place of the individual in this phenomenon and investigate the ways in which possession trance challenges our strongly held ideas of selfhood as unique and unitary; and finally, spinning off from that discussion, we will explore the ways in which possession trance promotes gender switching and certain types of gender ambiguity.

Possession by spiritual beings is a worldwide phenomenon. In her research on possession phenomena, Erika Bourguignon found some type of possession belief in 74 percent of the societies in her investigation pool of 488 cultures, and possession trance in 52 percent. While the highest incidence of possession phenomena was in the cultures of the Pacific rim and the lowest in North and South American Indian cultures, they were widespread among cultures of Eurasia, Africa, the circum-Mediterranean region, and among the descendants of Africa in the Americas. Those societies in which trance is most frequently interpreted as spirit possession were in Africa and areas influenced by Africa. Worldwide, possession phenomena are more likely to be found in agricultural societies than among hunter/gatherers, and the possessed are more commonly women than men. And although Western observers have often associated this phenomenon with mental illness, observers in those societies where it is common have developed ways to discriminate between possession phenomena and other altered states of consciousness (Bourguignon 1976, 31).

What is spirit possession? Vincent Crapanzano suggests the most liberal description. Spirit possession, he says, is "any altered state of consciousness indigenously interpreted in terms of the influence of an alien spirit" (Crapanzano 1977, 7). For the purposes of our discussion we can use Crapanzano's method of accepting as "real" those physical and psychological changes that are accepted by the participating group as legitimate spirit possessions. Santeros recognize that it is possible to fake a possession event, and they provide tests of the legitimacy of any particular such event. We, however, will not call the reality of these events into question; rather we will accept that possession occurs as described by participants.

As experienced in a Santería *tambor* (Sp., drum [ceremony]), spirit possession is a type of trance possession. I. M. Lewis in his classic *Ecstatic Religion* (1971) distinguishes between possession and trance. He suggests that trance is due "to the temporary absence of the subject's soul" (29), while possession is the "invasion of the individual by a spirit" (46). Although either state may happen independently, possession trance is a state wherein an alien spirit fills the space left empty by trance. When experienced in African and African-derived religious traditions, this alien spirit may be an Orisha, or the spirit of an ancestor, or the personality of a spirit guide. In religious language, this is a type of hierophany, a manifestation of the invisible into the visible world. Through this manifestation a being from the invisible world temporarily takes control of a visible body in order to experience the material world, communicate with devotees, and provide insight into the consciousness of the divine. Important to these actions is the presence of a community who can receive any communications and insights, since there is no direct communication between the invading spirit and the departed "soul." For the medium, the possessed person, there is an experiential "break" in existence during which another is incarnate in the medium's body.

Before we begin our analysis of this radical manifestation of the sacred as found in contemporary Orisha religion, I want to provide some descriptions of this phenomenon. The first piece describes a tambor held in the spring of 1993. The tambor was a ritual invocation of the Orisha given by a priest of Eleggua, the divine trickster, who was to be called from the invisible to the visible world by sacred drums and a type of call-and-response chanting. Two Orisha graced this event: Eleggua himself and Aganyu, who is the Orisha associated with the volcano. This was my introduction to the practice of Santería and the first time I watched the bodies of human mediums being invaded by sacred beings, to which I attribute a certain breathlessness of the account.

> Our host, Roberto, had changed into a pair of black pants accented with long red fringe, a red shirt, and a red and black hat—the colors of Eleggua. After some warm-up drumming, a rhythm to call Eleggua began. Roberto danced in the center of a circle formed by the crowd and the drummers and the lead singer. After a while the drumming and chanting got louder and more insistent. Suddenly there was a change— he was no longer Roberto but Eleggua. The drumming and chanting continued stronger as the singer called Eleggua to be firmly seated in Roberto's body. He chased Eleggua around the room, calling and chanting to him. Soon the glasses were thrown off, then the shoes, then the shirt unbuttoned. When it was determined that Eleggua was truly there, he was led into another room where he would be costumed in the appropriate attire. In the meantime Aganyu came down to possess another santero. His possession was neither as dramatic nor as turbulent as that of Eleggua, but finally he too was led to the back room.
>
> After a few minutes the Orisha were brought back and the real festivities began. It is hard to describe what happened for the next several hours. The two Orisha danced, talked to their devotees, . . . preached and danced some more. To an outsider who merely wandered in, it would

have looked like a really good party with a percussion group, a single male vocalist, and the crowd dancing and joining in the singing. But of course there was more to it than that. This was a religious service. Those two, who might be misidentified as overly enthusiastic partyers, were believed to be deities who were temporarily using the bodies of their followers in order to communicate with the rest of the congregation.

Several elements are necessary for a successful possession event. Orisha do not normally enter into persons unless called, and although participants are encouraged to communicate with their deities outside of the communal events, they do not normally engage in full trance possession except in the protected communal environment. In the context of Santería, the Orisha are allowed to invade only the bodies of those whose initiations have prepared them to receive their presence. If the uninitiated begin to exhibit signs of possession, they are removed from the environment of the sacred drums and called back into themselves.

In the Santería context, the possessed person has no memory of the presence of the Orisha and its actions and communications. Within the Santería community, the movement toward possession is characterized by temporary, often violent, physical changes. These are understood to be the priest's reaction to "invasion" by an alien spirit. Although possession is considered desirable and actually promoted by participation in the religion, the temporary absence of one's soul and the "vacating" of one's body are not easy. Once the possession is complete, the possessed person exhibits certain characteristics typical of the invading Orisha. These changes alert the remaining members of the group to the presence of the embodied Orisha.

Having looked at the phenomenon of possession from the point of view of an outside observer, I would like to share another account of possession trance, this time in the words of an accomplished medium. This excerpt comes from a film on the initiation ritual in the Brazilian religion of Candomblé. Candomblé is similar to Santería in many respects, including its foundation in the West African traditions. In this excerpt a woman attempts to describe her experience of possession trance. Whereas in the earlier account we looked at possession from the outside, here we hear the voice of the medium herself.

I feel this way when the Candomblé is playing . . . that the Orisha wants to get me, my legs tremble, something reaches up that takes over my heart, my head grows, I see that blue light, I look for someone to grab but can't find anyone and then I don't see anything anymore. Then everything happens and I don't see. Then I think that the Orisha must be something like wind, it comes towards you like a wind and embraces you. Like a shock in my heart, my heart beats as fast as the lead drum plays, my head grows, and it seems I see a blue light ahead of me and a hole appears in the middle of the room. Then I want to run, to grab someone, but people seem far away, out of reach. Then I don't see anything anymore. (Sarno 1980)

From their earliest beginnings, the Western philosophical and theological traditions have characterized the human person as a spiritual soul trapped within a material body. In their own ways both Plato and Augustine, to choose two widely recognized representatives of these traditions, valorized the spiritual at the expense of the material. After two thousand years of thought, we find the continuation of these ideas in Kant's theory of radical dualism. These characterizations of the human person have established a dichotomy that distinguishes between spirit and matter, the sacred and the profane, so that there is always a presumed chasm between these terms. In its most radical formulation there is an understanding that communication between the spiritual and the physical is impossible. With this formulation, religious experience becomes suspect and the touch of the divine is equated with madness.

Paul Ricoeur suggests that the history of the Judeo-Christian tradition is a constant struggle against the irrationality of sacred experience. In an article on manifestation and proclamation (1995, 55) he says that "one cannot fail to be struck by the constant, obstinate struggle against the Canaanite cults—against the idols Baal and Astarte, against the myths about vegetation and agriculture, and in general against any natural and cosmic sacredness—as expressed in the writings of the Hebrew prophets." This struggle was often expressed in the early Christian era as the conflict between iconoclasts and those who defended the use of religious icons (Baggley 1987, 23–25). Hundreds of years later, it could be suggested that differing views of the place of the word and the image, proclamation and manifestation, in Christian worship helped to fuel the Protestant Reformation. In spite of that history, as Ricoeur goes on to suggest, religious experience, the experience of hierophany, continues to enrich and inform religious traditions.

As we have seen, Santería practitioners have been able to preserve many of their traditions and re-create some of their forms of religious expression in the Americas. Among those preserved traditions is the use of drumming and dancing to communicate with the Orisha and to draw them into physical presence. It is during communal celebrations, like the tambor and the Candomblé described above, that the Orisha are made present to the community through the bodies of their devotees. The Orisha are made manifest to the community through the willingness of initiates to endure possession, to bring to consciousness that special state of mind that indicates one is "in the spirit." Whoever is empowered and willing to thus manifest the spirit does so, as Joseph Murphy says (1994, 184–85), "for the benefit of the community to allow others to share in the consciousness." Because one is normally entranced while possessed, one does not directly benefit from one's own possession. It is the community that benefits from one's willingness to become possessed, one's willingness to enter that altered state of consciousness.

Communal Mysticism

One of the features of the Afro-Diaspora traditions that make them different from European and Asian traditions is their communal nature. Nowhere in these traditions is there an understanding that one can or should leave the community in order to further one's spiritual development. Although one may encounter both the spirits and the Orisha in private, the community is required for many types of Afro-Diasporan religious expression. The community is necessary not only for an individual's personal religious development but for the very existence of the Orisha themselves: "The Orishas are made present by the action of the community and in the actions of the community. There are no Orishas without human beings" (Murphy 1994, 110). Within the mainstream Santería tradition it is during the communal celebrations, the tambores, that the Orisha are made present to the community through the persons of the santeros attending. Through spirit possession the gods, in the form of the Orisha, are brought into the community. Paraphrasing the description by I. M. Lewis (1971, 204) of possession cults in general, we can say, "What is proclaimed [in Santería and other possession cults] is not merely that God is *with* us, but that He is *in* us. [Santería is] thus the religion par excellence of the spirit made flesh." In addition, those santeros who are empowered to manifest the Orisha can only be "made" through human action, through the work of the community. It is only through the action of existing santeros that a devotee can be "made saint," imbued with the spiritual force that is identified as a particular Orisha, and it is only through the same community that an Orisha can be fixed into the various ritual objects of the religion. An individual priestess or priest cannot initiate new members into the community or fix the spirits. This means that if the community is unable or unwilling to confer such an initiation, no initiation is possible. At the same time, an Orisha is unable to call new children—that is, accept new devotees—without a community to initiate them. As Murphy says (1994, 180), "Its life as 'a' spirit depends on the service of its devotees." This interdependence between humanity and divinity is succinctly stated in the Yoruba proverb "Where there is no human being, there is no divinity" (180). In fact, as Lewis suggests (1971, 205), this dependence "celebrates a confident and egalitarian view of man's relations with the divine, and perpetuates that original accord between God and man which those who have lost the ecstatic mystery can only nostalgically recall in myths of creation, or desperately seek in doctrines of personal salvation."

As we have seen, the movement toward possession is characterized by temporary, often violent, physical changes. Once the possession is complete, the possessed person exhibits certain characteristics typical of the invading spirit—for example, a change of voice tone and speaking patterns, a movement from English to Spanish or Yoruba or another language, and unusual body postures. These changes alert the remaining members of the community that a spirit has arrived. In many cases, particularly in the case of Orisha possession, experienced participants recognize individual spirits by their particular characteristics and judge the authenticity of the possession according to how well these characteristics match community expectations.

If fully possessed, the person is entranced, unaware of his own or others' actions. Only in the presence of another can a spirit speak and be heard. In spite of the absence of the host personality, some or all of the communication from the spirit may be directed toward that person, and she must depend on the memory and goodwill of the other participants to convey the information from the spirit to her after her return. These communications are important, for they often involve requirements for the well-being either of the spirit or of its human host. Spirits whose requests are neglected can be expected to return later with a more strongly worded or more rigorous request.

Although trance possession, particularly that style of possession that characterizes Afro-Diaspora religions, is generally not included in traditional descriptions and analyses of Western and Eastern mystical experience, we can use those descriptions and methods to analyze these phenomena in order to see how closely they conform to our Western views of mysticism.

In his classic *The Varieties of Religious Experience*, William James proposes four characteristics of mystical experience. He suggests that such experiences are ineffable, noetic, transient, and passive. By *ineffable* he means these states are "more like states of feeling than like states of intellect" (James 1902, 380). "The subject of [the mystical experience] immediately says that it defies expression, that no adequate report of its contents can be given in words. It follows from this that its quality must be directly experienced; it cannot be imparted or transferred to others" (380). Mystical states are also *noetic*—experienced as states of knowledge, "states of insight into depths of truth unplumbed by the discursive intellect. They are illuminations, revelations, full of significance and importance, all inarticulate though they remain; and as a rule they carry with them a curious sense of authority for after-time" (380–81). These are the two principal characteristics of mystical experience. In addition, he suggests that such experiences are *transient*, normally lasting for half an hour to two hours at the most, and that they are *passive*, as "the mystic feels as if his own will were in abeyance, and indeed sometimes as if he were grasped and held by a superior power" (381). James objects to including "mediumistic trance" among mystical experiences, because "it may have no significance for the subject's usual inner life, to which, as it were, it makes a mere interruption. Mystical states, strictly so called, are never merely interruptive. Some memory of their content always remains, and a profound sense of their importance" (381).

That possession events are ineffable, transient, and passive does not seem open to question. Less obvious are their noetic quality and the requirement that the mystical experience have some significance for the subject's inner life. Yet I would argue that, taken within their cultural and religious environment, possession events also meet these two criteria. First, a review of that cultural milieu. European and Asian mystical experiences generally are solitary events: Teresa of Avila progressed through her interior castle alone; although Ramakrishna had spiritual teachers, his visions and other mystical experiences were internal; even St. Augustine's Ostria vision which involved his mother was essentially a personal event. While Teresa and Ramakrishna both lived in communities that supported their mystical activities, those communities were not *required* for the manifestation of their mysticism and in some cases were perceived to interfere with their interior religious development. Both of their traditions included the practice of long-term solitary religious living as helpful or even required for particular types of spiritual growth (Teresa 1961; Kripal 1992; Nikhilananda 1942; Augustine 1961). On the other hand, Afro-Diaspora religious expression, particularly a possession event, is usually part of a larger communal event. In the case of Santería, the community is required to initiate the devotee into the service of his or her deity and the community is required to call the Orisha or other spirit into the host, to protect the host during the event, and to receive the messages from the Orisha or spirit. Although a solitary possession is possible, it is understood that such an event provides less for both the host and the larger community and might actually injure the host, especially in the case of less experienced practitioners. Thus if we want to evaluate the noetic quality of the possession event, we have to evaluate it in the light of its collective qualities.

From the point of view of the medium, there is a radical break in perception. There is a realization that one's body has been used in unaccustomed ways, by an Other that can never be completely known. For the observing community too, there is a radical break as the body of the neighbor temporarily becomes home to a radical Other, to a sacred being whose presence demands attention. As the ritual concludes, as the drummers stow their instruments and the cooks begin to serve the food that has been prepared, each participant returns to his or her own being, changed in a greater or lesser degree by the experience of the divine incarnate. For the community, if not for the individual, the words and actions of the spirit do have a noetic quality. There is an understanding that the pronouncements have an authority beyond that of the host personality. Requests and commands from an Orisha are not only accepted, they maintain their authority for "after-time" and their fulfillment is expected. Unpleasant or unwelcome news from an Orisha must be accepted and acted upon, not only for one's own well-being but also for the well-being of the community.

In addition to the benefits to the community, identification with and possession by an Orisha or other spirit carries with it a presumed benefit for the host. Murphy says (1994, 85), "The Orishas are independent, personal spiritual beings who empower all life. Santería is the development of the relationships between human beings and Orishas." As discussed earlier, the relationship between the human and spirit worlds is one of mutual and reciprocal service. Marriage is a widely used metaphor for the relationship between an initiate and his spirit. In describing the shamanic relationship, Lewis says (1971, 190): "If the shaman is contractually bound as mortal partner to a divinity, that deity is equally tied to its human spouse. Both are inseparably conjoined: each possesses the other." Similarly, Murphy tells us (1994, 94), to be a iyawo "is to be married to the spirit, with all the mutual rights and obligations of marriage. Throughout the temporary one-year novitiate that constitutes *iyawoage*, the junior 'bride' is beholden to the spirit husband, a subordinate but reciprocal relationship of mutual service." This is hardly an indication of a relationship that has no significance for one's inner life; rather it portends a radical transformation of one's inner nature so one can partake of the divinity and manifest it to the rest of the community (185).

In *Mysticism: Sacred and Profane* (1957), R. C. Zaehner suggests that religious mysticism involves union with God or some other principle; it is a "unitive experience with someone or something other than oneself" (32). In Christian mysticism "the mystic *knows* that God is in him and with him; his body has literally become a 'temple of the Holy Ghost.' This is no longer a dogma accepted on faith, but, the mystic would allege, an experienced fact" (31–32). Accordingly, "the whole purpose of [a strictly religious mysticism] is to concentrate on an ultimate reality to the complete exclusion of all else; and by 'all else' is meant the phenomenal world or, as the theists put it, all that is not God" (33). Participants in spirit possession could be said to have a special type of unitive experience. Although it may not be obvious to the possessed individual, during the possession event he or she *becomes* the possessing Orisha. Much like the Christian mystic who experiences God as a fact, the community of the possessed experiences its god in the body of the possessed person. There is no requirement that one believe in the Orisha or even in the idea of spirit possession to recognize this presence; the physiological and psychological changes exhibited by the possessed show the presence of the Orisha or spirit to the community. Again, one might object that the possessed person does not have the direct experience of being an Orisha, but within this community *everyone* has the experience of meeting the Orisha face to face because the opportunities for possession are shared among the community. One may meet *and* be an Orisha within the course of a single evening, and over the course of a lifetime of such interactions one can experience both sides of that relationship many times.

The use of the marriage metaphor also encourages one to experience in a conscious way (outside the trance situation) oneself as the Orisha. As self and other become blurred, one is encouraged to develop the mutual relationship with one's Orisha guides so that the "spirit is not the conscious self, but something greater which may subsume the self, overcome its borders and direct the whole person" (Murphy 1994, 191). This type of "working" of the spirit may be compared to the Christian soul's experience of entering the outer and mid-level mansions of Teresa's castle, while the intimate relationship of the fully crowned santero with his or her Orisha may more closely resemble a soul's spiritual betrothal and marriage described in Teresa's sixth and seventh mansions (Teresa 1961). In both cases the mundane life outside the ritual event is changed and shaped by experiences within that event. A single encounter with an Orisha either while being possessed or as a participant in a tambor may not noticeably change one's thoughts, perceptions, or actions. However, repeated interactions will require one to make changes in order to maintain the developing relationship. These changes will include designating space for the Orisha in one's home, dedicating time to maintain that altar and communicate with its habitants, and participating in other ritual events, both public and private. As Teresa explains, when one enters the outer mansions one can maintain one's old life, but as one moves deeper into the interior castle, one must enter into a new life. So it is for practitioners of Santería: the initial interactions and requirements may be minimal, but as one forms a relationship with these beings, one is required to enter into a new way of life, not by leaving the "world" as Teresa did but by incorporating elements of ritual and practice into the everydayness of one's existence.

Thus, I suggest that spirit possession as practiced within this community can be included within the types of religious experience we call mystical. Although it has traditionally been excluded from discussions of religious mystical experience, spirit possession certainly contains many of the elements present in other types of mystical experience. The most significant difference between the santero's experiences and those of traditional mystics is the use of possession trance. The mystical experiences within many spiritual traditions include trance events as they are defined here, but most do not include the possession of the mystic by an alien entity. In addition, unlike many Western and Eastern mystical experiences which not only do not require a supportive community but may even reject communal activity, Santería religious experience requires the presence of a supportive community all along the spiritual path. Although an individual may do much developmental work at home or in another type of religious environment, it is only through the community that the presence of spiritual beings can be recognized.

Sources of the Self

Bodies have offered endless material for philosophical and theological ruminations. For Edith Wyschogrod, saintly bodies provide the canvas for a working out of ethical theory. It is in the presence of the body of the Other, represented by its face, that the self becomes an ethical subject since, as she says (1992, 232), "Once a face is apprehended, it addresses and solicits a relationship with the perceiver an-iconically, not as an image, but as weight or pressure that compels one to see the other as destitute," as demanding radical altruism. Possession trance causes a radical break in our understanding of bodies and minds, for what was (and will be again) the body of the neighbor is temporarily a sacred body invaded and controlled by the mind, the consciousness of a sacred being. While the body of the neighbor may demand altruism, the sacred body cannot be seen as destitute, to use Wyschogrod's terminology. Whatever our relationship to the person of the neighbor, while entranced his body and its invading spirit require worship—and present a field for divine revelation. Embodied

Orisha preach, teach, heal, comfort, chastise, and bless the community both as a whole and as individuals and small groups. Some Orisha enjoy their temporary embodiment eating, drinking, dancing, and playing with their devotees.[1] Like a well-trained horse, the medium must give control over to the possessing Orisha, and often he returns to find his body bruised and his clothes soiled. As we say in Texas, he has been "rode hard and put up wet."

Traditionally, Western philosophy has posited for each individual a continuous if not unitary self. Although one might not agree with William James that "I am the same self that I was yesterday" (1981, 316), there is still an understanding that we remain known to ourselves even as we move through a multiplicity of experiences and temporal phases. When I sleep and wake, if I become unconscious, even if I am subject to multiple personality disorder, both common sense and philosophical analysis suggest that a continuity of being passes through me. However, possession trance, as framed by Santería practice, suggests that what to all appearances is Roberto is actually the presence of a spiritual entity; that through the materiality of his body an Orisha has been incarnated and is participating in the world of matter. Through spirit possession the gods, in the form of the Orisha, are brought into the community. For the community, what was the face of the neighbor has become that of the divine Other. Because each initiate is a potential medium, each may participate in any particular event either as embodied Orisha or as a member of the enabling community.

In the Western mind, spirit possession is most commonly regarded as "the ante-chamber of the asylum" or "an institutionalized madhouse for primitives" (Lewis 1971, 179). Vincent Crapanzano suggests that even in the Western world, where "possession no longer 'occurs,' it serves nevertheless as a very powerful metaphor for the articulation of that range of experiences in which the subject feels 'beside himself,' not fully responsible for his own condition" (Crapanzano 1977, 7). However, full possession trance, as described in the preceding examples, is more than merely a metaphor for an unusual experience. Rather it is a penetration of the visible world by beings that are wholly Other. In her analysis of saintly altruism, Edith Wyschogrod (1990) says that the "saint's relationship to the Other generates a paradox bound up with saintly self-emptying." In the cases she describes, either the "Other is swallowed up by the self as an object of utility, desire, or representation and becomes part of the self" or there is a "total emptying without replenishment" so that "there is no subject to engage the Other." In either case, "the alterity of the Other disappears, is reduced to the homogeneity of the Same" (33–34).

Santería provides an opposite example. In its rituals the Self is overtaken by the Other. Although the body is emptied of human subject, the sacred Other fills the emptiness so that engagement with the observing community is possible. Alterity between the medium and the sacred Other is maintained, homogeneity avoided. The sacred Other never becomes the selfsame subject and never becomes merely an object of utility, desire, or representation. Communication between the visible and invisible worlds is established through the actions of the enabling community. It is from within the ranks of this community that the medium is chosen. At the beginning of the ritual, each initiate is an individual, a Self. But as the ritual progresses, one (or more) of these Selves is overtaken by an Other and is temporarily transformed into this Other. And even though the individual's Self is absent and cannot engage that Other, the community can. The possessed cannot communicate directly with the possessing Orisha, but the community stands ready to engage the Other on its own behalf and on behalf of its possessed neighbor. Roberto will never see the face of his Orisha mirrored in his own face, yet at another time his presence within the community may enable him to see that Orisha in the face of another medium.

During the possession event the medium maintains his status as the Other whose face demands radical altruism, especially since the community as a whole has accepted the responsibility for the well-being of his body during the trance event—for in this he is truly destitute and in need of protection during the absence of his "self." At the same time, the Orisha who is made present through possession is a sacred and absolute Other who calls the community to a discourse that extends beyond the Self and the Other, preempting the needs of the medium in the service of the community in whole and in part. While ministering to the needs of the community, the Orisha also makes demands on it, demands that can only be framed as revelation, as the concrete manifestation of the desires of the invisible beings made visible during the possession event.

Gender Crossing

As with the initiation event, the marriage symbology used in describing Orisha possession represents the relationship one must have to the Orisha, which is as a wife to sacred husband. Possession draws on the "natural attitude" toward gender and sexual relations to suggest that mediums, regardless of their own anatomical sex, gender, or sexual orientation, all act in a wifely manner to passively receive the invasion and dominion of their spirit-husbands. It is suggested that women are better mediums because they "naturally" accept this sort of invasion and domination and are the paradigmatic vessels of divinity. Similarly, those homosexual men who accept penetration as part of their sexual practice are also considered "naturally" adapted to spiritual penetration. We can, however, suggest that all mediums are gendered female in that all must perform in a wifely manner in order to complete their transformation into embodied Orisha. Not only does priestly work participate in the womanly activities of caregiving and reproduction; it also participates in the penetration and dominion of priestly bodies by their spirit-husbands. Possession events are expressive displays of the Orisha as royalty and gods, and they are the forceful displays of the power that the Orisha as spirit-husbands can assert over their priestly wives. If women stereotypically are passive, submissive, and amenable to subjugation, Santería priests in their role of possession mediums are correspondingly compliant to the desires of their possessing Orisha, giving over their bodies to the absolute control of the possessing entity.

However, it is the possession event itself that presents the best opportunity for the radical gender crossing found in Santería. During possession the priest is expected to fully exhibit the behaviors attributed to the possessing Orisha. Because no attempt is made to gender-coordinate priests and Orisha-husbands, there are many priests who differ in gender from their possessing Orisha, yet they are expected to make the (to us) radical transformation necessary to fully enact the gendered behaviors of those Orisha. Thus priests of Ogun are expected to exhibit his facility with a machete, while priests of Oshun are expected to be charming and seductive—regardless of the anatomy of the priest involved. Although priests may exhibit some of the characteristics of their Orisha-husbands outside the context of possession, it is while possessed that they are most fully expected to act in a manner consistent with the archetype represented by the possessing deity. Several scholars (for example, Pérez y Mena 1998, 21) have suggested that being possessed by a female spirit or Orisha calls a man's sexuality into question, since he acts in a stereotypically feminine manner during the possession event, but I have not found that to necessarily be the case.

As noted in the description of the Santería possession event, costuming behavior is one of the markers of possession used by the community to denote the presence of an Orisha. Once an Orisha has gained complete control of the priestly body, that body is removed from the main ritual arena and clothed in appropriate apparel. If a known medium has been hired to "dance the Orisha" on the assumption that possession will occur, an appropriate outfit will have been commissioned and await its Orisha owner. For male Santería initiates and for female initiates who embody male Orisha, this outfit is typically knee breeches and a silk shirt in the colors of the Orisha, while santeras who embody female Orisha will wear a silk gown in the appropriate colors. Traditionally these costumes are in the style of the colonial Spanish elite, although they are decorated with both African and European elements.[2] If a complete costume has not been prepared, the medium will be given *paños* (Sp., kerchiefs) in the Orisha's colors and whatever other accouterments are available.

As Wendy McKenna and Suzanne Kessler suggest, clothing and other gender attributes serve in the day-to-day world as signifiers of gender and hidden anatomical features. Calling these markers "cultural genitals," they suggest that observers often find it disconcerting when the markers of one gender are appropriated by the other. Those of us who have been acculturated in a Western European-based society find the appropriation of female cultural genitals by anatomical males particularly disconcerting, while female appropriation of male apparel provokes less discomfort. Thus it seems "natural" that women embodying male Orisha should wear pants or breeches, but men should never wear skirts, regardless of the gender of the possessing Orisha. That this is necessarily a natural extension of Yoruba cultural behavior is called into question when one looks to the costuming behavior of Candomblé devotees in similar situations. Like Santería, Candomblé is the reinterpretation of Orisha religion in a New World colonial environment. Developed in Brazil, particularly the state of Bahia, Candomblé shares many of the cultural traditions brought by enslaved Yoruba in the late eighteenth and early nineteenth centuries. Like Santería devotees, Candomblé practitioners dress their possession priests in costumes from the colonial period. However, Candomblé devotees often put all of their mediums in the traditional full skirt, heavily starched petticoats, and lace blouse of colonial women (Wafer 1991, 18).

As we suggested in chapter 3, among the precolonial Yoruba the possession priesthood was fundamentally the domain of women. Most such priests were anatomically female, and those who were not generally appropriated the hair styles, clothes, jewelry, and cosmetics of women (Matory 1994, 7). Although not transvestites in the traditional sense, as they were not attempting to convince observers that they were women,[3] these priests constructed themselves as "wives" of the Orisha through a variety of performative actions including the use of womanly attributes and cultural genitals. While this tradition of female-dominated priesthood continued in both Cuba and Brazil, it seems to have been more rigorously maintained in Brazil, where most Candomblé houses continue to be headed by women. Although the contention of Ruth Landes (1947) that only women were allowed to be mediums was probably an overstatement even at the time of her research, it does highlight the female dominance of Candomblé. Given this strong tradition of female leadership, it is not surprising that anatomical males who are called to the priesthood within Candomblé may be required to take on some female cultural genitals.

However, in Cuba it appears that Western abhorrence of male-to-female cross-dressing conquered the inclination to dress the priests according to their role as Orisha-wives or to dress the embodied Orisha as appropriate for their nominal genders. Thus all male Orisha are dressed in pants, but only those female Orisha who possess anatomically female bodies may wear appropriate (albeit Westernized) cultural genitals. Apparently among Cuban, and later American, practitioners the dressing of anatomical males in female clothing pushes the feminization of the priesthood too far. Whereas male possession priests in Africa often appropriate female clothing and other attributes, and Brazilian practitioners also appropriate female clothing in ritual contexts, in the Cuban-based Orisha religion male-to-female cross-dressing, even when it is partial and in the service of the Orisha, is too radical. The priest may be constructed as female both in terms of the possession event itself and in respect to the Orisha that has possessed him, but the appropriation of female clothing by male priests presents this situation in perhaps too strong and open a manner.

CHAPTER 6 · Sacrifice and Violence

Along with divination and possession trance, the use of blood sacrifice distinguishes Santería and other African-based religions from many mainstream traditions. In spite of the 1992 Supreme Court decision overturning the antisacrifice laws, the killing of animals in conjunction with religious activity remains one of the most problematic aspects of Santería practice. In this chapter I want to discuss the place of sacrifice within the larger Santería worldview, but I also want to call into question some of the underlying assumptions regarding sacrifice, religion, and violence.

This chapter has been developed in the shadow of the September 2001 attacks on the World Trade Center in New York City and the Pentagon in Washington, D.C., and the subsequent wars in Afghanistan and Iraq. Some of its earliest portions were already on my computer when the Twin Towers fell. This has made me especially aware of the interactions between religion and violence in the larger American landscape. Throughout the period immediately following the attacks, religious acts, including church services, public prayers, and both public and private religious rituals, proliferated, swelling in response to terrorist events and the subsequent wars, declining during the lulls between events. Churches reported larger crowds on the Sunday after the September 11 attacks than they would expect even during such days of high church attendance as Christmas and Easter. Religious and pseudoreligious songs ("Amazing Grace," "God Bless America") and rhetoric (commercial signs proclaiming God Bless America and United We Stand, the flying of American flags, the wearing of red-white-and-blue ribbons) permeated the society. Although the imagery was primarily patriotic and Christian, there was also token Jewish, Islamic, and other minority religious content invoked. Within days the president proclaimed a War on Terrorism and troops began to move into position to attack those believed to have instigated or supported these attacks. Originally dubbed Operation Infinite Justice and quickly renamed Enduring Freedom, this buildup to war was focused not only on traditional military forces but also on special-operations forces, small elite units whose mission would be to get "the enemies of freedom" who "sacrific[e] human life to serve their radical visions." All the peoples of the world, every nation, every region was told, "Either you are with us, or you are with the terrorists." In his address to a joint session of Congress and the American people a week and a half after the attack, President Bush proclaimed that the outcome of this war between "freedom and fear, justice and cruelty" was certain because "God is not neutral" between the forces of civilization and of terrorism.[1] A year and a half later, as the war in Iraq was commencing, George Bush and Saddam Hussein both used the discourse of religious sacrifice to prepare their respective constituents for the impending conflict. Both invoked the name of God/Allah; both proclaimed the justice of their cause and called on God/Allah to help defeat their opponents.[2]

The connections between religion and violence, including all types of sacrifice, have a long history of scholarly concern. Because Santería (along with other African-based religions) engages in rituals of sacrifice that include the immolation of animals, an exploration of sacrifice and other types of religious violence through the lens of African-based religions may provide new insights into these activities. In this chapter I will summarize some of the vast literature of religion and violence, then I will suggest that the standard approaches to the issues of sacrifice and violence in religion are flawed by their Indo-European ethnocentrism and that the perspectives of other religions and cultures, like Santería and the Yoruba traditional religion, can enhance our understanding of violence in human society. Whereas Christianity and Judaism are no longer sacrificial traditions and thus must approach blood sacrifice from a theoretical stance, santeros continue to participate in a sacrificial tradition in which natural and manufactured goods, plants, and animals are regularly offered to the deities as part of religious practice. By exploring sacrifice through the lens of a tradition in which blood sacrifice is still an essential feature, I hope to refocus our understanding of this important religious concept.

Sacrifice also has a gender element that is often ignored in the literature but has been brought to the fore by some feminist scholars. In general, those scholars who have done a gender analysis of sacrifice suggest that sacrificial rituals are male dominated and male oriented (Sered 2002, 13, 15). Although not gender neutral, the Santería ritual context provides for the participation of women in sacrificial rituals in ways that appears exceptional. In the final portion of this chapter I will continue our analysis of gender by considering the ways in which gender operates within the Santería sacrificial milieu and consider what the inclusion of women in sacrificial rituals says about the place of women and sacrifice within Santería.

One of the problems in talking about sacrifice is that the term denotes many different types of activity, and conversations easily slip from one meaning to the other. When scholars discuss sacrifice, they could be referring to human and animal sacrifice in "primitive" religion, or the (non)sacrifice of Isaac and its actuality in Christ's sacrifice, or sacrifice outside the Judeo-Christian context—animals, first fruits, and so on—as found in religious traditions around the world. Or they could be referring to self-sacrifice in the service of God or humanity, or sacrifice in the pseudoreligious sense, such as the "sacrifices" of those who die in military action, the "self-sacrifice" of police and firefighters, the sacrifice of "innocent" lives in wars and terrorist attacks and other meaningless deaths, or the sacrifices made by parents for their children or by employees for their employer, or the sacrifices "we all" have to make toward the war effort or some other communal good. Because of the intimate connection between religion and "sacrifice," even secular calls for sacrifice are often framed by religious rhetoric. In this chapter, however, I will limit my discussion to more explicitly religious sacrifices, focusing particularly on blood sacrifice and its meaning in the context of Santería practice, and will leave to others the extension of these notions into other contexts.

Religion and Violence

Religion and violence can be connected in several different ways. Many prominent theorists have suggested that religion was born out of the violence inherent in early human society. According to these views, religious activities were developed either in response to a primal or originary violent act or as an effort to refocus violence away from the primary social group, thereby diluting random or intragroup violence. This refocusing might have taken the form of scapegoating, allowing the violence to be enacted upon an individual or group outside the community, or of sublimation, channeling violent tendencies into activities more beneficial to the community. Several theories posit that the originary violent event(s) involved a murderous act against a prominent member of the community. In these theories the original murder was redefined, sublimated, or "forgotten" by the participants and their descendants, but can be rediscovered by a close reading of the appropriate texts. As we shall see below, Freud, Girard, and Burkert each have proposed a variant of such theories.

Approached from another angle, much of literature detailing the relationship between religion and violence comes together by way of sacrifice, particularly human sacrifice but other blood(y) sacrifices as well. Ritual killing, especially when it involves human victims, has inflamed the scholarly imagination for generations. Although there are several sacrificial stories in the Hebrew Bible,[3] almost all the theological work on these issues invokes the story of Abraham's (aborted) sacrifice of his son Isaac in Genesis 22. In this story a lone man, obeying the voice of God, leaves home, climbs a mountain, and prepares to immolate his only son, in spite of the promise made by that same God that this son would provide a continuous line of descendants as numerous as the stars in the sky (Gen. 15:5, 22:17). After testing Abraham's resolve to obey this most hideous of commands, God relents, stops Abraham's deadly hand, and provides a ram in the place of the sacrificial son. In Christian theology Isaac's brush with death at the hand of his (loving) father is understood to prefigure the sacrificial death of Jesus which serves to redeem humanity from the wrath of his heavenly Father. For some, when God stopped Abraham's hand, He was also stopping all human sacrifice among his chosen people. However, animal sacrifice continued among Abraham's and Isaac's descendants. With the building of the Temple, Hebrew sacrifices became more communal and public, and the victims were limited to common domestic animals.

Sacrifice in the Hebrew Bible typically is described by the term "holocaust," wherein the sacrificial victim is killed, the blood is drained and offered on the altar, and then the body is placed in the fire as a burnt offering, the smoke of which is deemed "pleasing to God."[4] This biblical sacrificial model with its total destruction of the victim, and accounts of ancient Greek and Vedic sacrificial rites, continue to inform descriptions of ritual sacrifice in spite of the fact that in many circumstances sacrificial events do not follow these forms. In fact, the more common sacrifice involved not the complete destruction of the victim but the sharing of the victim between God and the people by way of a sacrificial meal (Dunnill 2003, 83).

As anthropologists began describing the religious ceremonies of the peoples they studied, they often framed their ethnographic descriptions with such inflammatory words as "horrible," "frenzied," and "orgiastic." These accounts suggested both that ritual violence was an integral part of "primitive" religions and that such violence could occur only in an environment of irrationality and the loss of the normal inhibitions against killing—as if irrational or religious-inspired violence could be found only amid these so-called primitive religions.

When rituals found outside the Christian complex were compared with European religious services, particularly sedate Protestant Christian liturgies, there emerged a developmental view of religions that suggested that earlier, more primitive religions engaged in wild, irrational practices including bloody sacrifice but that more highly developed religions practiced a more restrained ritual form epitomized by the highly ritualized and symbolic form of Christian sacrifice. Thus in his article on violence in Mircea Eliade's *Encyclopedia of Religion* (1987, 15:271), Samuel Klausner can suggest that, when the religious ecstasy that precipitates religious violence is replaced by formal, rational law and/or contemplative mysticism, religion can overcome the violent tendencies of society.

Many scholars have also suggested that religion may either reduce or enhance the violent tendencies within a social system. In what is perhaps his most famous quotation, Karl Marx described religion as "the opium of the people,"[5] while Sigmund Freud suggested that the major motivators of man, particularly aggressive tendencies, are sublimated in religion. From a sociologist's viewpoint, Emile Durkheim proposed (1915, 258) that primitive religion serves to maintain common social values through the common experience of "psychical exaltation, not far removed from delirium." Although Marx was thinking of European Christianity (Marx and Engels 1964, 41–58), both Freud (1950, chap. 4) and Durkheim (1915, bk. 2, chap. 7) invoke frenzied ritual in their analysis of primitive or originary religious activity. While Marx urges that the proletariat (the people) reject the anesthetizing qualities of religion and overthrow those who have been oppressing them, Freud and Durkheim suggest that religion can be overcome with increased "civilization" or emotional development.

One cannot discuss religion and violence without mentioning the work of René Girard. In his book *Violence and the Sacred* he says that sacrifice is the most crucial, fundamental, and commonplace of religious rites and that it accounts for the totality of human culture including language, kinship systems, taboos, codes of etiquette, patterns of exchange, rites, and civil institutions. He suggests that sacrifice was developed in response to the mechanism of mimetic desire—that is, the desire to imitate a model or mediator who becomes one's rival as one approaches the mutually desired object. In multiple originary events Girard postulates rivals who displace their rivalry onto a third (innocent) party whose death (murder) becomes the original sacrifice. As those deaths are re-created, all memory of rivalry and rejection are erased and only the beneficial effects of the "sacrificial" death are remembered. This displacement, he goes on to suggest, triggered human linguistic, conceptual, and symbolic systems—that is, religion and culture. Girard's theory of the origin of religion is similar to the one Freud develops in *Totem and Taboo,* except that it postulates multiple originary events and replaces Freud's father with a surrogate victim. In both cases, a primeval event lies behind all subsequent religious and cultural behaviors.

The historian of Greek religion Walter Burkert also looks back to a primordial event for the origins of sacrificial rites. Unlike Girard, who uses primarily literary sources, Burkert creates his theory out of a close reading of Grecian sources and accounts of Paleolithic hunting cultures. Burkert suggests that in spite of the pervasiveness of sacrifice in ancient Greek culture it was anomalous and no longer understood by those performing the rituals. After reading the work of Karl Meuli, who noticed similarities between certain aspects of Greek sacrificial practice and the practices of Paleolithic hunters, Burkert developed his theory of ritual and religion. According to Burkert, human society had to change when early hominids began to develop a hunting culture. Because of the requirements hunting imposed on our prehuman ancestors, they had to develop new types of relationships, particularly new male-male and male-female relationships. As part of this redefinition, intraspecific aggression was projected onto the prey, whose death became the focal point of hominid ritualization. According to Burton Mack, Burkert proposes that hunting rituals eventually "gave rise to the full range of articulations that we understand to be mythic or symbolic, articulation characteristic of religion" (Hamerton-Kelly 1987, 26). According to Burkert, behind Greek religion and its sacrificial practices, indeed behind all religion, are the rituals of the hunt.

In 1983 Girard and Burkert joined together with the historian of religion Jonathan Z. Smith for a discussion of religion, violence, and sacrifice that resulted in the book *Violent Origins* (Hamerton-Kelly 1987). Although "winking" in his essay to let us know he is less than serious in his intent, Smith proposes yet a third hypothesis of human development and sacrificial rites. Noting that "animal sacrifice appears to be, universally, the ritual killing of a domesticated animal by agrarian or pastoralist societies" (197), Smith suggests rather than being characteristic of "primitive" societies, sacrifice is primarily a product of "civilization." He goes on to outline the hypothesis that sacrifice developed in conjunction with and as "a meditation on domestication." Like the breeder, the sacrificer is engaged in selective killing and is intimately concerned with the physical and behavioral characteristics of the chosen animal. Furthermore, he suggests, where there are native articulations of sacrifice, they generally revolve around issues of "gift-offering-display and/or pollution removal" (197–99).

Although Smith repudiates the other scholars' focus on primitivism, all three seem to agree that while sacrifice, particularly blood sacrifice, may have been an essential part of earlier religious systems, it has been overcome or sublimated or in some other way has disappeared from contemporary religious practice (218). However, both Santería practice and current events suggest that certain forms of bloody sacrifice persist. Animal sacrifice continues to be one of the most controversial aspects of Santería practice. Santeros believe that the giving of natural and manufactured items to the Orisha or to the ancestors is essential for human well-being. The fact that sometimes these goods include the lifeblood of living beings is a fundamental part of their religious practice.

Ebo Eje, Blood Sacrifice

Without Ogun no deity can be worshipped on earth.

Traditional Yoruba saying

In the early 1990s the city of Hialeah, Florida, passed a series of ordinances that made it illegal "to unnecessarily kill, torment, torture, or mutilate an animal in a public or private ritual or ceremony not for the primary purpose of food consumption."[6] Since the city allowed the killing of animals for a host of other reasons, "'even if you're tired of taking care of them,' as long as the purpose was not sacrifice," these ordinances appeared to be an effort to suppress the Church of the Lukumí Babalu Ayé, a local Santería congregation. The congregation decided to fight the ordinances as a violation of their First Amendment right to freedom of religion. Ernesto Pichardo, one of the founders of the Santería church, said, "Animal sacrifice is an integral part of our faith. It is like our holy meal" (Greenhouse 1993). At the hearing before the Supreme Court, Douglas Laycock, a law professor at the University of Texas, argued, "The only way to show that sacrifice is 'unnecessary' to the Santeria followers is to prove that Santeria is a false religion" (Greenhouse 1992). However, the legitimacy of Santería as a religion was never questioned as part of the hearing. In the Court opinion overturning the city's ordinances, Justice Anthony M. Kennedy, quoting the 1981 ruling in *Thomas v. Review Board of the Indiana Employment Security Division*, said, "Although the practice of animal sacrifice may seem abhorrent to some, 'religious belief need not be acceptable, logical, consistent, or comprehensible to others in order to merit First Amendment protection.'"[7]

Although animal sacrifice is one of the most controversial aspects of Santería practice, sacrifice, the giving of natural and manufactured items to the Orisha or other spiritual beings, is viewed by santeros as essential for human well-being. As J. Omosade Awolalu says in describing Yoruba beliefs and practices, "Sacrifice is the *sine qua non* in African traditional religion" (Awolalu 1979, 108). Through sacrifice, it is believed, one restores the positive processes in one's life and acquires general well-being. One gives to the Orisha and the ancestors what they need and want in the expectation that they in turn will give what one needs or wants. This is not viewed as "bribing" or "buying off" the Orisha; rather it is the mutual exchange of ashé necessary to maintain the balance of the cosmos. "The orishas offer health, children and wisdom; human beings render sacrifice and praise. Each needs the other, for, without the *ashe* of the *orishas*, human beings would despair of their God-given destiny and turn on themselves. And without the *ashe* of sacrifice, the *orishas* would wither and die" (Murphy 1993, 15).

According to Santería belief the Orisha are powerful beings, but they are not immortal. They depend on the continued devotion of their human "children." One of the most important forms of devotion is the "feeding" of the Orisha through the sacrifice of appropriate animals and the offering of their blood to the Orisha. Like all living things, the Orisha must eat. If they were not fed, not honored, they would cease to exist, as the gods of many ancient religions have ceased to exist. Through the sacrifice of plants and animals, Santería priests and priestesses effect the movement of ashé through the cosmos, between the visible and invisible worlds, and maintain the cosmic balance.

Many types of items are offered to the Orisha, including money, fruit, liquor, candy, palm oil, knives, mats, deer antlers, seashells, honey, molasses—anything that might appeal to a particular Orisha. When one's life is at stake or the community is celebrating an initiation, the sacrifice also includes the blood of animals. All types of sacrifice, but particularly animal sacrifice, serve to remind the participants of the delicate balance of the universe. As principally city-dwellers, we forget that something must die—be it a cow or a chicken or a carrot—to make our lives possible. We have become unconscious of the trees that died to give us this book, the cow, the wheat, the tomato, the potato that died for our cheeseburger and fries. When our grandparents wanted chicken for Sunday dinner, they went out into the yard, chose a chicken, killed it, plucked it, and cooked it; we, on the other hand, pick up a daintily wrapped package from the supermarket. Santeros value the lives of animals, but they value the lives of humans more. When the religion requires the sacrifice of an animal, it is offered to the Orisha or the ancestor with respect, then it is killed quickly and with as little pain as possible. They understand what the animal has given and are grateful.

It is required that humans perform this most important function. The Orisha and ancestors, having passed from the visible world, are no longer able to perform these rituals for themselves, while plants and animals lack the ability to enact their own offering. It is believed that the Orisha and the ancestors are fed and honored through such sacrifice, while the humans, animals, and plants are elevated spiritually and moved toward the fulfillment of their individual destinies. Such offerings are essential for the continued existence of all beings. Since the Orisha and ancestors "eat" only the blood of the sacrificed animal, the meat is generally cooked and served to the community as part of the religious feast. Through such meat the devotees share in the ashé of the Orisha.

Sometimes, however, when an animal is sacrificed as part of a ritual cleansing, it is believed to have absorbed the problems, dangers, and bad luck of the person being cleansed. In such a case the body is disposed of without being eaten. One of the arguments presented by the City of Hialeah against the Church of the Lukumí Babalu Ayé was that the discarding of such animal carcasses was a public health hazard. This practice of discarding animals throughout the city has presented problems to officials not only in Hialeah and Miami but also in New York, Los Angeles, and other cities with a concentration of Santería practitioners. However, as Justice Kennedy suggested, these cities have to find a way to regulate the "disposal of organic garbage" that does not unnecessarily burden the practitioners of Orisha religion (Greenhouse 1993).

Another concern is presented by the ASPCA (American Society for the Prevention of Cruelty to Animals). They suggest that Santería sacrifice is less humane than the killing in licensed slaughterhouses. They suggest that animals die slowly and painfully and that they are often kept in filthy and inhumane conditions before the ceremony. However, santeros contend that their methods are no more cruel than other types of legal slaughter, that the animals are killed quickly and cleanly, that they are generally eaten, and that the animals used are ordinary fowl and four-legged animals commonly available preslaughtered at the grocery store. As the religion moves into the mainstream, we might expect some sort of compromise between practitioners and officials that allows santeros to practice their religion, including engaging in sacrifice, legally and humanely.

Animal sacrifice, however, is just a small part of the much larger definition of ebo (sacrifice or offering) in the religion. As Awolalu (1979) suggests, sacrifice in its most general form is the relinquishment of something precious for a particular purpose (134). Among the Yoruba no one would come forward in worship without some type of offering, no matter how small or simple (108). Among santeros, such offerings might include water, rum, dried fish, honey, molasses, lengths of cloth, cowry shells, or money—all common objects of everyday life. Orisha religion among both the Yoruba and santeros is focused on the preservation and continuation of life. Devotees depend on the Orisha for their prosperity and good health. They understand that gift giving, both at the time of requests for assistance and in thanksgiving for assistance rendered, helps to solidify the connection between themselves and the Orisha.

Of all the theories of sacrifice, violence, and religion, Jonathan Z. Smith's slightly metaphorical rationale, although less fleshed out than others, seems to more closely describe Santería practice. Smith suggests that animal sacrifice, rather than being the result of sublimated violent tendencies or a ritualized form of hunting, is connected to animal domestication and gift giving. Santeros speak of "feeding" the Orisha or "giving" an animal to an Orisha. Sacrifice is part of an exchange of ashé between the visible and invisible worlds that revivifies both the giver and the recipient. Although framed according to the formulation *do ut des* (I give in order that you may give), these offerings are not viewed in a purely mechanistic fashion. Rather, many sacrifices are seen as ways to solidify the relationship between deity and devotee so that help may be solicited and expected in times of need.

The rituals themselves are not the frenzied or irrational events suggested by a reading of the literature of sacrifice but are controlled performances that balance the heat of blood with cool water, song, and prayers.[8] Animals are dispatched in an efficient and orderly fashion that is designed to please and vivify the Orisha. Because sacrificial animals are often prepared and cooked for the community, the sacrificial arena includes, in addition to the corral designed to hold the animals until the sacrificing priest is ready for them and the actual sacrificial site, spaces set aside to convert the raw carcasses into a feast. In these spaces, devotees skin goats and sheep, pluck chickens, and separate those parts of sacrificed animals destined for presentation back to the Orisha (the *acheses* or sacred portions) from the meat and the offal. Finally, the kitchen staff must cook the acheses for the Orisha and prepare the meat for the santeros and their guests. All of this activity, some sacred and some more mundane, belies any characterization of the proceedings as a wild Dionysian frenzy. As John Dunnill suggests in his analysis of biblical sacrifice (2003, 86), Santería sacrifice follows the pattern of "a feast shared with an honored guest, who is given the best portions." Dunnill suggests that the most usual form of sacrifice worldwide, rather than being characterized by the type of violent action described by Girard and Burkert, was generally a "celebratory" ritual in which "death is swift, unemphasized and relatively painless, with no hostility expressed" and in which the offering was "wholly or largely consumed by the offering community" (83). This idea that sacrifice is intimately connected with feasting and communal celebration is essential to our argument, and we will return to it below.

Sacrifice and Gender

One way of analyzing sacrifice is through the lens of feminist theory and gender analysis. Susan Sered (2002) says, "Cross-culturally, animal sacrifice is one of the most dramatically and consistently gendered ritual constellations" (13), and all analysis of gender and sacrifice is premised on the "striking observation that . . . sacrifice, and especially animal sacrifice, is . . . almost always a male dominated and oriented ritual activity" (15). Sered develops a series of models of blood sacrifice, five based on the literature on gender and sacrifice, one on her own research in Okinawa. As a group, her models suggest that sacrifice serves in some way to maintain patriarchy, the systematic control over women by men as a group, or to emphasize men's control of or association with death.

Sacrifice in the Orisha traditions, however, does not seem to follow any of Sered's models. In fact, I will suggest that it also does not follow the women-are-to-life-as-men-are-to-death dichotomy that seems to underlie most analyses of gender and sacrifice. Although both Yoruba and Cuban societies are hierarchical and patriarchal, the Orisha religion as it developed in Cuba is unusual among the sacrificing religions in that both men and women actively participate in sacrificial rituals.[9] On the one hand, it is difficult to suggest that sacrifice in Orisha religion functions in the service of patriarchal control. On the other hand, although women participate in sacrifice, it would be incorrect to assume that there is no gender differentiation in these rituals; while all participants are circumscribed by certain regulations and restrictions, there are more limitations on women than on similarly placed men. However, before we can analyze the ways in which men's and women's participation is different, we need to examine the specifics of Santería sacrifice.[10]

Both men and women participate as sacrificator,[11] the person on whose behalf a sacrifice is offered, and both male and female Orisha are recipients of sacrifice without distinction. These are important differences between Santería and other sacrificing religions. In these two ritual roles, that is, as sacrificator and as the recipient of sacrifice, there are *no* gender distinctions. All people, male and female, youngsters, the middle-aged and the elderly, may have sacrifices made in their name, and all may stand in the site of sacrificator without distinction. Analogously, all Orisha receive sacrifice without respect to any categorization to which they may be subject. Whether an Orisha is considered male or female, young or old, *funfun* (peaceful) or a warrior, all receive blood sacrifice as part of their rituals. Similarly, both male and female animals are sacrificed. However, individual distinctions are made among the Orisha, each of whom has very specific preferences regarding the species and characteristics of the animals offered in sacrifice.[12] For example, Eleggua likes black roosters, Obatala likes white male and female goats and white hens, Shango likes rams and red roosters, and Oshun likes castrated male goats and brown hens. However, all the animals of the barnyard are potential sacrificial victims.

Traditionally, the right to wield the sacrificial knife was limited to a small group of men initiated to the Orisha Ogun. In the Candomblé houses of Brazil, that is still the case. However, in Cuba both men and women are entitled to undergo this initiation and gain the right to use Ogun's blade. María Towá, one of the first oriaté in Havana, was known as the Queen of the Lukumi in the early twentieth century. She prevailed upon the *achogun*, the priests whose initiations allowed them to perform blood sacrifice, to initiate her into their cult, threatening to exclude them from the religious community if they refused. Subsequently she gave others this new initiation, which has come to be called *cuchillo* (Sp.), *pinaldo* (Yr.), or knife. All new oriaté must receive this initiation so that they have the authority to perform all portions of Orisha rituals, but other santeros and santeras may receive it as well.[13]

Although men and women can equally serve as sacrificator, the rules for men and women functioning as sacrificer, the person actually performing the ritual, differ in different sacrificial circumstances. Only initiated priests are allowed to perform sacrifices. If noninitiates need sacrifices performed on their behalf, they need to solicit the help of a priest, who can be either male or female. Sacrificial animals are divided into two categories: "feathers" (birds such as chickens, doves, and pigeons, sometime called "two-legs") and "four-legs" (goats, rams, and the like). All initiated priests can sacrifice animals of the "feathers" type, but an additional initiation, the cuchillo, is required to sacrifice four-legged animals. This initiation, which completes earlier Ogun initiations and gives one the right to use a knife (Ogun's tool) in sacrifice, is considered the fulfillment of one's kariocha or priestly initiation. Both men and women can receive both kariocha and cuchillo without distinction. However, premenopausal women do not generally exercise their right to act as a sacrificer, and postmenopausal women usually defer to men if appropriately initiated men are available to perform a sacrifice.

Looking at the sacrificial arena in Santería through the lens of gender analysis shows that, although women are not automatically excluded, it would be incorrect to say that gender is not a category of consideration. My analysis of the anomalies will be divided into two parts. First, I will consider how the inclusion of women in sacrificial rituals suggests that Santería practitioners operate under a different worldview than that encountered in the overwhelming majority of the literature on sacrifice. Then I will consider the rationale(s) for excluding certain categories of women from acting as sacrificers in spite of their right to do so.

Although Santería sacrifices can be performed for a variety of reasons and in conjunction with other rituals, they are almost always framed according to a vocabulary of food and nutrition. Sacrifices are said to "feed" the entity to whom they are offered. Devotees may be advised by a diviner to feed one or more Orisha, objects from an ancestor shrine, their ori (through the medium of their physical head), or even the earth. Orisha icons are fed as part of initiation ceremonies in order to vivify them and imbue them with the presence of an Orisha. Orisha and ancestor icons may be fed in order to strengthen them, in thanksgiving for petitions granted, or as part of a supplicatory ritual. The earth is fed in order to pacify its hunger with the blood of the victim rather than that of the sacrificator. Although the remains from sacrifices whose primary purpose is healing or the removal of negative influences are generally discarded, in most cases the carcasses of the sacrificed animals are cooked and used to feed the ritual participants. In these cases the blood, as the repository of the life force or ashé of the sacrificial victim, along with certain body parts called acheses that are imbued with ashé, are given as food to the receiving entity, while the flesh is fed to the ritual community, invoking an imagery of mutual feasting and celebration. In large sacrificial rituals such as initiations, much of the work of the feast falls to women. Not only may they participate in the actual sacrifice but women are generally responsible for some or all of the butchering and most of the cooking of the sacrificial meal. Often male/female differentiation continues in the butchering arena, as men may be responsible for processing the carcasses of four-legged offerings while women are responsible for processing the chickens and other "feathers." However, as soon as bodies are converted into meat, they are generally turned over to women for their final processing in the kitchen. Even in cases where the flesh of the sacrificial victim is not used to feed participants, all rituals end in a communal meal.

This parallel work of feeding the Orisha and ritually feeding the participants suggests an ideology of ritual practice that places it within the realm of female rather than male labor. Rather than an ideology of patriarchy, the overcoming of women's "pollution" and misbehavior, or the enactment of one's spiritual rebirth into the realm of the male (categories suggested by Sered's analysis), within Santería we find a valorization of feminine virtue and action. Although men may hold the knife that actually draws the blood of the sacrificial animal, it is women's labor of cooking and feeding that is metaphorically enacted both in the ritual room and in the kitchen. All of these activities, from the initial care of the livestock awaiting sacrifice to the actual sacrificial event to the cleaning and cutting up of the carcasses to the preparation of dishes for both visible and invisible beings, are part of the stereotypical responsibilities of women as caregivers, as those responsible for the care and feeding of their households.

Here we are reminded that all initiates not only are iyawo-Orisha during their initiation process but on some level continue as the "palace women" of their Orisha throughout their lives. Among the Yoruba both men and women cook and care for themselves, but the majority of such activity falls to adult women. A woman is responsible for feeding herself and her children, and generally a man's wives will rotate the job of feeding their husband (and any visitors to the household), although all of this activity may fall to the youngest of a man's wives. Even men who buy their meals in the market rather than being served at home are ultimately depending on a woman's labor for their food (Oyewùmí 1997, 55–58).

In Cuban and American societies, women continue to be primarily responsible for the feeding of their households. When we hear American women bragging about the cooking done by their husbands and boyfriends, it only emphasizes how extraordinary that activity is. Although public cooking, done by chefs and other professional cooks, may be dominated by men, domestic cooking continues to be seen as primarily the domain of women. Thus I want to suggest that the incorporation of the terminology of "feeding" into the sacrificial arena invokes a stereotypic female activity regardless of the gender of the sacrificator and sacrificer.

Both contemporary santeros and olorisha from the mid-nineteenth century use the terminology of "work" to describe their interaction with the Orisha.[14] One does not worship the Orisha so much as one works with and for them. An analysis of the work performed in the service of the Orisha reveals that much of it in other contexts would generally be attributed to women, from reproductive labor to the maintenance of the physical and emotional household, including feeding its inhabitants. Just as Yoruba wives provide new lineage members to the household of their husbands while engaging in both domestic and economic activities in support of themselves and their children, santeros "birth" new devotees and new Orisha icons through initiation while engaging in the maintenance of their religious families and monitoring the health and well-being of all its members both visible and invisible. Most Santería rituals are focused on enhancing the physical, emotional, and spiritual welfare of the extended religious family, including casual clients who are not active members of the community but come seeking help unavailable elsewhere. Based on the diagnosis of a divination session, the priest may prescribe any number of sacrificial activities. Many types of offerings may be required of the petitioner. In addition to the raw and processed materials that can be purchased from the appropriate vendors—fruit and flowers, cloth, candles, *herramienta* (Sp., tools, the metal or wooden implements of the Orisha)—these offerings can also include the cooking of special dishes for presentation to the Orisha in either their natural or domestic locations. Although both men and women participate in these activities, we can suggest that cooking, as the emblematic female occupation, has a special place in this religious work.[15]

But womanliness is not universally valorized within Santería, and the roles of male and female priests cannot be completely conflated in respect to sacrifice. Here women's potential for reproductive activity is used to limit their ritual participation. Menstruation taboos are sometimes used to limit women's full participation as Santería priests. Such a taboo proscribes premenopausal women from using Ogun's knife even after they have received the appropriate initiation and discourages postmenopausal women from sacrificing unless no qualified man is available. When questioned, elders often frame premenopausal restrictions in terms of "blood calling to blood." On the one hand, it is hypothesized that menstrual blood, even if the woman is not actively bleeding, is so strong that it will overpower the sacrificial blood and somehow negate the sacrificial aims. Or, on the other hand, that the heat of sacrificial blood will overpower a woman's own natural cycle and cause excessive, perhaps fatal, blood flow. Santeros are also known to use a vocabulary of pollution, suggesting that a woman of menstrual age, particularly during her cycle, may so taint the process that her ritual participation must be circumscribed.

Still, we should not automatically assign a Eurocentric notion of pollution to menstruation taboos. As Eugenia Herbert suggests in conjunction with menstruation taboos surrounding African iron culture, notions of pollution may refer to "things out of place" rather than some sort of absolutely impure or corrupting substance. Menstrual blood may be considered "out of place" at sacrificial rituals because it represents the failure to conceive. The blood produced by such failure can be understood as essentially different from the blood of sacrificed animals, which is a vitalizing power (Herbert 1993, 86). Since blood sacrifice is generally performed in the service of life, as part of healing rituals and initiations and the like, a theory of sympathetic magic in which "like calls to like" would discourage the presence of someone associated, even temporarily, with the failure of life. In a context in which every symbolic effort is made to support the life-giving purpose of the ritual, a menstruating woman would be discouraged from participating because her ashé works against the goal of the ritual itself rather than reinforcing it. Although the net result is the same—the exclusion of menstruating women from a ritual—and both explanations draw on theories of sympathetic magic, menstrual taboos that focus on fertility (or its absence) are based on an entirely different view of the female body than those that see menstrual blood as somehow "dirty" or polluting. In this more Africanized view, women during their reproductive years are identified totally with their sexuality and reproductiveness, such that the state of their reproductive abilities becomes the most important criterion framing their participation in ritual activities. Thus prepubescent girls, nursing mothers, and postmenopausal women are all seen as the most ritually stable representatives of anatomical females because all are assumed to stand outside the arenas of sexuality and reproduction. According to this view, women in all of these states are exempted from the fluctuations of the menstrual cycle and participation in sexual activities.[16]

Although one might consider menopause another kind of failure of fertility, Eugenia Herbert suggests a different rationale for the lifting of taboos on postmenopausal women. In her 1993 book *Iron, Gender, and Power* she ranges over a wide swath of sub-Saharan Africa exploring the nuances of iron technology. The basic conclusion of her book, however, is summed up in its cover art: an *edan* pair (*edan òsùgbó*, also known as *edan ògbóni*) bookend the text (see also fig. 44). The edan, a pair of male and female figures cast in bronze with a bronze chain linking them together, are the symbol of power of the Ogboni (Osugbo) society. Traditionally the Ogboni was a secret society of elderly men and women who played an important political and judicial role among the Yoruba people. Although the figures that form the edan usually have pronounced male and female sexual characteristics, they may also mix genitalia and other gender attributes (Herbert 1993, 31–32). Regardless of their form, the edan represent the sexual symmetry achieved by men and women who are beyond their reproductive years. Yet the edan represent more than essential gender complementarity; they also represent the power embedded in seniority. In old age, Herbert says, gender differences dissolve such that male and female interests intersect (238). As Oyewùmí suggests in the opening pages of her book (1997, xiii), ranking within Yoruba society depends first and foremost on seniority determined by relative age. Old men and women are treated differently from their younger counterparts and more similarly to each other (Herbert 1993, 221), because age represents an accumulation of spiritual power, wisdom, and impartiality shared by aged men and women (231–32). While younger women are totally identified with their sexuality and reproductive ability, older women are identified with both the benevolent mother and the witch (225). Only those with strong witchcraft substance can bear living children, raise them to adulthood, and live long enough to see their children and grandchildren.[17] Older women (and men) who support ritual events by their presence or participation can be seen as bringing their tremendous witchcraft power, their ashé.

However, these understandings of fertility and menopause are lost on contemporary American women who have been brought up with a different view of sexuality and menstruation. For many of these women, menstruation is neither a polluting event nor the failure of fertility. Rather their periodic flow is a natural event, no more extraordinary than breathing, eating, or sleeping, and not a reason to exclude them from any activities in which they wish to participate. Although menopause may be a more significant event in a woman's life, it too is seen as part of a natural process of life with little magical or religious significance.[18]

Since the restrictions on women's ritual participation and the use of the knife of Ogun are, like much of Santería ritual practice, customary rather than canonical, contemporary santeras often choose to ignore or circumvent these restrictions. Having lost the African view of women's cycles as markers of fertility and refusing to accept this natural process as polluting, many santeras silently protest these taboos by refusing to acquiesce to them and attending rituals regardless of where they are in their cycle. Similarly, women with the appropriate initiations choose to fully participate in sacrificial rituals without regard to their physical age or menstrual condition.

However, invoking contemporary feminist understandings of womanliness can leave santeras without religious support for these decisions. I would suggest another rationale for women's full participation in sacrificial rituals. If we move away from the conception of sacrifice based on a binary in which women represent life-giving while men represent life-taking, we can consider sacrifice not as a male-identified violent act but as one element in a larger ritual of feasting and celebration in which women at all periods of their lives can participate. When we conceptually incorporate sacrifice into the domestic sphere, all the steps in the preparation for a feast, including the selection and killing of the animals, can as easily fall within the purview of women as of men. Rather than suggesting that there is no difference between male and female roles and responsibilities, this approach brings sacrifice under the rubric that we are developing of Santería as a female-identified religious tradition, a rubric that valorizes rather than denigrates women's roles and activities. If the ritual of sacrifice is primarily about "feeding" rather than killing and violence, then women's participation as sacrificator and sacrificer is a natural extension of their other roles in the whole sacrificial event. Conceptually, sacrifice follows the pattern of a normal meal, ritualized to incorporate the participation of powerful invisible beings. A comparison between this type of ritual meal and the American holiday of Thanksgiving, which involves another sort of ritualized meal, can clarify our understanding. Stereotypically all of the preparations of the Thanksgiving feast fall to the women of the household. In the not-too-distant past, although the actual slaughter of the turkey may have been the responsibility of the men in the family, the mother would have purchased and raised the turkey chick and, after its death, cleaned and dressed and cooked it along with all of the other dishes deemed appropriate to the occasion. Today, when few people actually raise fowl in their backyards, it still falls to the women of the family to choose the carcass from among those offered by the butcher or grocer, prepare it, and present it to the assembled friends and family.

In a parallel move, a santera, with her many helpers, may select a live animal from among those offered by the farmer or his representative, care for it until the time of sacrifice, and then clean and cook the carcass for the assembled congregation. That dishes are prepared for both the living participants and the Orisha helps to maintain the connection between kitchen and ritual room. Whether or not a woman is actually handling the sacrificial knife, women are intimately involved with the entire ritual. As with Thanksgiving, the feeding of the assembled is rhetorically the most important element of the activity and the moment toward which all ritualized activity points.

Although in such an environment males may generally handle the actually killing and butchering of the animal while females handle the cooking and presentation of the ceremonial meal, this role separation is merely conventional and no longer a sacred limitation. Thus there is a possibility for unconventional behavior without jeopardizing the sanctity of the ritual itself. Once the conceptual prohibitions against women sacrificers are overcome, a variety of options are opened up. Women may choose to sacrifice for themselves, or they may employ the services of a male sacrificer to act on their behalf. Since larger animals require more strength, women may choose to sacrifice smaller animals such as fowl themselves but employ the services of men for larger animals like goats and pigs. In any case, their anatomical sex no longer serves as a limitation on their participation, while their gender role provides the most important focal point of the entire ritual process.

That [witches'] bird can hold a whip in its hand
It can hold a cudgel in its hand
It can hold a knife in its hand
It can become an orisha.

Yoruba song[1]

CHAPTER 7 · Witchcraft

It is not at all uncommon for outsiders to conflate Santería and other Afro-Cuban religious systems with *brujería* (Sp., witchcraft). Much of contemporary understanding of Cuban witchcraft is based on efforts of the
postcolonial elite in the Republican period to inscribe
onto their African and Afro-Cuban countrymen religious fanaticism and other disorderly behavior. The
term "witchcraft" along with the related terms "magic"
and "sorcery" are colored both by descriptions of the
European witch hunts of the early modern period and
by descriptions of certain beliefs and practices among
non-European peoples. Although in European cultures
witchcraft is often considered to be "consorting with
the devil," in African cultures it is believed that the mys-
terious powers to which human beings have access are
not necessarily associated with other beings, spiritual or
demonic. The source and location of these powers are
different in the two cultures, and these differences affect

the responses of these societies to the perceived exhibition of the powers. Both European and African views impact the ways we can approach the association of these phenomena with Santería and Orisha religion. Although scholars distinguish between witchcraft, magic, and sorcery,[2] both they and their sources often speak as though these three were similar or overlapping forces. I will use the term "witch" to describe all the practitioners of any of the magical arts and "witchcraft" as the result of that practice, without trying to draw strict boundaries between witchcraft, magic, and sorcery.

There is an enormous literature on both African and European witchcraft. In this chapter I will begin with a short description of the European witch hunts, narrowing our focus to the Spanish Inquisition in both Europe and New Spain (Mexico). Then I will look briefly at research on African witchcraft and the ways African understandings of witchcraft differ from European perceptions of witches and their works. An understanding of both of these approaches to witchcraft will help us to understand the ways in which the Orisha and their devotees can be associated with these unexplained phenomena. Finally, I will look at how concepts for these two disparate traditions have been combined into a contemporary vision of a world imbued with witchery.

Malleus Maleficarum: The European Witch Hunt

The tales of the European witch hunts are horrific.[3] Among other factors, Anne Llewellyn Barstow suggests, the manipulation of magical forces put the magic-worker in competition not only with the expanding male medical establishment but also with the Catholic clergy. Although theologians certainly don't frame it that way, transubstantiation, miraculous cures wrought by holy water and saintly relics, and the ritual of exorcism all bring the clergy into this magical realm and put them into competition with traditional magic-workers (Barstow 1994, 112).[4]

Most researchers agree that the majority of Europeans accused of witchcraft were "old, unattractive, disliked, and female" (16), although the percentages of men and woman accused and convicted vary across the European continent. "Originally seen as a useful member of the community ('a licensed and pledged midwife')," Barstow says, such a woman "became pariah ('a malefic and miserable woman')" (19). An essential feature of the witch trials was a belief in the reality of harmful magic (31). This belief was based on a belief in a variety of other types of magical abilities. The work of the village or urban healer in this period included activities we would characterize as both medical and magical: "healing, by both spells and potions, delivering babies, performing abortions, predicting the future, advising the lovelorn, cursing, removing curses, making peace between neighbors" (109). These women (and men) were believed to be able to manipulate magical forces because all of these activities were believed to require the power of magic (111). But such power can be used for both good and ill: the power to cure presumes the power to kill; cursing and removing curses are two sides of the same coin. Thus people feared the magic-worker, and it was that fear that religious and secular authorities turned against their victims (116–17).

Like the rest of Europe, Spanish villages had their own wise men and women, known as *curanderos*, who could, as Henry Kamen explains (1997, 269), "offer medicinal ointments, find lost objects, heal wounded animals, or help a girl to win the affections of her loved one. Cures might take the form of potions, charms, spells or simply advice."[5] However, when the curanderos were brought before the Holy Office, they were protected by two elements of the Spanish worldview. First of all, in Spain the inquisitors themselves questioned the *religious* nature of these activities. The Spanish inquisitors' primary interest was in "heresy," so popular superstition, sorcery, and activities like astrology, which did not fit neatly into the category of heresy, formed a marginal area of their investigations. In addition, since learned men and clergy dabbled in some of these areas themselves, particularly astrology, mere participation did not automatically implicate others in their eyes (269). Witchcraft, characterized by talk of flying through the air and copulating with the devil— the focus of the 1487 witchhunter's manual *Malleus Maleficarum* (Kramer and Sprenger 1928)—was seen by the Spanish inquisitors as "a delusion to be pitied rather than punished" (Kamen 1997, 270). Thus, although Spanish witches were subjected to a variety of punishments, few were murdered for their own or others' belief in their magic powers (Kamen 1997, 275; Barstow 1994, 92; Greenleaf 1969, 173).[6]

It was unlikely that the Inquisition affected most rural curanderos and their customers at all. Kamen suggests that vast areas of rural Spain were untouched by the Inquisition. For example, during the second half of the sixteenth century the tribunal of Catalonia made only sixteen visitations, and these were partial visits done in rotation. This meant, according to Kamen, that major towns may have been visited once every ten years, while people in rural areas may have seen an inquisitor only once in their entire lives. There were even places that were never visited by the Spanish Inquisition throughout the three hundred years of its history. Thus, he suggests, inquisitional activity was primarily an urban phenomenon (Kamen 1997, 280).

Only two classes of people were qualified for the stake under Spanish law:

relapsed heretics and the unrepentant. The "secular arm" of the city executed these, while others were punished in a ceremony called the *auto da fé* (act of faith), which involved public humiliation and penitence followed by a feast and festivities for the officials and spectators. Kamen provides accounts of several autos (203, 204, 207–10). Although heretics participated in the auto, their actual executions seem to have been accomplished in a less public location after the conclusion of the auto itself.

It was not until late in the inquisitional period that the Spanish inquisitors turned their eye from heresy toward other matters. In the late 1500s they began to recognize that a combination of formal religion and folk superstition permeated the lives of rural Spaniards. However, their campaign against these popular superstitions did not become significant until the seventeenth century (Kamen 1997, 256; Barstow 1994, 93).

Rather than focusing on witchcraft, Spanish thought at this time was dominated by issues of purity. *Limpieza de sangre* (purity of blood) began as a way of distinguishing between those whose ancestors had "always" been Christians and those whose ancestors had been Jewish or Muslim or had been disciplined by the Inquisition for some offense. Laws and regulations attempted to limit participation in the highest levels of society to honorable Old Christians, those with "pure" blood. According to these laws, if it could be proven "that an ancestor on any side of the family had been penanced by the Inquisition or was a Muslim or Jew, the descendant could be accounted of impure blood and disabled from the relevant office." Of course fraud, perjury, extortion, and blackmail were used to assure that only those without resources were penalized by these laws (Kamen 1997, 242).[7] Barstow says (1994, 93) that since this purity of ancestry was traced through family ties and religious orthodoxy, it was important that Christian Spanish women *as a group* not be demonized. In nineteenth-century Cuba impurity of blood was extended to mean "bad race," that is, African origin and slave status in either the present or previous generations (Stolcke 1974, 16–17). Thus religion and race were more important factors in these matters than imputed magical activity.

Two facts of particular interest to our analysis stand out from the witchcraft literature: relatively few people suffered death for witchcraft in the Spanish Inquisition, and although there were inquisitional courts in Central and South America there were *no* executions for witchcraft in Spanish America (Barstow 1994, 90, 201n13; Kamen 1997, 269–76).[8] Rather than concentrating on magic-workers, the Spanish Inquisition focused primarily on issues of religious heresy, specifically the secret practices of former Jews and Muslims, as well as on what was called Lutheranism, a generalized term for various Protestant beliefs.[9] Religious heterodoxy rather than witchcraft seems to have been the focus of the Spanish Inquisition in both Spain and her colonies. Witches and the practices associated with them were therefore less likely to be recognized and punished in Spain than in other portions of Europe. Unacceptable religious activity was closely defined by inquisitors as Jewish, Islamic, and Protestant beliefs and practices on the part of Christians, as well as indigenous practices by New World natives. Non-Islamic Africans seem to have been considered not to have any religion, or not to have a religion that came within the purview of the Inquisition and other religious authorities (Wood 1997; Palmié 2002, 229). Thus, according to Palmié, "the vast majority of cases involving Africans and their descendents entered into the [inquisitional] record under the rubrics of blasphemy or superstitious practice," not witchcraft or sorcery (230).

This made it possible for women and others in the Spanish colonies to continue witchcraft practices that included, in Barstow's memorable list, "healing, by both spells and potions, delivering babies, performing abortions, predicting the future, advising the lovelorn, cursing, removing curses, making peace between neighbors." When we think about healing in the colonial period, it is important to remember that, until the development of anesthesia and antibiotics, European medicine had little to offer the sick. Opium and hemp were known in ancient times, but general anesthetics were not discovered until the 1840s, and surgical procedures remained problematic until the advent of antibiotics in the mid-twentieth century. Although Louis Pasteur discovered in the nineteenth century that certain bacteria can kill anthrax bacilli and Alexander Fleming discovered penicillin in 1928, penicillin was not generally available until the early 1940s, when World War II stimulated additional research and production. Antibiotics did not come into general use until the 1950s. This means that until relatively recent times "healing, by both spells and potions," was the best medical care available not only to slaves, former slaves, and other members of the lower classes in the Americas but to rich and poor throughout the world.

Witchcraft in Africa

Research suggests that in West Africa witchcraft was deeply intertwined with the everyday world and was considered neither extraordinary nor awe-inspiring.[10] Barry Hallen and J. O. Sodipo, who approach the problem of witchcraft among the contemporary Yoruba from the position of philosophy of language, warn that, like many other concepts, the term "witch" cannot be directly translated between the European and Yoruba cultures (Hallen and Sodipo 1986, chap. 3). They suggest that the Yoruba word commonly translated as "witch," *aje,* rather than connoting a role or personal characteristic, refers to a special ability a person has in connection with the ori (destiny) chosen before birth. Thus, by their analysis, aje is a power that can be used for good or ill depending on the character of the person possessing it (112–13). Like Hallen and Sodipo's *onisègùn,* whom they characterize as herbalists, native doctors, and masters of medicine (10), the followers of the Orisha can invoke the powers of aje to support growth and life as well as to explain loss and misfortune.

The classic work on West African witchcraft, *Witchcraft, Oracles, and Magic among the Azande,* originally written in 1937, suggests that the Azande people of southern Sudan perceived witchcraft in a similar light: as a psychic act caused by a physical trait, a "witchcraft substance" in the body of the witch (Evans-Pritchard 1976, 1–4). Although any misfortune that could not be attributed to incompetence, breach of a taboo, or the failure to observe a moral rule was ascribed to witchcraft, only in the most egregious cases was there an attempt made to discover and punish the witch (13–18). Anyone could be a witch—could have witchcraft substance—so there was nothing remarkable about either being a witch or being bewitched by another (19). Since witchcraft is a physical substance one is born with, the Azande believed, it is possible for one person to bewitch another without knowing it; it is also possible that a person with witchcraft substance may keep it "cool" and never harm another (19, 49–50). Although those who exhibit unpleasant traits—a spiteful disposition, physical deformity, dirty habits—were not automatically regarded as witches, their names may have been more frequently placed before the witchcraft oracle and thus they may have been accused more often than their neighbors (52).

In his analysis of witchcraft among the Wimbum of Cameroon (2001), Elias Bongmba describes three different types of *tfu* (witchcraft). These include *bfiu,* which is a special skill that allows one to perform "extraordinary and spectacular things" such that one is perceived "as an especially powerful and gifted person" (22, 23); *brii,* which refers not only to a special ability that is generally malevolent but also to the person who possesses such a morally negative character (23–24); and *tfu* itself, which is often translated as "witchcraft" but which refers to a variety of activities whose common element is that they are carried out under the cover of darkness (24). Like the Azande, the Wimbum describe someone who has this power as having "witch-knowledge" (25) which is understood as "a hidden, non-hereditary, and non-purchasable force both men and women are born with" (25). Thus tfu is considered "an effective secret knowledge that can be intentionally deployed for the benefit of the practitioner, possibly at the expense of the victim" (25).

Although often perceived as a negative power, tfu can also have a positive meaning. Witchcraft knowledge, which is not distributed evenly throughout the population, may include the ability to "see" what those practicing evil tfu are up to. It is especially important that the *fon* or town leader have this power and thus be able to "see" what others cannot and to use the knowledge so obtained for the good of the people as a whole (30). The *nwe nshep*, commonly translated as "witch doctors," diviners, and other traditional healers, are also believed to have a form of witchcraft power that includes the ability to remove the illness and other bad luck that is the result of the evil tfu (32–35).

In a similar vein, Margaret Thompson Drewal (1992) says that there are three types of witch power among the Yoruba: white, red, and black. White witchcraft is beneficial, bringing prosperity and the good things of life; red witchcraft brings suffering, and black witchcraft causes death. She says that all witches can work all three kinds of magic, and powerful women can bring either prosperity or death, depending upon the type of witch power they deploy (178). Hallen and Sodipo (1986) summarize the popular stereotype of witchcraft among the Yoruba by saying that *aje*, the Yoruba term generally translated as "witch," refers to a "person who is anti-social and deliberately and destructively malevolent towards other members of his community." Generally identified as women, aje are believed to be members of *egbé* (associations) that meet at night and are capable of killing others, even their own children. However, as Hallen and Sodipo suggest, it is the fact that the aje have certain substances inside them, aje substance, that allows them to accomplish extraordinary things (102). Among the Yoruba as among the Azande, aje substance is a power that people have rather than a state of their souls or their personal selves. Every powerful person is assumed to have some aje; it is how one uses this power, how one behaves, that is important (105–7). Thus people with aje not only may be either men or women but also may be either good or evil, depending on their *iwa* (character) and their ori (destiny) (107–11).

Among the Yoruba the image of a witch is concise and dreadful. Witches are believed to transform themselves into birds at night so that they can perch near the houses of their victims and suck out their blood, causing illness or death (Thompson 1971, II/1). By sucking out their blood, the witches are believed to be eating the spirits of the individuals they have set out to destroy. This ability to transform themselves is a special quality of witches. Drewal says that some of the phrases used to describe women—*oloju meji*, "one with two

faces"; *abara meji*, "one with two bodies"; and *alao meji*, "one of two colors"—
all express their ashé, their power "to bring things into existence, to make
things happen." Since this power is both positive and negative, it is the power
of transformation, the power of the witches' aje to transform themselves and
to produce changes in others (M. Drewal 1992, 177). Robert Farris Thompson
(1971, 6/4) describes a seated image as a bearded figure with female breasts and
a swollen belly suggestive of pregnancy. He was told that this type of bearded
woman was, by definition, a witch because witches, like a bearded woman,
stand at the boundaries between categories. A bearded woman is a particularly
potent image, for not only does she embody the (female) powers of generation and sustenance, but her beard displays her (masculine) power and authority.

Another clue to this ambivalence is the euphemism used to refer to witches.
Among the Yoruba, to name something is to call it into presence. Rather than
do so in respect to witchcraft, they use the terms *eleye* (literally, "owner of
birds") and *awon iya wa* or *iyami* ("our mothers") as euphemisms to refer to
the aje. One implication is that those who are "our mothers" or witches by
night are also our mothers—and sisters, aunts, cousins, wives, co-wives—during the day. We can see this attitude expressed in the Gelede celebrations in
Ketu and other parts of southwest Nigeria. Thompson says that one of the
functions of the Gelede festival is "worship of the witches [and] honoring of
the devotees of the hot gods as messengers of the witches" (14/1). These gods
include Shango, Ogun, Sopona, and Eshu along with Orisha Oko.[11] The purpose of the festival is a *"confrontation with the gods as witches"* (italics in original)
and the appeasement of them through the "ultimate weapon," which is beauty.
The senior members of the Gelede cult are old women who command the
secrets of "the mothers" for the benefit of society, who work positive witchcraft on behalf of their sons and daughters and through them for their grandchildren (14/2).

Thus witchcraft power in different West African communities was seen not
only as a natural phenomenon but also as an ambiguous one, neither inherently good nor bad. Rather than being ethically marked a priori, witchcraft
power was understood to be dependent for its ethical quality upon the moti-
vations of the witch, who could use this power to help or hurt others. Melville
Herskovits could make the interesting comparison between the nature of
magic in the West African imagination and our own use of electricity and automobiles. Like magic, electricity and cars that are handled improperly not
only can be very dangerous; they also can be used to harm others purposely.
However, their helpful properties assure their continued presence in our lives.

In the same way, he argues, witch technology and magical charms, when handled with the proper controls, can be perceived as beneficial to society (Herskovits 1941, 73–74).

Older women particularly partake of this power. As Eugenia Herbert explains (1993, 225), during their reproductive years Yoruba women are defined by their sexuality and reproductive abilities, but older women are perceived as standing on the boundary between categories; although they continue to be benevolent mothers (and grandmothers), they are also perceived as witches with extraordinary power and authority. The older woman, in general, is particularly powerful in Yoruba society. Having married young, she often outlives her husband and his siblings. If she has successfully played her reproductive role, particularly if she has living sons, she comes into a position of indirect power and control within her husband's family. In addition, by outliving many of her peers, she will also have acquired her own direct power and control. Indeed, even without witchcraft, Herbert suggests, older women are a power to be feared (238). Not only are older women seen as witches, but so are priestesses, wealthy market women, and female titleholders—all of which are positions of acquired power (M. Drewal 1992, 177–78). However, postmenopausal women are seen as especially powerful (179), since living to old age is considered to be the result of extraordinary good luck, and such luck is associated with strong witchcraft powers.

Although both men and women can have witchcraft substance, in Africa as well as Europe, negative witchcraft is stereotypically associated with women. In his discussion of Yemoja (Yemaya), Thompson cites Judith Hoch-Smith (1978, 265) to suggest that the use of witchcraft by African women is a way of militating against total male dominance. Witchcraft lore suggests that great secret power is lodged in women who can choose to use that power to support or destroy the institutions of society (Thompson 1983, 74). Margaret Thompson Drewal (1992) says men believe that, when women get possessed, their spirits (emi) leave their body and are transformed into birds. They say that in this form women can "gather and hold secret meetings in the treetops" (172). Men also believe that "powerful women always gain access to men's secrets" because their spirits can go where women themselves are forbidden (180).

All of the Yoruba riverine goddesses are famed for their witchcraft. In fact, with the exception of Obatala, every Orisha is somehow associated with witchcraft, magic, or sorcery. Both Yemaya and Oshun are recognized as "mother of the witches" (Apter 1992, 113; Edwards and Mason 1985, 67, 78). Thompson suggests (1971, 14/3) that Gelede, the masquerade of western Nigeria, honors Yemaya who, as the mother of witchcraft, is the leader of the birds of the night who not only punish but also give children and a long life. Images of birds are important in the Yoruba iconography of witchcraft. Witches are conceived as night birds that perch on the trees of the market and cause troubles while others sleep. Nevertheless, birds also have positive images. Yoruba crowns are surmounted by one or more bird images. These birds represent the ashé (herbal medicine) placed in the crown itself. In recognition of the association between birds and women as witches, the birds invoke the role of the *iya kere*, one of the royal wives, who is in charge of the crown and places it upon the king's head each time he wears it. Second in rank only to the king's official mother, the iya kere not only has charge of the royal regalia but can choose to withhold the crown and other symbols of power from the king. Because she can prevent the king from performing his royal duties, she is one of the most powerful persons in the palace. The birds represent the power of women in general to either protect or destroy the person who wears the crown. These birds suggest the roles women have in supporting the king himself as well as women's relationship to witchcraft (Drewal, Pemberton, and Abiodun 1989, 38; Johnson 1921, 63–64).

Although both men and women could be endowed with witchcraft substance, in the popular understanding women, particularly older women, are especially strong witches who may use their power for either good or ill. As the ability to ward off the afflictions of daily living and to benefit one's self and one's family are considered characteristics of witchcraft power, doing well, raising many healthy children and grandchildren, and living to see the second or third generation are all indications of strong witchcraft power. Since witchcraft power is itself morally ambiguous, whether it is used for good or ill depends completely on the moral condition of the person wielding it. Thus older people are especially feared as they are believed to have especially strong witchcraft power that they have had a lifetime to learn to wield according to their will.

Brujería

Ideas about magic and witchcraft have had an unstable position in western European thought. Although, as Anne Barstow (1994) says, in "the sixteenth century, many—especially among the elite—began to hold a new belief, namely, that such supernatural power came from the devil, who bestowed it chiefly on women in return for their absolute obedience to him" (20), by the eighteenth century most Europeans had joined their Mediterranean neighbors in discounting the possibility of magic-working. The growth of the Enlightenment and its scientific method called the possibility of witchcraft and magic into question. Thus the Inquisition withered away as fewer and fewer people, either elites or commoners, believed in the supernatural powers witches were claimed to have wielded (Barstow 1994, 31, 92; Kors and Peters 2001, 392–94). However, the Republican period in Cuba (1902–58) saw a rise of purported brujería or witchcraft activity, particularly among its African and African-heritage population.

Stephan Palmié suggests that the disappearance and murder of the toddler Zoila Díaz in 1904 was the beginning of a witchcraft hysteria among the white Cuban middle and elite classes. According to newspaper accounts from the time, several elderly Africans including Domingo Bocourt, a "locally known *brujo*," assassinated *la niña Zoila* in order to use portions of her body for sacrificial or curative purposes (Palmié 2002, 211). As other supposed ritual child murders were reported in the Cuban press, the term *brujería* came to be associated with what Palmié calls "Afro-Cuban cultural otherness" (212), so that soon in a "long overdue 'crusade against brujeria'" the Cuban police were raiding the sites of Afro-Cuban cult activity and confiscating any ostensible ritual paraphernalia found there (213). As Palmié suggests, this modern witch craze was focused mainly on male Afro-Cubans and the cults of Abakuá and Palo Monte (214). However, as membership in these societies often overlapped with that of Regla de Ocha (Santería), practitioners of all the Afro-Cuban religions came under suspicion as practitioners of brujería and *hechicería* (sorcery).

In contradistinction to their sixteenth-century ancestors, the twentieth-century Cuban elite saw African-based witchcraft activity not as "a mistaken belief in satanic powers" or as "a matter . . . of madness" (Barstow 1994, 92) but as actual effective behavior. As Fernando Ortiz put it in his (in)famous *Los negros brujos* (1906, 169–70),[12] "all the more so since, in truth, the brujos [do] practice witchcraft; hence the fact that for reasons of atavism there are incredulous and relatively cultivated people who manifest a certain anxious respect for the embós [magical preparations] and oracle of the most savage African witchcraft" (cited in Palmié 2002, 216). In an effort to relieve Cuba of the taint of "blackness" brought on by the importation of enslaved Africans, social scientists like Ortiz worked with the police to identify and eradicate African-based brujería through the extermination of its practitioners (Palmié 2002, chap. 3). Although partially rehabilitated during the *afrocubanismo* movement that flourished between 1928 and 1940 (Matibag 1996), African-based religious practices in Cuba continue to be tainted by their associations with the notion of brujería.

Santería Witchcraft

Contemporary Santería practice in the United States conflates many of these European, Cuban, and African ideas of witchcraft in interesting ways. On the one hand (and in line with African sensibilities), all of the Orisha, and by extension all santeros, are understood to be imbued with a certain ability to subtly affect the visible and invisible world, to use "magic" to change lives and fortunes and to control natural phenomena. On the other hand (expressing a European understanding), witchcraft is perceived as an essentially malevolent force. Seldom have I heard of anyone directly accused of witchcraft, yet vague notions of witchcraft being used against individuals fill the air: "Someone is doing witchcraft against you" or "You need to protect yourself against witchcraft." The idea that witchcraft is everywhere is very African. Perceptive people guard themselves against the witchcraft of others, and many develop an arsenal of tools and powers to control the ever-present witch forces.[13] Moreover, in modern Santería the Orisha themselves are seen as powerful "witches" that can be invoked against the witchcraft of others. Although no one would admit doing witchcraft against another, positive magic for healing, for wealth, for the love of another, for all the good things of life are an essential part of the religion, and many casual conversations among practitioners include discussions of "recipes." These are spells and workings, generally based on a form of sympathetic magic, designed to enhance the lives of the practitioners or their clients.

Many people first come to the religion of Santería in search of physical, emotional, or interpersonal healing. Through divination and ebo (sacrifice) the priest attempts to nudge the individual's life back into the best manifestation of the ori received at birth. Magic performed for personal or family betterment is seldom perceived as evil or as the work of witchcraft. However, santeros believe that malevolent forces permeate the environment and may harm those who are weak or unprotected. Often an ongoing regimen of offerings, spiritual baths, and other minor rituals is prescribed to strengthen the client's ashé and protect against ubiquitous bad luck. When plagued by interpersonal, job, or love problems, divination can discover the cause and recommend a cure. Although it is not uncommon for clients to want to know from whom their bad luck emanates, such information is seldom forthcoming unless a direct question is asked. For the most part, the identity of the "witch" is unimportant; rather, securing the goodwill and protection of the petitioner's ancestors, spiritual guides, or the Orisha is enough to overturn malevolent forces, whether of spiritual or material origin.

I have never heard a contemporary Santería practitioner prescribe a ritual *instead of* a visit to a physician or hospital, unlike some healers whose work is at odds with Western medical practice. Rather, good results can be expected when rituals are performed to enhance and strengthen the work of a medical team. Clients who come to a practitioner with the thought that through the "magic" of Santería they might circumvent the Western medical system are rapidly disabused of that notion. Santería healing generally works in conjunction with rather than in opposition to other medical practices.[14] As Hallen and Sodipo suggest, only one with powerful aje can conquer powerful witchcraft, so, in spite of any protestation to the contrary, strong and effective santeros are perceived as having/being powerful witches who can direct the witch powers of the Orisha for good or ill.

Witchcraft and Theodicy

In its classical formulation, theodicy asks the question, Why is there suffering in a world ruled by a morally good God? Although the term was coined in the seventeenth century by the philosopher Gottfried Leibniz (1646–1716), the challenge of juxtaposing God's goodness and power against the experienced reality of suffering has plagued the ethical monotheisms from the beginning. Perhaps we find its most succinct formulation in the words of the philosopher David Hume (1711–1776): "Is he [God] willing to prevent evil, but not able? then he is impotent. Is he able, but not willing? then he is malevolent. Is he both able and willing? whence then is evil?" (Hume 1948, pt. 10, 66).

Although religions such as Santería that don't postulate a single, just, all-powerful deity aren't plagued by the contradictions inherent in this "trilemma"[15] of classical theodicy, they continue to ask the basic questions of theodicy: Why do good people suffer while the wicked prosper? Why do innocent children suffer and die? Why does the whirlwind destroy one house and leave its neighbor standing? Why in any catastrophe are some destroyed while others survive? And most basically: Why me? Why must *I* suffer? Why do *my* children sicken and die? Why can't *I* find the path in life I deserve?

Orisha philosophy provides a two-pronged answer to human suffering based on its ideas of personal destiny and the conflation of African, European, and creolized American witchcraft. In pursuit of the ideal of a long, fulfilling, prosperous life filled with family and friends, free from illness and disease, one must work within one's chosen destiny to obtain the best life possible. If one has chosen badly or is attempting to work outside the framework of one's destiny, life will encompass a series of difficulties. On the other hand, it is also possible for powerful beings from both the visible and invisible worlds, including the Orisha, the dead (both personal and nonspecific), and evil persons, to throw up obstacles in one's path, thus thwarting the chosen destiny.

As Segun Gbadegesin suggests (1991, 50–51), choosing a destiny is like picking a lottery number; in the absence of complete information and in spite of the best of intentions, one may choose badly and one's destiny may be "full of worms." Sometimes, however, because one has forgotten the fullness of the chosen destiny, one may focus on some portions of life and ignore others and miss that fullness. A story is told of a middle-aged man whose life was full of troubles. As a farmer he was hopelessly inept. Each year he had to borrow seed yams from his neighbors in order to plant. Being such a poor farmer, not only was he unable to pay back his debt, the next year he had to borrow more seed yams. Because of his lack of prosperity, he could not attract a wife and thus had no children, no family. In a society in which being a "big man" with a large family and an entourage is the ideal (Barber 1981), this man saw himself a complete failure. Discouraged, he went deep into the forest intent on ending his misery by killing himself. There he met a young man, perhaps Eleggua, perhaps the personification of his own ori, who persuaded him to return to the village and delay his death for one week. Thinking that one week could not make any difference in his resolve, he turned his back on the forest and returned to his village. It happened that, while he was in the forest, the old king had died. So while he was traveling back to his home, the village elders, the kingmakers, were meeting to choose a new ruler for the community. As he approached his village, a group of the high-ranking men rushed out to meet him. "Where have you been? We've been looking for you. Come with us," they said as they rushed him to the center of the village and began the ceremony that would install him as their new ruler. Within the week, the man who had seen himself as an utter failure had become the new king with all the tokens of prosperity, including the promise of wives and children. In spite of his failure as a farmer, the village elders saw that he was a good-hearted man, wise and compassionate, one whom they wanted to have absolute authority over the village.

This story tells us several things about the workings of destiny. It tells us that the fullness of one's destiny may not be obvious until later in life. It tells us that failure in one aspect of life does not necessarily portend failure in all aspects. It tells us that one may not see the fullness of one's own character: while the farmer focused on his failures, the rest of the village focused on his virtues. It also tells us that one's destiny may entail misfortunes and afflictions in the course of working itself out. Perhaps his misfortunes were instrumental in the development of the characteristics desired by the kingmakers. Without those misfortunes, he might not have been such a desirable candidate for kingship. Nevertheless, hard work and *iwa pele* (good character)—along with divination and sacrifice—will help one to manifest one's best destiny. Perhaps if this man had sought divination instead of taking his destiny into his own hands, he might have been prepared for his change in fortune.

Be that as it may, we are not the only beings who can have an effect on our destiny. The Yoruba concept of witchcraft provides other explanatory rationales for the hardships in life. It is understood not only that every person is born with a certain level of ashé but that other visible and invisible beings have the power to affect human life. Thus in the worst case one's life may be cut short by the malevolent actions of others in the visible or invisible world. Our fellow human beings can affect our destiny in both material and nonmaterial ways. Envy and greed may work against us at the material level as our enemies attempt to cause us suffering and pain. Some people may actually engage in unconscious witchcraft of the sort suggested by Evans-Pritchard's Azante. In addition, those who are cognizant of their powers may also choose to attack us through conscious witchcraft. Conversely, we may consciously or unconsciously engage in witchcraft behavior that can affect the destiny of others. The idea that one can both influence the lives of others and deflect their malicious attempts to influence ours forms the core of much of the literature of Santería. Thus we find that many popular books are filled with recipes and spells. One can find spells to win the love of another, to get a job, to have children, to repel an unwanted suitor, to punish a wayward spouse or gain control of an associate, to win the lottery or come into money, or to protect one's self and one's loved ones from the machinations of others. Because such spells and workings don't depend on the intervention of the Orisha or the ancestors, they generally come under the umbrella of brujería. They are not really a part of Santería per se, although santeros may recommend and even engage in these activities. Santeros (and other practitioners of African-based religious systems) often consider themselves and are often perceived by others to be especially strong practitioners of these sorts of witchcraft. All conscious witchcraft, whether for good or ill, depends on being able to use certain types of witchcraft powers. Within the Santería worldview one's natural witchcraft power is fortified and intensified by the ashé gained as part of one's initiations. Although few santeros would articulate it in just such a manner, they understand that they are the owners of certain powers (we would say that they are aje, the owners of witchcraft power) that can be used for good or ill and that can be used to deflect the "witchcraft" of others.

Invisible beings may also bring pain and suffering into one's life. There are no inherently malevolent beings in the Santería cosmos, but, like human beings, most of the denizens of the invisible world, including spirits of the dead and the Orisha, are considered to be morally ambiguous. Thus santeros believe that, just as people in the visible world may not always act in our best interests, beings in the invisible world also may not always act in our best interests. Invisible beings are commonly divided into three categories—the Orisha, one's own ancestral spirits, and other spirits of the dead—with a perceived moral hierarchy among these groups. The Orisha generally act in the best interests of their devotees. Ancestral spirits, while favoring their descendants, are understood to be more or less moral depending on their level of ethical development while alive. Other spirits, whose behavior is not affected by any prior familial relationship, are more ambiguous. Because none of these beings is understood as innately good or evil, when misfortunes are identified as the result of the actions of these beings, one of two scenarios is generally suggested. Either another person in an act of malicious witchcraft has sent the invisible being, often a nonancestral spirit, to do harm, or an invisible being is seeking attention.

When invisible beings, particularly the Orisha and ancestral spirits, are desirous of ritual attention or wish to promote behavior change in their devotees or descendants, they may communicate their desires through dreams or through synchronous events. But people are often "hard of hearing," and it is only when their troubles precipitate a visit to a diviner that they are able to hear the message in an unambiguous way. Divination might indicate that one has strayed from the path of one's chosen destiny, or is being subjected to material witchcraft by another, or is being sent an escalating series of misfortunes as messages from the invisible world. Depending on the diagnosis, one may need to align one's life and destiny more closely, or fortify personal defenses against witchcraft, or establish, reestablish, or strengthen relationships with the Orisha or the ancestors.

Santería Healing

As we saw in chapter 3, divination within the Santería complex involves not only identifying the causes of the client's misfortunes but also recommending a treatment, a course of action designed to mitigate the situation. A major portion of the work done by many santeros in the course of their religious practice is the diagnosis and healing of physical, mental, and interpersonal ills. Their clients may include members of their own religious family, casual participants in the religion, or outsiders who "use" Santería as an alternative or supplement to conventional medical, psychological, or personal counseling services. They are part of a long and broad tradition. In medieval times, as Barstow wrote, the practice of the local magic worker consisted of "healing, by both spells and potions, delivering babies, performing abortions, predicting the future, advising the lovelorn, cursing, removing curses, making peace between neighbors." Among the Yoruba a visit to the diviner and/or herbalist, both of whom were depositories of strong ashé, provided healing of physical and mental ailments. In Cuba the witch-hunters were also hunting healers. According to public understanding at the time, the black brujos used the blood of their victims to effect cures for aged former slaves (Palmié 2002, 211). Although delivering babies and performing abortions have been appropriated by conventional medicine, contemporary santeros continue to engage in other types of magical healing rituals, predicting the future, advising the lovelorn, removing curses and making peace among neighbors, and providing physical and mental solace to their clientele. When the diagnosis is witchcraft, santeros, like their African colleagues, generally do not try to identify the source of a problem but instead try to counteract the evil influences, strengthen the client, and protect him or her from further malignant intrusions. In the case of serious disease, a santero would not deny the causative role of bacteria, viruses, or bad lifestyle. However, the santero would also understand that we are all exposed to bacteria and viruses and perhaps unhealthy lifestyles. Why this particular person has succumbed to this particular disease at this particular time is the focus of the divinatory investigation. As a consequence you'll hear a santero say, "Well, you've been cursed," and then go on to describe a series of rituals that are aimed at counteracting the curse rather than at identifying its source.

Healing rituals may call on the Orisha or the client's ancestors or other spirit guides. They may use both external and internal herbal remedies, or they may require ritual baths or initiation into religious practice. Clients may be asked to make offerings to spirits or Orisha or to make major or minor lifestyle changes. All of these healing activities are focused on the movement of ashé, of strengthening the client's personal power and moving him or her along the path of best destiny. Moreover, all of these healing activities require some sort of sacrifice on the part of the clients. They may be required to purchase the ingredients for prescribed rituals (a sacrifice of time and money), or to forsake certain behaviors or activities (a sacrifice of personal autonomy), or even to participate in the ritual feeding of an Orisha or other invisible being (a blood sacrifice).

Our modern scientific worldview doesn't allow for any of these activities to be effective. Although research has shown that prayer in conjunction with conventional medicine enhances healing, the types of activities performed by santeros in the course of their healing work are generally discounted, and practitioners may be prosecuted for fraudulent behavior. However, anecdotal evidence provided by clients suggests that they find these activities helpful.

Santería practitioners often distinguish between the concepts of healing and curing. As generally understood, "cure" refers to a restoration of health—a complete recovery from whatever disease plagues the patient. Although it is possible that a religious ritual might effect such a complete restoration of health, cures are generally understood to operate at the level of the physical and to be the province of orthodox Western medicine with its reliance on sophisticated drugs, diagnostic tests, and machines. Healing, on the other hand, implies a restoration to wholeness that has a wider range of implications. While a cure can be claimed only when the patient has been returned to some assumed ideal human condition free of disease and its complications, healing ranges over the whole physical, psychological, and spiritual landscape in an attempt to bring the patient into a balanced relationship with himself and his environment. A client may be considered healed when he or she makes peace with the physical, mental, or spiritual affliction, even though a cure has not been effected. For example, a visit to a santero is unlikely to cure AIDS, but the healing rituals might enable the sufferer to live a full and rich life in spite of, or perhaps even because of, the disease.[16] The work of the santero may heal whether or not the client is cured. This is not to say that such healing can't be accomplished through other, more conventional means (a visit to a psychiatrist or social service agency, for example). For many, however, it is the santero who provides these sorts of healing benefits.

Witchcraft and Gender

Stephan Palmié suggests that African-based traditions of Ocha (that is, Orisha religion, Regla de Ocha, Santería) and Palo (Reglas de Congo, including Palo Monte and Palo Mayombe) together with the European tradition of Kardecian spiritism (Espiritismo in Spanish) evolved together in Cuba to form a moral continuum along which spirits of the dead, ancestral spirits, and the Orisha may be classified as increasingly more enlightened and ethical beings. According to this moral map, Palo spirits (the nonancestral dead) are "darker, tormented and potentially malicious beings" who, having been captured, bought, exploited, and abused, work for their priests as "mystical entrepreneurs and mercenary healers." As slaves who can impose no moral conditions on their activity, they are morally ambiguous actors who do as they are commanded. Palo rituals are characterized as violent, uncouth, and generally uncivilized (192, 193–94). The Orisha, on the other hand, are seen as highly evolved spiritual beings who are conceived according to an ideology of kinship. Thus interactions between the Orisha and their devotees are often formulated in the idiom of gift exchange (173), while their ritual events are seen as stately, even royal displays (163–68).

Even though the Orisha may generally be considered morally superior to both humans and spirits, it is incorrect to suggest that they are unambiguously so. While both the literature and casual conversations with practitioners suggest that the Orisha are "good" and can only be called upon to perform benevolent work—in contrast to the spirits of the dead, especially those spirits worked by paleros, who are often perceived as "bad" or available to perform malicious witchcraft for a petitioner—santeros generally understand that all of the Orisha are powerful witches whose power can be utilized according to the moral propensities of the devotee invoking them. Santeros may call Palo "crude . . . but powerful . . . , violent but fast and effective" because it deals with the dead and the uncultivated landscape rather than with divine beings who inhabit socialized spaces (164), but such characterizations ignore the place of the warrior Orisha who live on the boundary between the village and the forest and are also associated with the uncultivated bush.

Ogun the blacksmith, Ochosi the hunter, and Eleggua the messenger and trickster have been combined in the Americas to form a trinity known as Los Guerreros, the Warriors. Unlike most of the other deities, these Orisha are less likely to be imagined according to an idiom of "awesome royal authority" than one of "embodiment of brute force," as Palmié describes the Orisha and Palo spirits respectively (164). In the home of the santero, they are physically separated from the remaining Orisha and sit by or behind the devotee's front door so that they can guard the boundary between public and private space and be poised to defend the inhabitants of the house. Other Orisha may be conceived of as royalty, but these Orisha are generally thought of as workers, with a rough appearance and manners much like those often attributed to Palo spirits. Not only are Los Guerreros violent and powerful but, like Palo spirits, they also may be dangerous to work with. It is said that Ogun will turn on his devotees if the power of his bloodlust is not satisfied. Car accidents, gunshot wounds, and surgery are all methods by which Ogun can exact his revenge. By the same token, Eleggua, in his form as the trickster, is known to turn an unsuspecting devotee's malevolent actions back on the perpetrator.

Although the other Orisha (including Shango and Oya, who are also considered warriors, albeit of a more refined nature) are commonly invoked to "fight" for their devotees, all of the Orisha, even Obatala the emblematic *funfun* and peaceful Orisha, have warrior aspects that can be called upon when necessary. To suggest, for example, that Oshun is only the gentle sweet ingénue, queen of the sweet water and mistress of all the good things of life, is to miss the full power of her archetype, which also posits her as *iyalode*, the leader of the aje, the witches that meet at night to wreak havoc on their enemies in the community. Similarly, to limit Yemaya to an image of the gentle and affectionate mother is to misapprehend the power of the fierce mother both in respect to her children and to those who may threaten them.

In chapter 3 we looked at the way the female-dominated Orisha cults were denigrated vis-à-vis the male-dominated priesthood of Ifá because of their potential for irrational and irresponsible behavior in the absence of hegemonic control; in Stephan Palmié's work we find a similar denigration of Ocha vis-à-vis Palo because of its refined and civilized nature. When Palmié says that practitioners support the view that "ocha and palo stand to each other like religion and magic, expressive and instrumental forms of human-divine interaction" (193), he is invoking a wide range of anthropological literature dealing with both the relationship between religion and magic and that between expressive and instrumental forms of religiosity. By juxtaposing Ocha and Palo as religion and magic, he places the two forms in moral opposition according to the formula articulated by Emile Durkheim (1915, 57–63) that, although magic and religion appear to be similar in that both rely on beliefs and rites, on myths and dogmas, and both seek technical and utilitarian ends, they are diametrically opposed in that religious adherents are always bound together in a "single, moral community" while practitioners of magic lack any such community. In the first portion of this characterization, by putting Ocha in the category of religion while relegating Palo to the realm of magic, Palmié's statement is making certain moral claims about the work of the two religious complexes appearing to valorize Ocha by placing it within the legitimating moral category. However, the second portion of the statement undercuts this valorization by ascribing instrumentalist forms to Palo while relegating Ocha to expressive ones and thus genderizing the two traditions.

Although generally "magical" systems are treated less sympathetically in the literature than "religious" ones, in this case Palo is consistently described as crude but powerful, the site of instrumental and masculinist activity, juxtaposed to an expressive Ocha dominated by women and by "overly refined" (read homosexual) men (Palmié 2002, 164). Whereas Ifá-centric rhetoric fo-

cuses on the intellectual qualities of its priesthood and practices, Palo emphasizes the "manly"—the bold, courageous, powerful, amoral—quality of its
magical work. That both of these systems deny membership to homosexual
men highlights their chauvinistic natures. Women and homosexual men
caught in the Ifá-Ocha-Palo continuum can find themselves disparaged both
for being too close to nature and emotional and for being too cultured, refined, and elegant—not cerebral enough to engage in the study of Ifá and not
brutal enough to work effectively with the powerful spirits of the *nganga*
(ritual pot). That a single person may be an initiate in all three of these systems
does not negate the common ascription of incompatible attributes to practitioners of the three systems.

The popular stereotype among both Europeans and Africans that witches
are predominantly women also leads us to question the position of women in
the cultures of early modern Europe, Yoruba Africa, and contemporary
America. Anne Llewellyn Barstow (1994), after characterizing the stereotypical witch of the European witch hunts as "old, unattractive, disliked and female" (16), tells us that, while some wealthy women were accused, generally
witches were "of the poorer sort" (26), "uppity women—women given to
speaking out, to a bold tongue and independent spirit" (27). Many held a
certain authority within their communities, for such a woman was often a
"healer, midwife, advice-giver, fortune-teller, spell-lifter," one to whom people
turned in time of need (29). Women visionaries were especially suspect, both
to their neighbors and to the inquisitors, since it was understood that malevolent spirits easily deceived them. It was also thought that women were more
tempted to these activities as a way of achieving attention and power in a society that generally left them powerless. Similarly, among the Yoruba there is a
tendency to conflate the categories of aje and women. Popularly witches are
thought to be women, generally older women, who meet in secret assemblies
and prey on the bodies of non-witches. By nature these women are thought to
be inherently antisocial and deliberately and destructively malevolent people
who use their witchcraft substance to the detriment of the larger society.

In both the African and the European case, male witches are believed to be
especially powerful. Those who can identify and prosecute witches (often
called "witch doctors" in the literature) are also seen as more powerful still.
The discussions of Hallen and Sodipo (1986) with the onisègùn—the herbalists, native doctors, and masters of medicine—eventuated in them not only
admitting that they had aje power but also suggesting that they were especially
powerful aje who used their witchcraft powers to achieve good ends—including identifying and contesting the power of "evil" witches (107). Such an

analysis completely contradicts the commonly held perception that all those with witchcraft power are evil or at best amoral. However, underlying the onisègùn's proclamation of themselves as power aje who use their witchcraft powers for good ends is the implication that the "evil" witches against whom they battle are the malevolent women that form the stereotype of the aje.

Although witchcraft is often seen as the special province of women, men who appropriate witchcraft activity to themselves tend to valorize their own witchcraft capabilities as more ethically or powerfully wielded. Thus Hallen and Sodipo's onisègùn saw themselves as benevolent and eminently moral persons far from the commonly held image of aje as malevolent women, while Palmié's informants suggested that a strong (masculine) priest was able to keep the great power of his nganga and the spirits that reside there under his control. And although Palmié suggests that the distinction between Ocha and Palo is based on "bad indigenous sociology of religion," since the Orisha may also exhibit some of the worst characteristics of the muertos in the nganga, including immorality and a mercenary tendency, nowhere does he overturn his earlier valorization of paleros as especially strong spiritual workers relative to the more effeminate santeros. Hence we are left with the notion that, although "witch" is a female appellation, men who engage in witchcraft activities are more potent than their female counterparts.

CHAPTER 8 · Conclusion: A Distinction without a Difference

In chapter 2 I suggested that just as the male was normative for Christian saintliness, to such a degree that Christian women had to repudiate their female nature in order to achieve true spirituality, in Santería religious practice the ideal for both men and women is formed by qualities associated with being female. Santería is thus a female-based religion, valorizing female virtues and practices so that, in spite of being embedded within patriarchal cultures, the female rather than the male is normative.

As we have seen in subsequent chapters, Orisha worshippers use female roles and titles to suggest certain attributes and to perform activities associated with their religious practice. Although it is not necessary for santeros to repudiate their masculine nature in order to participate fully within Santería communities, it *is* sometimes necessary for them to be able to move into female roles as part of their religious practice. Similarly, women priests are sometimes required to move between gender roles, most obviously when they participate in possession activities but also at other points in their religious lives. That both men and women must move between roles embodying different conceptions not only of the Self but also of the sacred Other demands a view of the self that is fluid rather than fixed or unitary.

We have framed this fluidity in terms of gender because gender fluidity seems to be both the most radical and the most challenging concept for those of us coming out of a Western European philosophical environment. As Eugenia Herbert suggests, the African view of gender transcends the essentialist/constructionist debate described in chapter 2 through a both/and approach. While certain types of behaviors and attributes are understood to be essential features of the anatomical males or females, gender is understood to be constructed and relational, not a fixed category but rather one that varies according to the context (Herbert 1993, 224–25, 236). Thus from this African-based viewpoint one can suggest that femaleness and maleness each embodies certain characteristics that are important to religious practice while simultaneously suggesting that both anatomical males and anatomical females can (and should) exhibit those characteristics as part of ritual practice. That is, both men and women must sometimes take on the roles commonly attributed to the other anatomical sex while not repudiating their own anatomy (or, for that matter, their sexual orientation, which is another issue).

In analyzing this worldview it is important to understand that, although male and females roles are essentialized such that certain characteristics are assigned to one gender or the other, this genderizing is *not* normatively male. This African viewpoint does not consider women to be defective men (nor men to be defective women). Rather, man and woman are complementary pieces of a cultural whole and both have qualities that are necessary for the proper functioning of the world. At the same time, since gender is constructed according to the demands of the occasion, it is possible for one to move between gender roles independent of anatomy. This movement provides balance when an anatomically appropriate body is unavailable. Thus in the colonial Cuban situation, it was possible both for female priests to reestablish and reinvigorate their religious traditions in the absence of a significant number of male colleagues and for males to be incorporated into these revitalized traditions. This moves us from Oyewùmí's thesis that among the Yoruba "gender is a difference without a distinction" to a completely different theoretical/ideological base, one in which gender is a concept that is used to distinguish and characterize certain attitudes and practices but which is fluid and open to individuals regardless of their anatomical configuration, a distinction without a difference.

To say, as I have, that Santería is an essentially feminine religion that valorizes female attitudes and practice will challenge both religious insiders and scholarly outsiders. However, let us reconsider those portions of the religion in which gender is highlighted.

According to the basic cosmology of this tradition, everyone has a destiny for this life, and can be or do anything as long as it is supported by that destiny. Part of destiny is the body into which one is born. One can learn the contours of one's destiny through divination. Although Ifá divination is traditionally the domain of men, women priests can speak to their Orisha through the cowry shells. Cowry divination has become especially strong in the Americas, perhaps because of the leadership needs of women in environments in which Ifá was not available. Never able to establish itself in Candomblé, Ifá has become a strong force within Santería communities both in Cuba and in the United States. However, until recently Ifá has been the exclusive domain of straight men, leaving the development of much of Santería to women and gay men (without excluding other men). Although the initiation of women into Ifá may be changing the power dynamics within the wider Orisha traditions, it is unlikely that women will attain full equality in the foreseeable future.

In order to manifest one's best/highest destiny one needs to offer gifts and sacrifices to invisible beings. Traditionally sacrifice has also been the domain of men, but in Cuba women appropriated the initiations necessary to participate in sacrifice at all levels, including blood sacrifices. In a wider context, as discussed earlier, sacrifice can also be seen as "women's work," in that it participates in a rhetoric of care and feeding. Even in situations where women are excluded from the actual moment of bloodletting, they are important actors on the larger sacrificial stage. Although not necessarily gendered work, the transformation of a carcass into food for both the Orisha and the worshipping community continues the ideology of the feminine nature of priestly work.

Universally a new initiate in Yoruba-based traditions is given the title "iyawo" to indicate his or her new role as the wife of a spirit-husband. In this conceptual system, the Orisha are always gendered male relative to their priests, regardless of the anatomical characteristics assigned to them in the mythology. Although priests may reclaim their anatomical gender in the reproductive move of initiating new priests themselves, they always remain iyawo and are denominated as such whenever they themselves are the focus of ritual attention. That is, no matter how old one is in the religion, no matter how many years of initiation one has, when one receives a new initiation or is given a new Orisha one is denominated iyawo for the duration of that event. As the wives of the Orisha, priests not only serve as caregivers for the Orisha and their devotees/children, they also serve as the vessels for their head Orisha, most radically during possession events.

Santería is fundamentally a possession religion. Initiation gives one the right and sometimes the ability to embody the Orisha. Possession is associated worldwide with women because of their assumed lack of control and the ease with which they can move between psychological states. It is in the possession rituals that we can see most strongly that the female is normative for Santería. In the course of the possession event, the priest's personality is taken over and overshadowed by the Orisha so that he or she becomes the living, breathing embodiment of that deity and exhibits the gender attributes associated with it. Although male priests are regularly called upon to assume a metaphoric female gender, this is the only point in the practice of Santería where female priests usually assume a fully male gender, and that only when the possessing Orisha is male. However, since roles within the religion are fluid, roles nominally limited to males—that of sacrificer, for example—can be assumed by females when they have been given the appropriate initiations and have met other ritual requirements.

The fact that women are precluded from participating in certain aspects of the religion during their reproductive years or during certain portions of their menstrual cycle seems to argue against this thesis of female valorization. However, I have suggested that since these restrictions do not exclude women qua women, they need to be reconsidered. Contemporary women, calling on the ideology of equality between men and women, continue to challenge the exclusionary tactics of their male colleagues, often by looking back to the matriarchs who founded these traditions. In a cultural environment in which fewer and fewer women accept their reproductive and menstrual cycles as dangerous or polluting, women are becoming less willing to forgo participation in ritual activities because of their menstrual status. Following the work of Eugenia Herbert, I have suggested that underlying these restrictions is an ideology not of pollution but of fluctuations of power. From an African perspective, two different conceptions of women's power influence the restrictions on women's participation. On the one hand, there is an understanding of a woman's cycle as a fluctuating site of life-giving ashé such that the menstrual period can be seen as a failure of fertility that stands over against the fertility required for most ritual events. On the other hand, menopause is seen as the pinnacle of a woman's power and her achievement of seniority within the hierarchical system. Now she can no longer be excluded from any ritual role or capacity. As an exceptionally powerful member of the aje, who can be both the benevolent mother and a witch, the older woman is thought to contribute extraordinary ashé to any ritual in which she participates. Thus we can suggest that at base these requirements valorize women's unique reproductive capabilities and the positive accumulations of power that accrue to women over a lifetime.

Witchcraft is stereotypically associated with women, but in all the traditions we considered, both men and women could be called witches. While men's witchcraft is often seen as more powerful—witches are women, while those who can control witches are men—witchcraft power is not an intrinsically gendered characteristic. Nonetheless, witchcraft power is often associated with women's reproductive abilities. Thus, although both men and women can be witches, older women who have moved beyond their reproductive abilities through menopause are often considered to be especially potent witches who can aid or hinder the ritual activities of others. Cross-culturally, women are thought to have amassed secret power that can serve as a potent force for the continuation of society. This excess of power is often denominated as "witchcraft" in that it is ambiguous and can be used either for the betterment or detriment of individuals or groups. Although, as Claude Meillassoux has argued, "the great historical enterprise of man (male) has been to gain control of the reproductive functions of women" (quoted in Herbert 1993, 237), men have never been able to completely assimilate and appropriate women's power. Orisha traditions, especially Santería, as sites for the promotion of health, luck, strength, tranquility, and spiritual evolution—that is, all the good things in life—have long served as conduits by which women's power can be exercised by both anatomical males and females in the pursuit of these goals.

In Western psychology, men who take on female roles are generally assumed to be overt or latent homosexuals. Stephan Palmié says that men who are involved in Santería, particularly those who are crowned to female Orisha, are often assumed to be homosexuals. However, as I have suggested in chapter 4, the Orisha to which one is crowned may or may not have any relationship to one's personality, and even when there is a relationship between the individual and the archetype represented by the Orisha, sexual orientation may not be the most important feature of that relationship. It is common to find gay men crowned to such male Orisha as Shango, Eleggua, Ogun, and Obalata, straight men crowned to the female Orisha Oshun, Yemaya, and Oya, and straight and lesbian women crowned to any of these.

Having said that, it is important to note the strong participation of gay men and lesbians in this religion. It is estimated that between 30 percent and 50 percent of all santeros are gay men and lesbians. Thus it is not at all unusual to find a preponderance of homosexuals at any ritual or ceremony. I have suggested that homosexuals, particularly gay men, might be drawn to this religion because of its openness to all types of people and the variety of roles open to practitioners. There are many roles and positions within the religion. One might be drawn to serve the Orisha by becoming a diviner or a cook or the godparent to many others or a medium who easily embodies the Orisha or the artisan who makes the clothes and necklaces and other accouterments of the Orisha or the artist who designs and builds the *tronos* (thrones) for each event. Rituals require many hands, and everyone can find a place both during rituals and during other periods. Few of these roles are gender specific, and none is exclusive. This means that one may participate in whatever manner suits one's skills and inclinations (assuming always that one has received the proper initiations). Many people find this fluidity of roles liberating and empowering. Particularly women and gay men, who might find themselves blocked from participation in other religious systems or in other portions of their lives because of their anatomy or sexual orientation, can find their place within this religious system and can rise to the highest positions of authority. This is particularly true in oriaté-centered houses that have eschewed the authoritative leadership of a babalawo. Although these communities have been little studied by scholars, they encompass a large percentage of Orisha practitioners. In the absence of the strong male leadership provided by the babalawo, openings are available for both women and gay men to assume positions of authority. Additionally, in the less homophobic environment that is more typical of oriaté-centered communities, gay men can exhibit their own special gifts for the benefit of the community.[1]

Ifá-Centrism

Many religious traditions have encoded within their mythology the idea that once the tradition had belonged to women but for a variety of reasons sometime in the mythological past it was appropriated by men, who continue to hold on to their positions of power. Ongoing changes in the Orisha traditions in the Americas suggest that the community of babalawo, in its self-understanding as the high priests of the religion, is attempting to consolidate its influence within the religion and deny the position of women we have been tracing. As early as the 1980s a group of Cuban babalawo created a cultural religious group called Ifá Ayer, Ifá Hoy, Ifá Mañana (Ifá Yesterday, Ifá Today, and Ifá Tomorrow), and in the 1990s babalawo both on the island and in the United States began to develop officially recognized organizations of their brotherhood (Vélez 2000, 93–94). George Brandon has done a survey of the changes in what he calls Afro-American religion in the United States between 1959 and 1999. He describes these organizations as "a reticulate network that overlaps at times with other religious groups" and is "strongly hierarchical at the local level, yet largely acephalous at higher levels" (Brandon 2002, 151–52). The basic unit of Santería, as he correctly describes it, is the house—*ilé* in Yoruba, *casa* in Spanish—organized around a single priest and all the priests, godchildren, and uninitiated followers he or she has managed to gather under his or her authority (152). Although any one devotee may be associated with a particular house, each initiate is also caught up in a web of relationship based on the initiatory relationship of his or her initiator (Clark 2003a). The organizations that Brandon documents stand mostly outside these traditional relationships in that the members may or may not be related by initiation. These organizations include churches (the best-known of which is the Church of the Lukumí Babalu Ayé in Hialeah, Florida), town organizations (for example, Oyotunji Village) and *egbe*—a Yoruba term for a guild, club, or society. Among the Yoruba an egbe may be composed of all the practitioners of a particular trade or profession, all those selling in a particular market, or members of any other group with a common interest that transcends lineage concerns. As they have developed in the New York City area, egbe are associations of priests with the same primary Orisha. Thus all of those crowned to Yemaya, for example, have formed such a voluntary association, meet regularly to share religious knowledge, perform rituals focused on their titular Orisha, and plan and present public religious and cultural activities focused on Yemaya (Brandon 2002, 155–57).

On a national level, Orisha devotees have developed a variety of organizations that often cross not only initiatory lineages but also a wide range of religious traditions, with practitioners of different West African–based traditions coming together for their mutual benefit. Practitioners of traditions that do not usually recognize each other's initiations and thus do not allow each other to participate in their religious rituals can join together for certain types of training and support. Participants in these organizations include not only the various Orisha-based traditions, such as Santería, Lukumi, and what Brandon calls Orisha-Voodoo in the United States, but also practitioners of Brazilian Candomblé and Haitian Vodou and their many variants, as well as priests in Orisha, Ifá, Akan, and Vodou traditions from Africa. For the most part the principal activity of these groups has been the organizing of national and international conferences that emphasize academic, ritual, and philosophical discussions (Brandon 2002, 161–62). Finally, the Orisha, or at least their followers, have begun to colonize the Internet. Quite a few Web sites, mailing lists, and Usenet groups have been developed over the last fifteen years. Local, national, and international organizations have developed Web sites, as have individual practitioners, vendors of goods and services, scholars, and other interested individuals. Outsiders wishing to learn more about these traditions as well as devotees soliciting information and companionship can find like-minded individuals through the World Wide Web (163–64).

As Brandon suggests, all of these groups draw upon existing cleavages in the larger society that tend to separate individuals according to racial, ethnic, economic, class, or other characteristics. Because of the acephalous nature of Orisha practice beyond the house level, no individual or group of individuals has the power or authority to regulate the activities of individual practitioners or the groups they have created. In many ways, contemporary Orisha practices are reminiscent of precolonial African practice in which individual cults and groups of cults functioned under the umbrella of a common cosmology and ties of kinship and friendship but without any recognized shared leadership (164–67). However, as Brandon is careful to point out, most Santería practitioners are not affiliated with any group beyond their individual houses and most do not feel that what Brandon calls the segmented reticulate structure of the larger community is inherently weak or divisive. Many priests see the efforts to organize extrahouse groups at the regional, national, or international level as foreign to the concepts of a Santería that is properly nonhierarchical and nondoctrinal (168).

As both María Teresa Vélez (2000, 93–94) and Brandon (2002, 168, 169–70) suggest, these efforts toward institutionalization within the religion seem to be part of a multifaceted campaign to gain recognition within American society and thereby provide a basis for a mutually respectful interaction with mainstream religious groups. This harkens back to Peel's research (1990) and the many parallels between the "pastor" and the babalawo in nineteenth-century Yorubaland that led to their mutually respectful interaction. The contemporary movement toward legitimation within the larger American society seems to be following a similar trajectory. However, when we realize that most of these groups are organized and led by men, many of whom are babalawo, while the majority of Orisha worshippers are women and gay men, we need to

stop and question who are the winners and who are the losers in this movement toward institutionalization.

I believe that Brandon hints at the answer when he suggests that a concern
for gender roles has propelled women to seek a greater degree of gender equality than has traditionally been found in Cuban-based traditions. He specifically suggests that women within Santería have been denied certain rights and
privileges that are now being extended through the development of new roles
with Ifá. However, the initiations of women into Ifá traditions, institutionalized as *iyanifá* (Yr., mother of Ifá) or *apetebi* (Yr., consort of the babalawo),
as they are being defined in the U.S. context continue to be "matters of contro-
versy and contentions between women and babalawos within the Yoruba revi-
talization movement as well as between Cuban babalawos and santeras"
(Brandon 2002, 161).

When the role of babalawo is put forward as the highest priesthood within
Orisha religion, it would be surprising if women devotees in the United
States, who have watched their sisters fight for full equality in other patriarchal
religions, did not campaign for full equality in that tradition. The valorization
of Ifá has led American women, particularly African American women, to
pursue Ifá initiations in a push toward gender equality. The contention that
women cannot "see Odu" and receive the highest level of initiation, however,
means that they are kept at the lower initiatory levels within Ifá. Just as women
in other traditions have discovered a stained-glass ceiling limiting their full
participation in those traditions, the iyanifá and apetebi are discovering that
they are still excluded from full initiation into the traditions of Ifá. And, as
Brandon says, these initiations continue to be controversial in the wider
Orisha community.[2]

However, we must distinguish the Ifá cult as it has developed alongside
Santería and in contradistinction to it from Santería proper as exemplified by
oriaté-centered communities. The Ifá cult continues to exhibit the same hegemonic claims and male domination that Peel noted in its earliest interactions
with Christian missionaries, and it continues to stand over against the female-
dominated cults that tend toward a diversity of beliefs and practices (Shaw
1990, 343, citing Peel 1990). Within Ifá and the Santería communities dominated by babalawo, women (and gay men) are systematically excluded from
full participation. Still, as I have suggested, Santería proper is both female-
oriented and female-normative and thus more welcoming both to women and
to gay men.

Women are again being trained as oriaté, and as the population ages more and more, santeras will discover that the menstrual limitations imposed on fertile women no longer apply to them. Historical research is also working in favor of the increased participation of women. Contemporary santeras are discovering that many of the founders of their tradition, the leaders of the earliest communities, were women, and they are beginning to counter current "traditions" limiting their participation with older traditions that not only valorize "womanliness" in the abstract but provide strong role models for participation on all levels.

Notes

Chapter 1

1. Although I will generally include brief translations of foreign words the first time they are used in the text, more complete definitions are available in the glossary.

2. Each of these names invokes a certain historical or political position. For example, "Lukumi" is used in the literature as a synonym for "Yoruba" in naming the African people. It has also been appropriated by some religious practitioners to describe practices that are more authentically "African." Although the word *lukumí* is often translated as "my friend" and described as the greeting offered to companions in Cuba, the designations Lukumí, Ulcami, or Ulkamy were used on early maps of West Africa for the kingdom of Oyo (Hair, Jones, and Law 1992, 2:633n19; J. Mason 1996, 77). I will generally favor "Santería," as it is the designation favored by the communities in which I work.

3. Miguel "Willie" Ramos's thesis offers perhaps the best summary of the history of the peoples who developed Orisha religion in the Americas (Ramos 2000, chaps. 1–2). See also Johnson 1921; R. Smith 1988; Law 1977; Ortiz 1921; Cros Sandoval 1975; Howard 1998; Cabrera 1975.

4. This description of Afro-Cuban cabildos is based on the work of George Brandon (1993, 70–74) and David Brown (1989, 39–68; 2003, pt. 1).

5. See my article "Orisha Worship Communities" for an analysis of the changes in worship structure between Africa and Cuba.

6. As David Brown's account points out (2003, 17–18), the transition that eventuated in contemporary Orisha practice was "characterized by significant discontinuities: . . . the religion's founders and later exponents were historically self-conscious individuals who strategically positioned themselves socially, carefully selected, implemented, and disseminated the knowledge they possessed, and collaborated in setting up 'commissions' of specialists and elders for this purpose."

7. Chapter 3 of Stephan Palmié's *Wizards and Scientists* details the Republican period.

8. The descriptions of God from a Christian perspective in this section draw heavily on the analysis of the term "God" by Francis Schüssler Fiorenza and Gordon D. Kaufman in *Critical Terms for Religious Studies*.

9. My article "¡No Hay Ningún Santo Aquí!" discusses the lack of anthropomorphic images on contemporary altar displays. However, Joseph Murphy is looking into the explosion of Orisha figures, particularly those found on the Internet (personal communication, 2000). This seems to be one of the ways a European propensity for human figures is beginning to infiltrate Orisha communities in the United States.

10. See my article "Orisha Worship Communities" for a discussion of Yoruba worship communities and how those communities changed in the New World.

11. "Santería Altar Displays as Memory Palaces." Paper presented at annual meeting, American Academy of Religion, Comparative Studies in Religion Section and African Religions Group, Nashville, November 2000.

12. That is, the threat of death by lightning, death by plague, the judgment of the ancestors, death by the sword, and death by whirlwind all failed to persuade the women to return.

13. There is an extensive literature on sacrifice. However, Susan Sered's "Towards a Gendered Typology of Sacrifice" offers one of the best overviews while providing a useful typology by which to analyze the various cultural types. In addition and of special interest for my analysis are René Girard's classic *Violence and the Sacred*, William Beers' *Women and Sacrifice* , Nancy Jay's *Throughout Your Generations Forever*, and Carolyn Marvin and David Ingle's "Blood Sacrifice and the Nation."

14. I discuss the difference between curing and healing more fully in "Healing Rituals in the Suburbs: African-Based Healing among Middle-Class Americans." Paper presented at annual meeting of American Academy of Religion, African Religions Group and Religion, Medicines, and Healing Consultation, joint session, Atlanta, November 2003.

15. Allan Kardec (1804–1869, born Léon-Dénizarth-Hippolyte Rivail) was a French scientist who developed the spiritualist practice known as spiritism or Espiritismo.

Chapter 2

1. Obatala has both male and female paths. Some people say that Eleggua has both male and female paths, although most santeros are at a loss to identify any female paths of Eleggua. Inle is sometimes considered androgynous, male half of the year and female the other half, or a forest deity half of the year and a water deity the other half. Olokun is worshipped as a male deity by Bini and Yoruba peoples living along the Nigerian coast and as a female deity in Ile-Ife. Hence there are two different Orisha named Olokun, one male and one female (J. Mason 1996, 2).

2. The principal examples of this phenomenon are Shango, who is represented by St. Barbara, and Obatala, represented by the Virgin of Mercy (Virgen de las Mercedes).

3. Although gay women are not treated as a special group within Santería, (openly) gay men are often subjected to the same ritual limitations as women.

4. A parallel analysis of Candomblé is beyond the scope of this project, but it is interesting to note that, although there is no babalawo tradition in Candomblé, both drumming and large-animal sacrifice are limited to specially initiated men in these traditions.

5. For example, Portia in *The Merchant of Venice*. Joan of Arc provides an interesting, if ambiguous, example in that, although she took on masculine clothes and attributes, she never attempted to hide her anatomy or "female nature."

6. The 1982 Sydney Pollack film *Tootsie*, starring Dustin Hoffman, provides an excellent exploration of the trials and tribulations of an anatomical male attempting to take on the gender of a woman.

7. Edward Said's *Orientalism* (1979) provides one of the best scholarly approaches to the genderizing of international relations. D. H. Hwang's play *M. Butterfly* (1989) provides an entertaining presentation of the same issues.

8. My summary of these positions is based on Anne Klein's excellent description of this debate in the introduction to her *Meeting the Great Bliss Queen*, 1–11.

9. In Boyarin (1998, 119). These verses are: Gen. 1:27–28: "And God created the earth-creature in His image; in the image of God, He created him; male and female He created them. And God blessed them, and God said to them: Reproduce and fill the earth" and Gen. 5:1–2: "This is the book of the Generations of Adam, on the day that God created Adam in the image of God He made him. Male and female He created them, and He blessed them, *and called their name Adam*, on the day He created them" (italics in Boyarin).

10. In Boyarin (1998, 119). These verses are Gen. 2:7, 20–23: "And God formed the earth-creature of dust from the earth and breathed in its nostrils the breath of life, and the earth-creature became a living being. And the earth creature gave names to all of the animals and the fowls of the air and all of the animals of the fields, but the earth-creature could not find any helper fitting for it. And God caused a deep sleep to fall on the earth-creature, and it slept, and He took one of its ribs and closed the flesh beneath it. And the Lord God constructed the rib which he had taken from the earth-creature into a woman and brought her to the earth-man. And the earth-man said,

this time is bone of my bone and flesh of my flesh. She shall be called wo-man, for from man was she taken."

11. This story can be found in the *diloggun* divination system in odu *Osa Meyi* (9–9), quoted in Bascom, *Sixteen Cowries*, 231–32.

12. Oyewùmí would strongly object to the conflation of the roles of wife and mother. She characterizes "wife" as a four-letter word in much of Africa because it symbolizes relations of subordination between any two people. However, as she says, "*Mother* is the preferred and cherished self-identity of many African women" (Oyewùmí 2000, 1096).

13. I am not the first or only person to question Oyewùmí's characterization of Yoruba culture as without gender categories. Although they appeared too recently to be adequately included in this book, see for example Olajubu, who says (2003, 9) that "gender classifications have always existed among the Yoruba but may be transversely manipulated, as is the case in social structures and the ritual space in religion," and Peel, who suggests (2002, 163) that "there is abundant evidence that many aspects of nineteenth-century Yoruba life were profoundly shaped by gender."

14. Although priests of certain Orisha are proscribed from initiating priests of certain other Orisha, the proscriptions are generally not gender related.

Chapter 3

1. Bascom (1960) presents a similar view of the soul in Yoruba belief systems. He suggests that these beliefs are common not only among practitioners of traditional religion but also among those who practice Islam or Christianity (401). Although there are minor differences between the beliefs as outlined by Bascom and by Gbadegesin, in general their two accounts agree.

2. Although individual persons/devotees/priests may be male or female, in this account I will often favor the female with the understanding that, unless it is noted otherwise, everything that is said pertains to both.

3. For a summary of Jung's concept of Self, see Samuels, Shorter, and Plaut, *A Critical Dictionary of Jungian Analysis*, 135–37.

4. See John Mason's *Four New World Yorùbá Rituals*, "Dídà Obì (Kola Divination)," 76–92, or Lydia Cabrera's *El Monte*, 379–91, for a detailed description.

5. While both scholars and practitioners say that there are 256 possible combinations in both diloggun and Ifá, one elder pointed out that in actuality, since it is possible to throw a zero (no shells mouth up), in diloggun there are 281 possible combinations (Olumide, personal communication, December 1999). However, throws beginning with zero indicate such extreme danger for both the diviner and the client that many oriaté will abort the divination session without generating the second number (Chango Ladé, personal communication, June 2003).

6. It is interesting to note that even Olodumare the great god requires the services of Orunmila the diviner. Throughout the Yoruba divinatory texts, every level of society, from the simplest plants and animals to the deities, consults with diviners.

7. Although some sources say it was possible for women to learn Ifá divination (Abimbola 1997, 86–87; Bádéjo 1996, 91), few African women could combine such training with the rigors of exogamous motherhood. In misogynistic Cuba, this practical reality hardened into the rule that not only women but also gay (womanly) men were barred from initiation as priests of Ifá.

8. Portions of this section and the next section were originally published as "You Are (Not) Shango: Jungian Archetypes in Contemporary Santería" in *Wadabagei: A Journal of the Caribbean and Its Diaspora* and are used with permission.

9. Stephan Palmié in *Wizards and Scientists* suggests that among the santeros with whom he did his work, men whose ruling Orisha is female are always suspected of being at least latent homosexuals (345n54). However, an informal survey of the communities with which I am familiar and discussions with elders within those communities produced too many counterexamples—that is, gay men with virile Orisha and straight men with female Orisha—to make such a universal statement.

10. However, although each priest is made the priest of a single Orisha, he or she is also initiated into the worship of a total of five to seven Orisha as part of the initiation. See my article "Orisha Worship Communities" for a fuller description of this phenomenon.

11. J. Lorand Matory (1994) discusses an Ogun cult group that also does not engage in possession trance and also bars women from membership. This, however, is not a universal characteristic of Ogun cults as it is for the Orunmila cult.

12. See J. Lorand Matory's *Sex and the Empire That Is No More* for an analysis of this phenomenon.

13. See, for example, Farrow 1926; Lucas 1948; Ìdòwú 1994; Karade 1994, 6; Murphy 1993, 175; Brandon 1983, 77.

14. This description of the place of the babalawo within Santería is based on traditional, conservative practice. In spite of the fact that it is considered extremely unorthodox, there are babalawo in the United States who directly participate in all aspects of Orisha initiation, much to the consternation of many traditionalists.

15. María Towá and Efuche, two other important women, are discussed in chapter 6, "Sacrifice and Violence."

16. It was through the work of the famous oriaté Obadimeji, who trained only other men, that the role of oriaté became male-centered (but not exclusively male) as it is today (Ramos 2000, 105).

Chapter 4

Portions of this chapter were originally presented to the American Academy of Religion, African Religious Groups and Religions in Latin America and the Caribbean Group, and the Society for Philosophy in the Contemporary World, and have benefited greatly from their responses.

1. *Iyawoage* is a mixed Yoruba-Spanish word referring to the extended initiation period that begins with the initiation itself and concludes with the dismantling of the first birthday altar a year later. It is only after the completion of the iyawoage and his

reintegration into the secular community that the new priest is considered "fully crowned."

2. See Michael Mason's account of a warrior's initiation in "I Bow My Head to the Ground" and Marta Vega's account of her experience in *The Altar of My Soul* for such personal accounts.

3. Although both men and women are initiated as Santería priests, I will prefer the masculine in the following account in order to focus our attention on the gender ambiguities of the *iyawo* experience.

4. *Asiento* and *kariocha* are the Spanish and Yoruba terms for this priestly initiation that is also call a "crowning."

5. See, for example, the feminist analyses of Buddhism by Rita M. Gross (1993) and Anne Klein (1994).

6. Although, as Palmié points out (2002, 164), both men and women participate in both traditions, as we shall discuss in chapter 7, "Witchcraft," Palo is often characterized as *cosa de hombre* (Sp., a man's thing) and seen by women as having an overly macho atmosphere, while Ocha is perceived as more refined and thus attractive not only to women but also to its many homosexual adherents.

Chapter 5

1. Here there is a radical difference between Candomblé and Santería. In the Candomblé tradition, the Orisha are typically stately and royal, hardly deigning to recognize their devotees; in the Santería tradition, the Orisha are more earthy manifestations who not only bless their devotees with their presence but consistently interact with them, often while enjoying their own embodiment.

2. For descriptions and analysis of similar costumes worn as part of the initiation ritual, see Flores-Peña and Evanchuk, *Santería Garments and Altars*, 13–26.

3. For a discussion of the degrees of identification possible with clothing metaphors, see Joseph, *Uniforms and Nonuniforms*, 18.

Chapter 6

1. All quotes are from President George W. Bush's address to a joint session of Congress and the American people, September 20, 2001, at: http://www.whitehouse.gov/news/releases/2001/09/20010920-8.html or http://www.rnc.org/news/read.aspx?ID=1326 or http://archives.cnn.com/2001/US/09/20/gen.bush.transcript.

For an analysis and comparison of the religious rhetoric of George Bush and Osama bin Laden, see Bruce Lincoln's excerpt (2004) from his book *Holy Terrors: Thinking about Religion after September 11*.

2. See, for example, George W. Bush's speech of March 19, 2003, as the United States launched into war, at: http://www.whitehouse.gov/news/releases/2003/03/20030319-17.html or www.cnn.com/2003/us/03/19/sprj.irq.war.bush.transcript and a summary of Saddam Hussein's speech of March 20, 2003, at: http://www.cnn.com/2003/WORLD/meast/03/20/irq.war.saddam.transcript/.

3. Of particular interest to feminist scholars is the story of Jephthah's daughter (Judges 11), but see also the sacrifices of Esau and Jacob, and Abraham's aborted sacrifice of Isaac (or, in Islamic literature, of Ishmael).

4. Although the meaning of this word has been extended to describe the genocide of European Jews and others by the Nazis during World War II, some authors prefer not to use it because of its association with sacrifice that is pleasing to God, which the destruction of the Jewish people certainly was not; see, for example, Pfau and Blumenthal 2001, 199n1.

5. See Karl Marx's "Contribution to a Critique of Hegel's *Philosophy of Right:* Introduction," in Marx and Engels, *On Religion* (1964, 42).

6. Portions of this section were originally published as "Santería" in *Sects, Cults, and Spiritual Communities* and are used with permission.

7. Justice Anthony M. Kennedy in *Church of Lukumi Babalu Aye, Inc., v. Hialeah,* 508 U.S. 520 (1993).

8. Most sacrifice within the Santería tradition is performed in private and is not generally open to the gaze of noninitiates, so little information about sacrificial practices is available. See John Mason's *Four New World Yorùbá Rituals* for the only description of these rituals written by an initiated priest.

9. Although Candomblé practitioners generally use the services of a male sacrificator, the practitioners of Vodou, like santeros, seem to allow both men and women to participate as both sacrificators and sacrificers.

10. It is important to note here that, unlike gender-based divination limitations, the limitations on women's participation in sacrifice are not generalized to include gay men.

11. The terms "sacrificator" and "sacrificer" follow the lead of Veena Das in "Language of Sacrifice."

12. Information about Orisha food preferences, both animal and nonanimal, can be found in John Mason, *Ìdáná Fún Òrìṣà: Cooking for Selected Heads.*

13. See http://www.ochareo.com/history.htm. There are several conflicting versions of this story. David Brown (2003, 101, 109–10) credits Efuche, a priestess of Ochosi who is known in some circles as *la reformista de la religión* (the reformer of the religion), with several reforms including instituting the *pinaldo* ritual.

14. See Peter McKenzie's *Hail Orisha!* for a description of Yoruba religious practices in the mid-nineteenth century.

15. We can also suggest that shopping, another female-identified activity, holds an important place in Santería religious practice. Often the first thing one must do after a divination session is to acquire the materials for the prescribed offering. This may require visits to the supermarket, florist, *botánica*, and other retail establishments.

16. Sexual activity with nursing women is generally scandalous in West African societies. Of course, these categorical statements ignore the facts that nursing may not completely suppress a woman's menstrual cycle and that both prepubescent and postmenopausal women may be sexually active.

17. We will discuss Yoruba notions of witchcraft and witchcraft substance in more detail in chapter 7.

18. The vast literature aimed at convincing modern women of the "magical" qualities of menstruation and menopause attests to the foreignness of this concept.

Chapter 7

1. Robert Thompson (1971, 1412) has quoted and translated this song from Pierre Verger, "Grandeur et décadence du culte du ìyàmi Òsòròngà: Ma mère la sorcière chez les *yoruba*," *Le Journal de la Société des Africanistes* 35 (1): 141–243.

2. For example, Evans-Pritchard (1976, 1) describes a witch as one who can do harm psychically. That is, "a witch performs no rite, utters no spell, and possesses no medicines," while sorcerers require magical rites in order to call evil on their neighbors. Although he says that the "Azande distinguish clearly between witches and sorcerers," the two types are often conflated even in his text.

3. There has been an epidemic of research analyzing the phenomenon of European witch-hunting of the late medieval and early modern periods. This account relies heavily on the work of Anne Llewellyn Barstow. Barstow begins her feminist analysis of the European "witchcraze" with a survey of the literature on this phenomenon (1994, 1–13). Newer works that discount Barstow's misogynistic stance—e.g., Robin Briggs' *Witches and Neighbors* (New York: Viking, 1996), which focuses on the "disliked" aspect of those accused of witchcraft rather than on their "female" aspect—do not significantly change my own analysis of this phenomenon in relation to Santería.

4. It is interesting to note that the Catholic Church still supports ninety-five exorcists in France alone. Exorcist-priests suggested in the late 1990s that the demand for their services has risen steadily with "the approach of the millennium . . . cultural dislocation, the erosion of traditional religion and the rise of sects and cults dealing in spiritism" (Simons 1998).

5. Although the general understanding of *curandero* is "healer," my contemporary dictionaries also include the translations "witch doctor," "charlatan," and "quack."

6. The most severe punishment listed by Richard Greenleaf (1969, 173) for sorcery in Mexico was two hundred lashes and exile to Spain, where the accused was to wear a sanbenito (penitential garment) during his five-year term in the galleys. Although a term in the galleys could be deadly, it was considered a more humane punishment than burning.

7. These laws were enforceable into the nineteenth century. Kamen (1997, 253) quotes Lea, *Inquisition of Spain,* as saying that conversos, those whose ancestors had converted from Judaism or Islam, were still in 1858 "refused all public offices and admission to guilds and brotherhoods so that they were confined to trading. They were compelled to marry among themselves, for no one would contract alliances with them nor would the ecclesiastical authorities grant licenses for mixed marriages" (vol. 2, 314).

8. Irene Silverblatt's discussion of witchcraft accusations against Andean women presents a different face than that presented by Henry Kamen's work on Mexico. Although the earliest clerics, conquistadors, and administrators in what has become

Peru all agreed that indigenous religion was devil worship, by the seventeenth century the campaign against "idolatry, curing and witchcraft" had the "obvious political motive" of forcing "the Indian into the *reducciones*—all the better to evangelize, to maintain political control, to facilitate the collection of tribute" (Silverblatt 1987, 170, 175; see also all of chap. 9). Silverblatt's work is also in line with the thesis that incomplete conversion—that is, heresy—was the focus of the Spanish Inquisition, rather than witchcraft per se.

9. The analysis by Richard Greenleaf (1969) of Inquisition records in sixteenth-century Mexico confirms a similar interest in *judaizantes*, or crypto-Jews, and in "Lutherans" (Protestants of various stripes) as well as in bigamists and blasphemers. In both Spain and the colonies, adherents of the Jewish and Islamic religions who had never converted were exempted from the jurisdiction of the Inquisition, as they were not Christians (Kamen 1997, 18).

10. The literature on African witchcraft is significant and growing. Important for my analysis are E. E. Evans-Pritchard's classic *Witchcraft, Oracles, and Magic among the Azande* (abr. ed., 1976), Elias Kifon Bongmba's work describing witchcraft among the Wimbum of Cameroon (2001), and the excellent analysis by Barry Hallen and J. O. Sodipo (1986) of contemporary Yoruba witchcraft focusing on the problems in translating this African concept into a European language.

11. Thompson doesn't name these deities but rather speaks of "followers of thunder, iron, smallpox, and mischief." I have merely assigned the names commonly associated with these deities.

12. In much the same way that the *Malleus Maleficarum* functioned as the canonical text for late medieval and early modern witch-hunters in Europe, *Los negros brujos* served as the canonical text for witch-hunting in Republican Cuba (Palmié 2002, 217).

13. It is interesting to note that Ernesto Pichardo, the president of the Church of the Lukumí Babalu Ayé in Hialeah, complained that his political opponents on the Hialeah city council were perpetrating witchcraft against him as his animal sacrifice case made its way to the United States Supreme Court (Palmié 2002, 198–200).

14. Johan Wedel's *Santería Healing* and my own "Healing Rituals in the Suburbs" provide the most current analysis of healing within the Santería religious complex.

15. This terminology is from Green, "Theodicy."

16. See my "Healing Rituals in the Suburbs" for a more detailed analysis of healing and curing from a Santería point of view.

Chapter 8

1. This is not to suggest that no oriaté or oriaté-centered house exhibits homophobic behaviors and attitudes, merely that such behaviors and attitudes are less commonly found in such communities.

2. In the spring of 2003 the International Council for Ifá Religion, which claimed to be the umbrella body of all Ifá adherents around the world, withdrew the chieftaincy title of Yeye Araba from a certain Ms. D'Haifá because it was reported that she

was in possession of Orisa Odu, which would have given her a full Ifá initiation. According to the announcement posted on the Orisha Mailing List (the oldest of the online Orisha groups) and on the Web site of Miguel "Willie" Ramos, a respected oriaté and the president of the Templo Olorisha Lukumí de las Américas (TOLA), for any female to claim to own or keep or see Orisa Odu is an "abomination." However, without this final initiation one is not fully initiated into Ifá and one cannot initiate others into Ifá. See International Council 2003.

Glossary

aborisa (Yr.): To some contemporary practitioners, a person who has participated in the religion but has not undergone the *asiento* or *kariocha* ceremony.

acheses (Lk., parts imbued with *ashé*): Sacred portions; parts of sacrificial animal destined for the Orisha.

aiye (Yr.): Visible world, this world, the earth. Opposite of *orun*, the invisible world. Also *aye*.

Ajalamo (Yr.): Maker of heads/destinies.

aje (Yr.): Witch, witches; more correctly, one/those possessing witchcraft substance.

alaafin (Yr.): Ruler of the city of Oyo.

alejo (Lk., stranger resident in the House): A person who has received the first initiation of *ileki* or *collares*.

aña (Lk.): Drums.

Aña (Lk.): Spirit inhabiting sacred drums.

apetebi (Yr.): Female, ordained to her patron divinity, who serves the Ifá order.

ara (Yr.): Body.

ashé (Yr.): Power, energy, blessings; energy of the universe; ritual power. Also, empowered material.

asiento (Sp., from *asentar*, to seat, place): Initiation ceremony to make or crown a priest; placing or seating the Orisha in the head of the devotee.

auto da fé (Sp., act of faith): Disciplinary ceremony of the Spanish Inquisition. Also, *auto de fé*.

awon iya wa (Yr., our mothers): The witches. Also called *iyami* or *eleye*.

aworo (Yr.): Orisha priest. Sometimes translated "fetish priest" in eighteenth-century documents.

aya (Yr.): Wife.

ayaba (Yr.): Palace women; wives of the ruler.

aya-ile (Yr.): Women of the house; in-marrying wives.

aye (Yr.): Visible world. See *aiye*.

babalawo (Yr., father of secrets): Priest of Orula/Orunmila, the owner of the Ifá divination system.

babalosha (Yr., father of Orisha): Male priest.

bembe (Lk.): Drum ritual. Used interchangeably with *tambor*.

bruja/brujo (Sp.): Witch.

brujería (Sp.): Witchcraft.

cabildo (Sp.): Church chapter house, town council; in Cuba, social club for *gente de color*.

camino (Sp., road, path): Advocation of an Orisha. Some Orisha have many caminos, others only one.

cascarilla (Sp.): White chalklike material made from eggshells, used in rituals. Also called *efun*.

collar (Sp., necklace): Strand of colored beads representing an Orisha. Also called *eleke* or *ileki*.

cuchillo (Sp., knife): Ritual that bestows the right to sacrifice animals with a knife. Considered the culmination of the priestly initiation of a *santero/-a*. Also called *pinaldo*.

curandera/curandero (Sp.): Healer.

diloggun (Lk., from Yr. *medilogun*, sixteen): Divination system using sixteen cowry shells.

ebo (Yr.): Sacrifice; offering or work given to Orisha or egun.

ebo eje (Yr.): Blood sacrifice.

efun (Yr.): White chalk used in rituals. Also called *cascarilla*.

egun (Lk.): Ancestor. Sometimes used interchangeably with *muerto*.

Egungun (Yr.): Spirit of the ancestors honored in ritual masquerade.

Eleggua (Lk.): Trickster Orisha, guardian of the crossroads, one of the Warrior Orisha. Also known as Elegba, Elegbara, or Eshu.

eleke (Yr.): Bead; single strand of colored beads representing an Orisha. Also called *collar* or necklace.

eleye (Yr., owner(s) of birds): The witches. Also called *iyami* or *awon iya wa*.

Eshu (Yr.): Trickster Orisha often conflated with Eleggua.

Espiritismo (Sp.): Kardecian spiritism, developed by French scientist Allan Kardec.

fundamento (Sp., basis, foundation): The stones and tools enclosed in the altar containers that serve as residence for the Orisha.

funfun (Yr.): White; cool, peaceful.

gente de color (Sp., people of color): In Cuba, former slaves and their descendants.

Guerreros, Los (Sp.): The Warriors, a group of Orisha comprising Eleggua, Ogun, Ochosi, and Osun. Usually received as part of a single ritual of the same name.

hacer el santo (Sp.): To make the saint. See *asiento*.

herramienta (Sp., tool, set of tools): The metal or wooden implements of the Orisha.

Ifá (Yr.): Divination system, performed only by a *babalawo*, invoking the wisdom of Orula/Orunmila. Also, the Orisha Orula/Orunmila.

igbodu (Yr.): Sacred grove, site of religious activity.

ilé (Yr., earth, town, household): A religious family consisting of a *santera/santero* and all godchildren.

ileki (Yr.): Bead; single strand of colored beads representing an Orisha. Also called *collar* or necklace.

itá (Lk., from Yr. *itan*, story, history): Divination by *diloggun*, performed as part of *asiento*, telling the initiate's past, present, and future. Also *ita*.

italero (Lk./Sp., one who performs *itá*): A diviner trained in cowry shell divination. Although *itá* refers only to divination done in conjunction with initiations and other rituals involving the sacrifice of four-legged animals, the term *italero* is often used to denote anyone who reads the shells. Often conflated with *oriaté*.

iwa pele (Yr.): Good character.

iya (Yr.): Mother; also, title of any adult woman.

iya kere (Yr.): Royal wife, second highest ranking of palace women, keeper of royal paraphernalia.

iyalawo (Yr., mother of secrets): Title of female Ifá priest. See *iyanifá*.

iyalode (Yr., titled market woman): Head of marketplace. Sometimes used to designate leader of witches.

iyalosha (Yr., mother of Orisha): Female priest.

iyami (Yr., our mothers): The witches. Also called *awon iya wa* or *eleye*.

iyanifá (Yr., mother of Ifá): Title of female Ifá priest. See *iyalawo*.

iyawo (Yr., bride younger than speaker, wife): A new initiate of either sex.

iyawoage (Yr./Sp.): Yearlong liminal period after the *asiento*, during which one is subject to a long list of restrictions. Also, *iyaworaje*.

iyawo-Orisha (Yr., wife of an Orisha): Initiated priest.

Jakuta (Yr.): Thunder deity whose worship was assimilated into that of Shango.

jubona (Yr.): Second godparent at a Santería initiation. See *ojugbona*.

kariocha (Yr., to place the Orisha [on/in the head]): Priestly initiation.

limpieza de sangre (Sp., purity of blood): For a Spaniard, ancestry free of non-Christians.

Lukumi (Lk.): Creolized Yoruba language developed in Cuba; alternative name for Santería. Also *Lucumí*.

madrina (Sp.): Godmother.

matanza (Sp., slaughter): Sacrifice.

matrona (Sp., matron): Queen; female leader in a *cabildo*.

medilogun (Yr.): See *diloggun*.

muerto (Sp., dead person): Usually, the spirit of a dead person.

nganga (Kongo/Congo): Originally a priest in Central African traditions. In Cuba it became the name of the pot, and its component objects, which are the abode of the spirits of the dead, worked in the Regla de Congo.

oba (Yr., ruler): Title given to an *oriaté*.

Obatala (Yr., Ruler of the White Cloth): Wisest and oldest of the Orisha.

obi (Yr.): Kola nut; in Cuba and the United States, coconut pieces used for divination. Also, name of Orisha associated with coconut divination.

obìnrin (Yr.): Anatomical female.

Ocha (Lk., contraction of *Orisha*): The Orisha religion (see *Regla de Ocha*); its deities.

Ochosi (Lk.): Hunter Orisha, one of the Warrior Orisha. Also known as Oshosi, Ossoosi.

odu (Yr.): Letter or number determined by either *diloggun* or Ifá divination.

Ogun (Yr.): Orisha of iron, a blacksmith, one of the Warrior Orisha.

ojugbona (Yr., one who clears the road, eyes of the road): Witness, second godparent at a Santería initiation. Also *jubona*, *yubona*.

okàn (Yr.): Heart.

oko (Yr., husband): Honorific applied by a woman to all members of the lineage of her conjugal partner.

okùnrin (Yr.): Anatomical male.

Olodumare (Yr.): Great God, deity behind the Orisha. Olodumare is propitiated only through the Orisha. Also known as Olorun or Olofi, although in Cuba these are often considered separate members of a divine trinity reminiscent of the Christian trinity. Also *Olódùmarè*.

Olofi (Lk., supreme ruler): Title of Olodumare.

Olokun (Yr): Orisha of the depths of the ocean.

olorisha (Yr., owner of Orisha): Worshipper or devotee of the Orisha. In the Americas, priest of Orisha religion.

Olorun (Yr., owner of heaven): Title of Olodumare.

omo (Yr.): Child.

omo-ile (Yr.): Child of the house.

omo-Orisha (Yr.): Child of an Orisha.

onisègùn (Yr.): Herbalist, native doctor, master of medicine.

opele (Yr.): Divination chain used by a *babalawo*.

opon Ifá (Yr.): Ifá divination board.

ori (Yr.): Head; personal destiny, one's personal Orisha. Also, *orí*.

oriaté (Lk., head or ruler of the [divination] mat): Highly trained diviner and ritual specialist who presides over the initiation of Santería priests and other rituals.

Orisha (Yr.): Deity or deities of the Yoruba traditional religion and Santería. Also *orisa* or *orisa* (Yr.) and *oricha* (Sp.).

Orisha Oko (Yr.): Deity of farming who is associated in Yorubaland with the identification and control of witchcraft.

Orula (Lk.): Deity of divination, owner of Table of Ifá. Also known as Orunmila.

orun (Yr.): Invisible world, heaven, sky. Opposite of *aiye*, the visible world.

Orunmila (Yr.): Deity of divination, owner of Table of Ifá. Known in Santería as Orula.

Oshun (Yr.): Orisha of rivers and sweet water, love, children, and the pleasures of life. Also Ochun or Òsun.

Osun (Yr.): Protector Orisha, one of the Warrior Orisha.

Oya (Yr.): Orisha of the whirlwind, owner of the cemetery.

padrino (Sp.): Godfather.

palero (Sp.): Priest of Palo Monte and its related religions.

Palo (Sp.): Reglas de Congo, Central African–based religions in Cuba including Palo Monte and Palo Mayombe.

pataki (Lk.): Story or legend, usually associated with the *diloggun*.

pinaldo (Yr.): Knife. See *cuchillo*.

regla (Sp.): In religious sense, rule, order, way.

Regla de Congo (Sp.): Way/Rule of the Congo People; also known as Palo Monte and Palo Mayombe.

Regla de Ocha (Sp/Yr.): Way/Rule of the Orisha; also known as Santería.

santa/santo (Sp., saint, holy being): In Santería, a Catholic saint associated with an Orisha. *Santos* is often used as a generic term for the Orisha themselves.

santera/santero (Sp., maker or seller of saints): A Santería devotee; more properly, an initiated priest.

Santería (Sp.): Conventionally translated as "Way of the Saints," Orisha religion in Cuba and the United States. See also *Regla de Ocha, Lukumi*.

şe òrìşà (Yr.): To make, do, or work the Orisha. Pronounced "shay Orisha."

Shango (Yr.): Fourth king of Oyo, Orisha of thunder and lightning.

shekere (Yr.): Musical instrument, a gourd with beads or shells woven around it as noisemakers.

Sopona (Yr.): Orisha of smallpox. Also know as Babaluaiye or Obaluaiye.

tambor (Sp., drum): Drum ceremony to invoke the Orisha. Also called *bembe*.

traje del desayuno (Sp., breakfast dress): Gingham outfit worn by a new initiate before noon on the "middle day."

traje del medio (Sp., middle [day] dress): Fancy outfit worn by a new initiate during the public presentation on the "middle day."

trono (Sp., throne): Altar built to honor one or more Orisha or as part of an initiation.

Yemaya (Lk., Mother Whose Children Are Like the Fishes): Orisha of the ocean and maternal protection. Also called Yemoja (Yr.).

yubona (Yr.): Second godparent at a Santería initiation. See *ojugbona*.

Bibliography

Abimbola, 'Wande. 1976. *Ifá: An Exposition of Ifá Literary Corpus*. Ibadan: Oxford University Press Nigeria. Repr., Brooklyn, N.Y.: Athelia Henrietta Press, 1997.

———. 1997. *Ifá Will Mend Our Broken World: Thoughts on Yoruba Religion and Culture in Africa and the Diaspora*. Roxbury, Mass.: Aim.

———. 2001. The Bag of Wisdom: Ọṣun and the Origins of the Ifá Divination. In Murphy and Sanford 2001, 141–54.

Abiodun, Rowland. 1989. The Kingdom of Owo. In Wardwell 1989, 90–115.

———. 2001. Hidden Power: Ọṣun the Seventeenth Odù. In Murphy and Sanford, 10–33.

Abogunrin, Samuel O. 1989. Ethics in Yoruba Religious Tradition. In *World Religions and Global Ethics*, ed. S. Cromwell Crawford, 266–96. New York: Paragon House.

Afolabi (Clayton D. Keck Jr.). "As Long as They Don't Shove It down Our Throats—The Regulation of First Class Oloshas to Second Class Status." http://www.evilfagempire.com/orisha/shove.htm. Accessed February 4, 1999; site now discontinued.

Apter, Andrew. 1992. *Black Critics and Kings: The Hermeneutics of Power in Yoruba Society*. Chicago: University of Chicago Press.

Augustine, Saint. 1961. *Confessions*. Trans. R. S. Pine-Coffin. New York: Penguin.

Awolalu, J. Omosade. 1979. *Yorùbá Beliefs and Sacrificial Rites*. London: Longman. Repr. Brooklyn, N.Y.: Athelia Henrietta Press, 1996.

Bádéjo, Diedre L. 1996. *Òsun Sèègèsí: The Elegant Deity of Wealth, Power and Femininity*. Trenton, N.J.: Africa World Press.

Baggley, John. 1987. *Doors of Perception: Icons and Their Spiritual Significance*. London: A. R. Mowbray.

Barber, Karin. 1981. How Man Makes God in West Africa: Yoruba Attitudes Towards the Orisa. *Africa-London* 51 (3):724–45.

Barnes, Sandra T. 1980. *Ogun: An Old God for a New Age*. Philadelphia: Institute for the Study of Human Issues.

Barstow, Anne Llewellyn. 1994. *Witchcraze: A New History of the European Witch Hunts*. San Francisco: Pandora.

Bascom, William R. 1944. *The Sociological Role of the Yoruba Cult-Group*. Menasha, Wis.: American Anthropological Association.

———. 1950. The Focus of Cuban Santeria. *Southwestern Journal of Anthropology* 6 (1):64–68.

———. 1960. Yoruba Concepts of the Soul. In *Men and Cultures: Selected Papers of the Fifth International Congress of Anthropology and Ethnological Sciences*, ed. Anthony F. C. Wallace, 401–10. Philadelphia: University of Pennsylvania Press.

———. 1969. *The Yoruba of Southwestern Nigeria*. New York: Holt, Rinehart and Winston.

———. 1980. *Sixteen Cowries: Yoruba Divination from Africa to the New World*. Bloomington: Indiana University Press.

Beers, William. 1992. *Women and Sacrifice: Male Narcissism and the Psychology of Religion*. Detroit: Wayne State University Press.

Beier, Ulli. 1980. *Yoruba Myths*. Cambridge: Cambridge University Press.

Bongmba, Elias Kifon. 2001. *African Witchcraft and Otherness: A Philosophical and Theological Critique of Intersubjective Relations*. Albany: State University of New York Press.

Bourguignon, Erika. 1976. *Possession*. San Francisco: Chandler and Sharp.

Boyarin, Daniel. 1998. Gender. In Taylor 1998, 117–35.

Brandon, George. 1983. The Dead Sell Memories: An Anthropological Study of Santeria in New York City. Ph.D. diss., Rutgers University.

———. 1993. *Santeria from Africa to the New World: The Dead Sell Memories*. Bloomington: Indiana University Press.

———. 2002. Hierarchy without a Head: Observations on Changes in the Social Organization of Some Afroamerican Religions in the United States, 1959–1999, with Special Reference to Santeria. *Archives de Sciences sociales des Religions* 117:151–74.

Bremer, Fredrika. 1853. *The Homes of the New World: Impressions of America*. Trans. Mary Howitt. 2 vols. New York: Harper and Brothers.

Brown, David Hilary. 1989. Garden in the Machine: Afro-Cuban Sacred Art and Performance in Urban New Jersey and New York. Ph.D. diss., Yale University.

——. 2003. *Santeria Enthroned: Art, Ritual, and Innovation in an Afro-Cuban Religion*. Chicago: University of Chicago Press.

Butler, Judith. 1990. *Gender Trouble: Feminism and the Subversion of Identity*. New York and London: Routledge.

Cabrera, Lydia. 1975. *El monte: igbo, finda, ewe orisha, vititi nfinda: Notas sobre las religiones, la magia, las supersticiones y el folklore de los negros criollos y el pueblo de Cuba*. 4th ed. Miami: Ediciones Universal.

Canizares, Raul J. 1991. The Ethics of Santeria. *Journal of Dharma* 16 (4):368–74.

Clark, Mary Ann. 1998. Santería. In *Sects, Cults, and Spiritual Communities: A Sociological Analysis*, ed. William W. Zellner and Marc Petrowsky, 118–30. Westport, Conn.: Praeger.

——. 2000. Orisha Worship Communities: A Reconsideration of Organizational Structure. *Religion* 30 (4):379–89.

——. 2001. *¡No Hay Ningún Santo Aquí!* (There Are No Saints Here!): Symbolic Language within Santería. *Journal of the American Academy of Religion* 69 (1):21–41.

——. 2002. You Are (Not) Shango: Jungian Archetypes in Contemporary Santeria. *Wadabagei: A Journal of the Caribbean and Its Diaspora* 5 (1):105–35.

——. 2003a. Godparenthood in the Afro-Cuban Religious Tradition of Santería. *Journal of Religious Studies and Theology* 22 (1):45–62.

——. 2003b. Healing Rituals in the Suburbs: African-Based Healing among Middle-Class Americans. Annual meeting of the American Academy of Religion, African Religions Group and Religion, Medicines, and Healing Consultation, joint session, Atlanta, November.

Connell, R. W. 1987. *Gender and Power: Society, the Person, and Sexual Politics*. Stanford, Calif.: Stanford University Press.

Cosentino, Donald J. 1997. Repossession: Ogun in Folklore and Literature. In *Africa's Ogun: Old World and New*, ed. Sandra T. Barnes, 290–314. Bloomington: Indiana University Press.

Crapanzano, Vincent, and Vivian Garrison, eds. 1977. *Case Studies in Spirit Possession*. New York: Wiley.

Cros Sandoval, Mercedes. 1975. *La Religión afrocubana*. Madrid: Playor.

Das, Veena. 1983. Language of Sacrifice. *Man* 18 (3):445–62.

Deren, Maya. 1953. *Divine Horsemen: The Living Gods of Haiti*. London and New York: Thames and Hudson.

Drewal, Henry John. 1997. Yorùbá Beadwork in Africa. In *Beads, Body and Soul: Art and Light in the Yorùbá Universe*, ed. Henry John Drewal and John Mason, 13–85. Los Angeles: UCLA, Fowler Museum of Cultural History.

Drewal, Henry John, III, John Pemberton, and Rowland Abiodun. 1989. The Yoruba World. In Wardwell 1989, 13–43.

Drewal, Margaret Thompson. 1992. *Yoruba Ritual: Performers, Play, Agency*. Bloomington: Indiana University Press.

Dunnill, John. 2003. Communicative Bodies and Economies of Grace: The Role of

Sacrifice in the Christian Understanding of the Body. *Journal of Religion* 83 (1):79–93.

Durkheim, Emile. 1915. *The Elementary Forms of Religious Life*. Trans. Karen E. Fields. New York: Free Press, 1995.

Ebisi, C. Njideke. 1994. In Memoriam. In Ìdòwú 1994, vii–ix.

Edwards, Gary, and John Mason. 1985. *Black Gods—Orisa Studies in the New World*. Brooklyn, N.Y.: Yoruba Theological Archministry.

Eliade, Mircea. 1959. *The Sacred and the Profane: The Nature of Religion*. Trans. Willard R. Trask. New York: Harcourt Brace.

———, ed. 1987. *The Encyclopedia of Religion*. 16 vols. New York: Macmillan.

Evans-Pritchard, E. E. 1976. *Witchcraft, Oracles, and Magic among the Azande*. Abr. ed. Oxford: Clarendon.

Farrow, Stephen S. 1926. *Faith, Fancies and Fetich, or Yoruba Paganism*. New York: Macmillan. Repr., Brooklyn, N.Y.: Athelia Henrietta Press, 1996.

Fiorenza, Francis Schüssler, and Gordon D. Kaufman. 1998. God. In Taylor 1998, 136–59.

Flores-Peña, Ysamur, and Roberta J. Evanchuk. 1994. *Santería Garments and Altars: Speaking without a Voice*. Jackson: University Press of Mississippi.

Freud, Sigmund. 1950. *Totem and Taboo*. Trans. James Strachey. New York: W. W. Norton.

Garfinkel, Harold. 1967. *Studies in Ethnomethodology*. Englewood Cliffs, N.J.: Prentice-Hall.

Gbadegesin, Segun. 1991. *African Philosophy: Traditional Yoruba Philosophy and Contemporary African Realities*. New York: Peter Lang.

Gilligan, Carol. 1982. *In a Different Voice: Psychological Theory and Women's Development*. Cambridge, Mass.: Harvard University Press.

Girard, René. 1977. *Violence and the Sacred*. Trans. Patrick Gregory. Baltimore: Johns Hopkins University Press.

Green, Ronald M. 1987. Theodicy. In Eliade 1987, 14:430–41.

Greenhouse, Linda. 1992. High Court Is Cool to Sacrifice Ban. *New York Times*, November 5.

———. 1993. Court, Citing Religious Freedom, Voids a Ban on Animal Sacrifice. *New York Times*, June 12.

Greenleaf, Richard E. 1969. *The Mexican Inquisition of the Sixteenth Century*. Albuquerque: University of New Mexico Press.

Gross, Rita M. 1993. *Buddhism after Patriarchy: A Feminist History, Analysis, and Reconstruction of Buddhism*. Albany: State University of New York Press.

———. 2003. What Went Wrong? Feminism and Freedom from the Prison of Gender Roles. *Cross Currents* 53 (1):8–20.

Hair, P. E. H., Adam Jones, and Robin Law, eds. 1992. *Barbot on Guinea: The Writings of Jean Barbot on West Africa 1678–1712*. London: Hakluyt Society.

Hallen, Barry, and J. Olubi Sodipo. 1986. *Knowledge, Belief and Witchcraft*. London: Ethnographica.

Hamerton-Kelly, Robert G., ed. 1987. *Violent Origins: Walter Burkert, Rene Girard, and Jonathan Z. Smith on Ritual Killing and Cultural Formation*. Stanford, Calif.: Stanford University Press.

Hawkesworth, Mary. 1997. Confounding Gender. *Signs* 22 (3):649–85.

Herbert, Eugenia W. 1993. *Iron, Gender, and Power: Rituals of Transformation in African Societies*. Bloomington: Indiana University Press.

Herskovits, Melville J. 1941. *The Myth of the Negro Past*. Repr. Boston: Beacon Press, 1990.

Hoch-Smith, Judith. 1978. Radical Yoruba Female Sexuality. In *Women in Ritual and Symbolic Roles*, ed. Judith Hoch-Smith and Anita Spring, 245–67. New York: Plenum Press.

Horton, Robin. 1983. Social Psychologies: African and Western. In *Oedipus and Job in West African Religion*, by Meyer Fortes. Cambridge: Cambridge University Press.

Howard, Philip A. 1998. *Changing History: Afro-Cuban Cabildos and Societies of Color in the Nineteenth Century*. Baton Rouge: Louisiana State University Press.

Hume, David. 1948. *Dialogues Concerning Natural Religion*. Ed. H. D. Aiken. New York: Hafner.

Hwang, David Henry. 1989. *M. Butterfly*. New York: New American Library.

Ìdòwú, E. Bolájí. 1994. *Olódùmarè: God in Yorùbá Belief*. Memorial ed. New York: Wazobia. Orig. pub., London: Longmans, 1962.

International Council for Ifa Religion. 2003. D'Haifa Title Taken. http://ilarioba. tripod.com/media/pressrelifacouncil3–4–03.htm. Accessed November 5, 2004.

James, William. 1902. *The Varieties of Religious Experience*. Repr., New York: Penguin, 1982.

———. 1981. The Consciousness of Self. In *The Principles of Psychology*, by William James, ed. Frederick H. Burkhardt, Fredson Bowers, and Ignas K. Skrupskelis, 279–379. Cambridge, Mass.: Harvard University Press. Orig. pub., New York: Holt, 1905.

Jamison, Stephanie W. 1996. *Sacrificed Wife, Sacrificer's Wife: Women, Ritual, and Hospitality in Ancient India*. New York: Oxford University Press.

Jay, Nancy. 1992. *Throughout Your Generations Forever: Sacrifice, Religion and Paternity*. Chicago: University of Chicago Press.

Johnson, Samuel. 1921. *The History of the Yorubas: From the Earliest Times to the Beginning of the British Protectorate*, ed. O. Johnson. London: Routledge.

Joseph, Nathan. 1986. *Uniforms and Nonuniforms: Communication through Clothing*. New York: Greenwood Press.

Kamen, Henry. 1997. *The Spanish Inquisition: An Historical Revision*. London: Weidenfeld and Nicolson.

Karade, Ifá. 1994. *The Handbook of Yorùbá Religious Concepts*. York Beach, Maine: Samuel Weiser.

Kessler, Suzanne J., and Wendy McKenna. 1978. *Gender: An Ethnomethodological Approach*. New York: Wiley.

Klausner, Samuel Z. 1987. Violence. In Eliade 1987, 15:268–72.

Klein, Anne Carolyn. 1994. *Meeting the Great Bliss Queen: Buddhists, Feminists, and the Art of the Self*. Boston: Beacon Press.

Kors, Alan Charles, and Edward Peters, eds. 2001. *Witchcraft in Europe, 400–1700: A Documentary History*. 2nd ed. Philadelphia: University of Pennsylvania Press.

Kramer, Heinrich, and James [Jacob] Sprenger. 1928. *Malleus Maleficarum*. Trans. Montague Summers. Repr., New York: Dover, 1971.

Kripal, Jeffrey J. 1992. *Ramakrishna's Foot: Mystical Homoeroticism in the Kathamrita*: Las Colinas, Texas: Monument Press.

Landes, Ruth. 1947. *The City of Women*. Repr., Albuquerque: University of New Mexico Press, 1994.

Law, Robin. 1977. *The Oyo Empire, c. 1600–c. 1836: A West African Imperialism in the Era of the Atlantic Slave Trade*. Oxford: Clarendon Press.

Lawson, E. Thomas. 1984. *Religions of Africa: Traditions in Transformation*. San Francisco: Harper and Row.

Lea, Henry Charles. 1906–1908. *A History of the Inquisition of Spain*. 4 vols. London and New York: Macmillan.

Lemmon, Michael. 1998. Interview. http://www.voiceofthoth.com/Interview.htm. Accessed November 5, 2004.

Lewis, I. M. 1971. *Ecstatic Religion*. Baltimore: Penguin.

Lincoln, Bruce. 2004. The Rhetoric of Bush and Bin Laden. http://fathom. lib.uchicago.edu/1/777777190152/. Accessed November 5, 2004.

Lucas, J. Olumide. 1948. *The Religion of the Yorubas*. Lagos: C.M.S. Bookshop.

Mack, Burton. 1987. Introduction: Religion and Ritual. In Hamerton-Kelly 1987, 1–72.

Marvin, Carolyn, and David W. Ingle. 1996. Blood Sacrifice and the Nation: Revisiting Civil Religion. *Journal of the American Academy of Religion* 64 (4):767–80.

Marx, Karl. 1964. Contribution to a Critique of Hegel's Philosophy of Right. Introduction in *On Religion*, by Karl Marx and Friedrich Engels. Repr. of Moscow: Moscow Foreign Languages Publishing House, 1957. Orig. edition, Moscow: Deutsche Französische Jahrbücher, 1844.

Mason, John. 1985. *Four New World Yorùbá Rituals*. Brooklyn, N.Y.: Yorùbá Theological Archministry.

———. 1996. *Olóòkun: Owner of Rivers and Seas*. Brooklyn, N.Y.: Yorùbá Theological Archministry.

———. 1999. *Ìdáná Fún Òrìsà: Cooking for Selected Heads*. Brooklyn, N.Y.: Yorùbá Theological Archministry.

Mason, Michael Atwood. 1994. I Bow My Head to the Ground: The Creation of Bodily Experience in a Cuban American *Santería* Initiation. *Journal of American Folklore* 107 (423):23–39.

———. 2002. *Living Santería: Rituals and Experiences in an Afro-Cuban Religion*. Washington, D.C.: Smithsonian Institution Press.

Matibag, Eugenio. 1996. *Afro-Cuban Religious Experience: Cultural Reflections in Narrative*. Gainesville: University Press of Florida.

Matory, J. Lorand. 1994. *Sex and the Empire That Is No More: Gender and the Politics of Metaphor in Oyo Yoruba Religion*. Minneapolis: University of Minnesota Press.

McKenzie, Peter R. 1976. Yoruba Òrìsà Cults: Some Marginal Notes Concerning Their Cosmology and Concepts of Deity. *Journal of Religion in Africa* 8 (fasc. 3):189–207.

———. 1997. *Hail Orisha! A Phenomenology of a West African Religion in the Mid-Nineteenth Century*. Leiden: Brill.

Murphy, Joseph M. 1993. *Santería: African Spirits in America*. Boston: Beacon Press.

———. 1994. *Working the Spirit: Ceremonies of the Africa Diaspora*. Boston: Beacon Press.

Murphy, Joseph M., and Mei-Mei Sanford, eds. 2001. *Òsun Across the Waters: A Yoruba Goddess in Africa and the Americas*. Bloomington: Indiana University Press.

Neimark, Philip John. 1993. *The Way of the Orisa: Empowering Your Life through the Ancient African Religion of Ifa*. San Francisco: HarperSanFrancisco.

New York Times. 1993. Excerpts from Supreme Court Opinions on the Ritual Sacrifice of Animals. June 12.

Nikhilananda, Swami, trans. 1942. *The Gospel of Sri Ramakrishna*. New York: Ramakrishna-Vivekananda Center.

Ogungbile, David O. 2001. Ẹẹ̀rìndìnlógún. In Murphy and Sanford 2001, 189–212.

Olajubu, Oyeronke. 2003. *Women in the Yoruba Religious Sphere*. McGill Studies in the History of Religions, ed. K. K. Young. Albany: State University of New York Press.

Olupona, Jacob K. 1991. *Kingship, Religion, and Rituals in a Nigerian Community: A Phenomenological Study of Ondo Yoruba Festivals*. ACTA Universitatis Stockholmiensis, Stockholm Studies in Comparative Religion 28. Stockholm: Almqvist and Wiksell International.

Ortiz, Fernando. 1906. *Los negros brujos*. Repr., Miami: Ediciones Universal, 1973.

———. 1921. *Los cabildos afrocubanos*. Havana: La Universal.

Ortner, Sherry B., and Harriet Whitehead. 1981. *Sexual Meanings: The Cultural Construction of Gender and Sexuality*. Cambridge: Cambridge University Press.

Oyewùmí, Oyèrónké. 1997. *The Invention of Women: Making an African Sense of Western Gender Discourses*. Minneapolis: University of Minnesota Press.

———. 2000. Family Bonds/Conceptual Binds: African Notes on Feminist Epistemologies. *Signs* 25 (4):1093–98.

Palmié, Stephan. 2002. *Wizards and Scientists: Explorations in Afro-Cuban Modernity and Tradition*. Durham, N.C.: Duke University Press.

Parsons, Talcott. 1962. *Toward a General Theory of Action*. New York: Harper and Row.

Parsons, William B. 1997. Psychoanalysis and Mysticism: The Case of Ramakrishna. *Religious Studies Review* 28 (4):355–61.

Peel, J. D. Y. 1990. The Pastor and the Babalawo: The Interaction of Religions in Nineteenth-Century Yorubaland. *Africa* 50 (3):338–69.

———. 2002. Gender in Yoruba Religious Change. *Journal of Religion in Africa* 32 (2): 136–66.

Pérez y Mena, Andrés Isidoro. 1991. *Speaking with the Dead*. New York: AMS.

———. 1998. Cuban Santería, Haitian Vodun, Puerto Rico Spiritualism: A Multicultural Inquiry into Syncretism. *Journal for the Scientific Study of Religion* 37 (1): 15–27.

Pfau, Julie Shoshana, and David R. Blumenthal. 2001. The Violence of God: Dialogic Fragments. *Cross Currents*, 51 (2): 177–200.

Ramos, Miguel. 2000. The Empire Beats On: Oyo, Batá Drums, and Hegemony in Nineteenth-Century Cuba. Master's thesis, Florida International University.

Ricoeur, Paul. 1995. Philosophy and Religious Language. In *Figuring the Sacred: Religion, Narrative, and Imagination*, trans. David Pellauer, ed. Mark I. Wallace, 35–47. Minneapolis: Fortress Press.

Said, Edward W. 1978. *Orientalism*. New York: Pantheon.

Samuels, Andrew, Bani Shorter, and Fred Plaut. 1986. *A Critical Dictionary of Jungian Analysis*. London: Routledge and Kegan Paul.

Sarno, Geraldo. 1980. *Iawo: Initiation in a Gege-Nago Temple*. New York: Cinema Guild. Video recording.

Schoenfeld, Eugen, and Stjepan G. Mestrović. 1991. With Justice and Mercy: Instrumental-Masculine and Expressive-Feminine Elements in Religion. *Journal for the Scientific Study of Religion* 30 (4):363–80.

Scott, Joan W. 1986. A Useful Category of Historical Analysis. *American Historical Review* 91 (5):1053–75.

Segato, Rita Laura. 1995. *Santos e Daimones: O Politeísmo Afro-Brasileiro e a Tradição Arquetipal*. Brasília: Editora Universidade de Brasília.

Sered, Susan. 2002. Towards a Gendered Typology of Sacrifice: Women and Feasting, Men and Death in an Okinawan Village. In *Sacrifice in Religious Experience*, ed. Albert I. Baumgarten, 94–116. Leiden: Brill.

Sharf, Robert H. 1998. Experience. In Taylor 1998, 94–116.

Shaw, Rosalind. 1990. The Invention of "African Traditional Religion." *Religion* 20 (4): 339–53.

Silverblatt, Irene. 1987. *Moon, Sun, and Witches: Gender Ideologies and Class in Inca and Colonial Peru*. Princeton, N.J.: Princeton University Press.

Simons, Marlise. 1998. Shaded by Gargoyles, the Exorcist of Notre Dame. *New York Times*, June 15.

Smith, Jonathan Z. 1987. The Domestication of Sacrifice. In Hamerton-Kelly 1987, 191–205.

Smith, Robert. 1988. *Kingdom of the Yoruba*. 3rd ed. London: Currey.

Stolcke, Verena. 1974. *Marriage, Class, and Colour in Nineteenth-Century Cuba: A Study of Racial Attitudes and Sexual Values in a Slave Society*. Cambridge: Cambridge University Press.

Taylor, Mark C. 1998. *Critical Terms for Religious Studies*. Chicago: University of Chicago Press.

Teresa of Avila, Saint. 1961. *Interior Castle*. Trans. E. Allison Peers. Garden City, N.Y.: Doubleday, 1961.

Thompson, Robert Farris. 1971. *Black Gods and Kings: Yoruba Art at UCLA*. Los Angeles: University of California.

———. 1983. *Flash of the Spirit: African and Afro-American Art and Philosophy*. New York: Random House.

Vega, Marta Moreno. 2000. *The Altar of My Soul: The Living Traditions of Santería*. New York: One World/Ballantine.

Vélez, María Teresa. 2000. *Drumming for the Gods: The Life and Times of Felipe García Villamil, Santero, Palero, and Abakuá*. Philadelphia: Temple University Press.

Verger, Pierre. 1957. *Notes sur le culte des Orisa et Vodun à Bahia, la Baie de tous les Saints, au Brésil et à l'ancienne Côte des Esclaves en Afrique*. Dakar: IFAN.

———. 1966. The Yoruba High God. *Odu* 2 (2):19–40.

Wafer, Jim. 1991. *The Taste of Blood: Spirit Possession in Brazilian Candomblé*. Philadelphia: University of Pennsylvania Press.

Wardwell, Allen, ed. 1989. *Yoruba: Nine Centuries of African Art and Thought*. New York: Center for African Art.

Wedel, Johan. 2004. *Santería Healing*. Gainesville: University Press of Florida.

Whitmont, Edward C. 1991. *The Symbolic Quest: Basic Concepts of Analytical Psychology*. Expanded ed. Princeton, N.J.: Princeton University Press.

Wood, Alice Landru. 1997. Chains of Virtue: Seventeenth-Century Saints in Spanish Colonial Lima. Ph.D. diss., Rice University.

Wyschogrod, Edith. 1990. *Saints and Postmodernism: Revisioning Moral Philosophy*. Chicago: University of Chicago Press.

———. 1992. Does Continental Ethics Have a Future? In *Ethics and Danger: Essays on Heidegger and Continental Thought*, ed. Arleen B. Dallery and Charles E. Scott, 229–41. Albany: State University of New York Press.

Zaehner, R. C. 1957. *Mysticism: Sacred and Profane*. Oxford: Clarendon Press.

Index

Babalosha, 78, 164

Barstow, Anne Llewellyn (*Witchcraze*), 122, 141

Bearded woman, 128

Biblical pattern of sacrifice, 112

Bird images, positive, 130

Bocourt, Domingo, 131

Bongmba, Elias Kifon (*African Witchcraft and Otherness*), 126–27

Bourguignon, Ericka (*Possession*), 87

Boyarin, Daniel, 33, 78

Brandon, George (*Santería from Africa to the New World*), 5–6, 149, 150

Bremer, Fredrika (*Homes of the New World*), 7

Brown, David, 66

Brujería, 130–33

Buddha, 47–48

Buddhism, 4

Burkert, Walter, 107–8

Butter Bean and Itchy Bean, 48, 50

Cabildo, 6–7, 8, 164

Candomblé: compared to Santería, 158n1; description of possession, 89–90

Case Studies in Spirit Possession (Crapanzano), 87, 97

Celebratory rituals, 112

Christianity, 4; compared to Orisha cults, 65

Church of the Lukumí Babalu Ayé, 109, 110, 149

City of Women (Landers), 100–101

Clothing: "cultural genitals," 100–101

Colonial period, 125

Confessions (Saint Augustine), 90

Constructionist argument, 32, 84, 144

Costuming, 99–100

Crapanzano, Vincent (*Case Studies in Spirit Possession*), 87, 97

Cross dressing: Candomblé, 100; Western abhorrence of, 101; Yoruba, 100

Cuban Revolution, 14

Cuban witchcraft hysteria, 131

Cuchillo, 113–14, 164

"Cultural genitals," 29, 100

Curandero/a, 123

Curing: compared to healing, 138

Deren, Maya, 86

Destiny. *See* Ori

D'Haifá, 161n2

Díaz, Zoila, 131

Diffused monotheism, 11

Diloggun, 54–55, 164; compared to Ifá odu, 156n5; core practice, 69–70

Divination: coconut (coco), 54; cowry, 54–55 (*see also* Diloggun); healing, 136–38; Ifá, 55–56 (*see also* Ifá); priesthoods, 21–22, 64–65; types, 21, 49

Domestication: and violence, 108, 111

Do ut des ("I give in order that you may give"), 111

Doxis: in Santería, 19–20

Drewal, Margaret Thompson, 127

Drumming for the Gods (Vélez), 150

Dunnill, John, 112

Durkheim, Emile, 106–7, 140

Ebo, 49, 111

Ecstatic Religion (Lewis), 87

Edan ògbóni/edan òsùgbó, 118

Efuche, 159n13

Egbe (club), 149

Eleggua, 113, 165: association of, with witchcraft, 138, 139; description, 14; diviner, 69; possession by, 88–89

Eleye, 128, 165

Eliade, Mircea, 71

Embodiment: fluidity of, 22

Èmí (breath), 51

Èníyan (person), 51

Enlightenment, 130–31

Eshu, 165. *See* Eleggua

Espiritismo, 24, 138, 165

Essentialist argument, 32, 84, 144

Ethical quality: of witchcraft power, 128–29

European witchhunt, 122–23

Evans-Pritchard, E. E. (*Witchcraft, Oracles and Magic among the Azande*, 126

Expressive religion, 80–81, 140–41

Face of the Other, 96

Female. *See* Women

Feminists: theologians, 10; theory of sacrifice, 112

Ochosi, 16–17, 59, 166; association with witchcraft, 139
Odu of Ifá, 52
Oedipus, 47
Offerings, 110
Ogun, 16–17, 166; association with witchcraft, 128, 139; description, 17–19; and sacrifice, 113
Okàn (heart), 51
Oko, 42, 167
Older women: power of, 128, 129; ritual participation of, 147. *See also* Menopause
Olodumare, 40, 69, 167
Olódùmarè: God in Yorùbá Belief (Ìdòwú), 10
Olokun, 37, 167
Olorisha, 65, 167
Olupona, Jacob (*Kingship, Religion, and Rituals in a Nigerian Community*), 73
Omo-ile, 41–42
Omo-Orisha, 43, 76–77, 78
Oneself: as the Orisha, 95
Onisègùn, 126, 141, 167
Opele, 65–66
Opon Ifá, 69
Ori, 21, 51–54, 145, 167: choosing, 51–56; gender, 62; metaphysical self, 75; mutable, 61–62; theodicy, 134–5
Oriaté, 66–67, 167
Oriaté-centered houses, 66–67
Orientalism (Said), 155n7
Orisha, 35, 167: ambivalently ethical, 15–16; archetypes, 56–58; assigning to devotees, 57; blurred relationship between self and, 95; characteristics of, 11, 12, 13–14; dependence on human beings, 91–92, 109; developmental model, 84; ethical spirits, 139; feeding, 109–10; gay priests, 57–58; gender, 35–37, 57–58; guardian, 52, 103; Internet presence, 150; memorative web, 13; morally ambiguous, 139; relative gender, 145–46; self, 96–98; spirit-husbands, 99; theodicy, 133–34. *See also specific Orisha* — groups, 85: compared to Christianity, 65; movement toward legitimatization, 150–51; organizational structure, 149–50
Orisha Oko, 167: association with witchcraft, 128

Ortiz, Fernando (*Los negros brujos*), 131
Ortner, Sherry (*Sexual Meanings*), 30
Orula, 55, 69, 167
Orunmila, 167. *See also* Orula
Oshun, 37, 57, 113, 167: association with witchcraft, 129, 140; description, 18–19; diviner, 55; seventeenth Orisha, 39–40
Other, 96, 97, 98
Oya, 36–37, 167
Oyewùmí, Oyèrónké (*Invention of Women*), 20, 35, 78, 144–45
Oyotunji Village, 149

Palmié, Stephan (*Wizards and Scientists*), 80, 131, 138, 147
Palo Mayombe. *See* Palo Monte
Palo Monte, 24, 79, 167: compared to Ocha, 80–81, 138–39; gender, 63; instrumental and masculine, 140–41; spirits, 138–39; witchcraft, 131
Parsons, William, 30
Pasteur, Louis, 125
Peel, J. D. Y., 65, 282
Person: in Western tradition, 90
Philo: on gender, 33
Pichardo, Ernesto, 109
Pinaldo. *See* Cuchillo
Plato, 90; *Symposium*, 34
Possession: benefit for the host, 94; Candomblé, 89–90; characteristics, 88, 87, 89–90, 92; communal nature of, 91, 93–94; definition, 87; and gender crossing, 99; marriage metaphor, 94, 98–99; mystical experience, 96; and natural attitude toward gender, 98; noetic quality of, 93–94; penetration by the Other, 97–98; and revelation, 96, 98; in Santería, 89, 146; by spirit-husband, 98–99; trance, 87; unitive experience, 94–95; Western, 97; worldwide occurences, 87
Possession (Bourguignon), 87
Power: of older women, 129; of transformation, 127–28
Power dynamics: fluidity, 22; seniority, 118; Yoruba, 39
Praxis: in Santería, 19–20
Priest: divination, 21–22, 64–65; fetish, 65;

and relative gender, 145–46; spirit-wife/ husband, 84, 98, 100. *See also* Olorisha
Priestly womanliness, 81–83

Queen: in English, 40–41; in Yoruba, 41

Ramakrishna, Sri, 30
Radical altruism, 98
Radical dualism, 90
Ramakrishna, 93
Ramos, Miguel "Willie," 153n3
Regla de Congo, 168. *See also* Palo Monte
Regla de Ocha, 168. *See also* Santería
Reincarnation, Yoruba beliefs, 4–5
Religion: compared to magic, 140–41; moral-centered, 80; response to a primal violence, 105; ritual-centered, 80; and violence, 102–3
Republican period (Cuba, 1902–1958), 8, 131
Ricoeur, Paul, 90
Right to sacrifice, 113–14
Ritual: cleansing, 110; communal nature of, 91; comparison of Santería and Palo Monte, 139; feasting, 119; healing, 137; hunting and religion, 107–8; killing, 105; limitations on participation by women, 116–17; sacrificial, described, 111–12; work, 116

Sacrificator, 113
Sacrifice: animal domestication, 108, 111; basis of culture, 107; celebratory rituals, 115; denotation, 104; description, 106, 111–12; essential to human well-being, 109; feasting, 119; feeding, 114–15; feminist theory, 112; gender analysis, 22, 112, 114–20; gift-giving, 111; Greek, 106; holocaust, 106; human, 105; hunting culture, 107–8; inhumane, 111; male- dominated, 112; menstruation taboos, 117–18, 145–46; mimetic desire, 107; offerings, 110; right to, 113–14; ritual cleansing, 119o ritual celebration, 119; valorization of feminine, 115; Vedic, 106; war, 103; women's labor in, 115, 145; Yoruba, 109, 111
Sacrificer, 114
Sacrificial religions: compared to Christianity, 106

Sacrificial stories, 105
Said, Edward (*Orientalism*), 155n7
Saintly altruism, 97
Saintly bodies, 96
Salvational religious traditions, 64
Samsara, 77
Santería, 168; compared to Candomblé, 158n1; compared to Ifá, 65–67, 151; compared to Palo Monte, 80–81, 140; emotional characteristics of, 140–41; expressive and feminine, 140–41; female normative, 143, 145, 151; history, 5–8; Internet presence, 150; movement toward legitimatization, 150–51; national organizations, 149–50; organizational structure, 149–50; rituals, 138–39; possession, 146; witchcraft, 132–33
Santería (Murphy), 65–66
Santería from Africa to the New World (Brandon), 5–6
Santero/a. *See* Priest
Saturated Self (Gergan), 22
Scapegoating, 105
Scott, Joan, 30
Seniority: as power, 118
Şe òrìṣà, 19, 79, 168
September 2001 attacks, 102
Sered, Susan, 22, 112
Sex: definition, 28
Sex and the Empire That Is No More (Matory), 30, 75, 78
Sexual Meanings (Ortner and Whitehead), 30
Shango, 37, 57, 113, 168; association with witchcraft, 128, 140; description, 16–17; moral code, 16–17
Sharf, Robert, 73
Shaw, Rosalind, 65
Shell divination. *See* Diloggun
Shopona, 168; association with witchcraft, 128
Silverblatt, Irene (*Moon, Sun, and Witches*), 160n8
Smith, Jonathan Z., 108–11
Sodipo, J. O. (*Knowledge, Belief and Witchcraft*), 125–26, 141
Spanish Inquisition, 123–25; Africans, 125; Americas, 124–25
Spanish Inquisition (Kamen), 123

SPCA. *See* American Society for the Prevention of Cruelty to Animals
Spells, 135
Spirit-husbands, 84, 99
Spiritism. *See* Espiritismo
Spirits: moral hierarchy, 136; Palo Monte, 138–39
Stepping into the World ritual, 48
Studies in Ethnomethodology (Garfinkel), 20, 28
Subjectivity: in Western philosophy, 22
Sublimation: of violence, 105
Sympathetic magic, 50
Symposium (Plato), 34

Tambor (drum ritual), 88
Teresa of Avila, Saint (*Interior Castle*), 93, 95
Tfu, 126–27
Thanksgiving, 119–20
Theodicy, 133–36
Totem and Taboo (Freud), 107
Towá, María, 8, 113–14
Trance: definition, 87. *See also* Possession
Transvestism, 100; Western abhorrence of, 101

Unitary self, 97
U.S. Supreme Court, 108–9

Valorization: feminine, 115; Ifá, 151
Varieties of Religious Experience (James), 90
Vedic sacrifices, 106
Vélez, María Teresa (*Drumming for the Gods*), 150
Violence: religion, 102–3; scapegoating, 105; sublimation, 105
Violence and the Sacred (Girard), 107
Violent Origins (Hamerton-Kelly), 108

War, 103
Warrior Orisha, 127, 139
West Africa: witchcraft in, 125–30
Whitehead, Harriet (*Sexual Meanings*), 30
Wimbam people, 126–27
Witch: birds, 127–28; characteristics in Yoruba, 126; euphemism, 128; men and women, 141–42
Witchcraft: Abakuá, 131; as ambiguous, 128–

29; Andean, 160n8; attacks, 135; beliefs in twentieth-century Cuba, 131; destiny, 135; and Enlightenment, 130–31; European concepts, 122–25; explanation for hardships, 135; gender, 24, 141–42, 146–47; negative, 129; Palo Monte, 131; power of transformation, 127–28; Santería, 132–33; spells, 135; substance, 118, 126, 127; types of, 126–27; Warrior Orisha, 127; West African, 125–30; Western, 133
—power of: ethical quality, 128–29; fortification against, 135; older women, 129
Witchcraft, Oracles and Magic among the Azande (Evans-Pritchard), 126
Witchcraze (Barstow), 122, 141
Witch-knowledge, 126–27
Women: aje, 141–42; birds, 127–28, 129; bodies in Yoruba religion, 38; cabildo period, 7; equality, 150; feeding by, 115–16; limits on ritual participation, 116–17, 151; model for behavior, 84; natural mediums, 98–99; and negative witchcraft, 129; older, 128, 129, 147 (*see also* Menopause); and power, 147; witches, 141–42; and Yoruba religion, 38
Working the Spirit (Murphy), 91
Worship: as work, 19–20, 79, 116

Yemaya, 37, 57; association with witchcraft, 129–30, 140; description, 18; diviner, 55
Yoruba: description of household, 41–42; image of witch, 127–28; Lukumi, 6, 74; marriage and priesthood, 76; sacrifice, 109–10; types of witch powers, 127. *See also* Santería
Yoruba Beliefs and Sacrificial Rites (Awolalu), 109, 111

Wizards and Scientists (Palmié), 80, 131, 138, 147
Wood, Alice Landru, 125
Wyschogrod, Edith (*Saints and Postmodernism*), 96, 97

Zaehner, R.C. (*Mysticism: Sacred and Profane*), 94–95

Mary Ann Clark is an independent scholar and adjunct professor in the University of Houston system. Her recent publications include articles in the *Journal of Religious Studies and Theology* on godparenthood in the Afro-Cuban religious tradition and in the *Journal of the American Academy of Religion* on symbolic language within Santería.